THE
UNCROWNED CHAMPS

THE
UNCROWNED CHAMPS

HOW THE 1963 SAN DIEGO CHARGERS *WOULD* HAVE WON THE SUPER BOWL

DAVE STEIDEL

Foreword by Lance Alworth

CARREL BOOKS

Carrel Books may be purchased in bulk at special discounts for sales promotion, corporate gifts, fund-raising, or educational purposes. Special editions can also be created to specifications. For details, contact the Special Sales Department, Carrel Books, 307 West 36th Street, 11th Floor, New York, NY 10018, or carrelbooks@skyhorsepublishing.com.

Carrel Books® is a registered trademark of Skyhorse Publishing, Inc.®, a Delaware corporation.

Visit our website at www.carrelbooks.com.

10 9 8 7 6 5 4 3 2 1

Library of Congress Cataloging-in-Publication Data is available on file.

Jacket design by Tom Lau
Jacket photos courtesy of the San Diego Chargers

All helmet images that appear in the text are courtesy of the NFL and Craig Wheeler

ISBN: 978-1-63144-046-5
Ebook ISBN: 978-1-63144-047-2

Printed in the United States of America

Dedicated to the players of the 1963 Champion San Diego Chargers.

CONTENTS

CONTENTS

Bottom Row: (from left to right) Paul Maguire, Sam Gruneisen, Chuck Allen, Jerry Robinson, Frank Buncom, Bob Lane, Jacque MacKinnon, Walt Sweeney, equipment manager Tom Denman

2nd Row: Trainer Kearney Reeb, Dave Kocourek, Don Rogers, Earl Faison, Emil Karas, Ron Mix, Keith Lincoln, Gerry McDougall, Ernie Ladd, Ernie Wright, offensive line coach Joe Madro

3rd Row: Head coach Sid Gillman, defensive coach Chuck Noll, defensive line coach Walt Hackett, Bob Jackson, Sam DeLuca, Charlie McNeil, Pat Shea, Tobin Rote, Hank Schmidt, Bob Petrich, Bob Mitinger, George Gross, receivers coach Hugh Taylor, publicity director Bob Burdick

Top Row: Bud Whitehead, Dick Westmoreland, John Hadl, Dick Harris, Lance Alworth, George Blair, Wayne Frazier, Paul Lowe, Don Norton

PROLOGUE

In 1963, I was a San Diego Chargers fan, as well as a Chicago Bears fan. I watched and rooted for both teams to win their championship games that were played a week apart. The Little League team I played for at the time was the Downtown Youth Center Bears, so I felt I had some kind of bond with the Chicago team. I was also drawn to their "Monsters of the Midway," hard-hitting reputation. And even though the Bears quarterback Bill Wade looked three steps slower wearing his old-style high-top football shoes, he was my favorite player because I was also the quarterback for my Bears team.

Then there was the AFL and the Chargers. The glamor team of the league had those great powder-blue uniforms (although I couldn't appreciate them on my black-and-white television set) and also Lance Alworth, Paul Lowe, and Keith Lincoln speeding and weaving down the field on long scoring plays. They also had their own version of "monsters" in 6' 9" defensive tackle Ernie Ladd and 6' 5" defensive end Earl Faison leading their "Fearsome Foursome" while shoving people around almost at will. And of course, those lightning bolts on their helmets were just the thing that young football fans such as I were infatuated with.

Truth be told, I rarely saw the Bears play a game. I formed my opinion, as most kids did, by reading newspapers and magazines and collecting bubble-gum cards. The NFL league rule at the time was that only local teams' away games (my local team was the Philadelphia Eagles) could be televised. There was no national game of the week for the NFL either, so if you were going to watch a Sunday afternoon football game and your team was playing at home, the only thing available to you was the AFL game. I watched the Chargers every time they were on, and with the league presenting an early East Coast game and a late afternoon double-header game from the West Coast, the Chargers were on a lot. The only time I saw any smidgen of a Bears game this season was when the Eagles traveled to Chicago or an occasional highlight on the news.

The AFL was still relatively new and the NFL dwarfed it with media coverage and fan interest early on. The quality of play and personnel was mostly described as thin and the idea that any AFL team could compete in the NFL was thought of as ludicrous, or years away. It's funny how over those early years I never heard anyone debate whether the 1960 AFL champion Houston Oilers could have beaten the NFL champion Philadelphia Eagles, nor how the '61 and '62 AFL champion Oilers and Dallas Texans would have fared against the Vince Lombardi–led Green Bay Packers either. But bring up the 1963 football season and that is where the road separates and the debates begin. So intriguing was an AFL vs. NFL matchup that *Sports Illustrated* wrote about the fans desire for an interleague championship game and included legendary Hall of Fame quarterback Otto Graham speculating that the AFL champion San Diego Chargers could defeat their NFL counterpart Chicago Bears.

The AFL's stepsister treatment by the NFL partisan media, which seemed to slant nearly every story toward a superior NFL point of view, is now legendary. And the AFL's struggle for respectability at the time seemed so unachievable because of this bias that former AFL receiver Chris Burford described the league's effort for fair and objective treatment by the press as being like "pushing water up hill." It just wasn't going to happen, as sports writers of the day appeared to write with their minds already made up about the quality of the league before their fingers hit their keyboards. They described the new league as a bunch of rejects from other leagues and made up of over-the-hill veterans and second-rate college players. They even predicted that the league would not last beyond their second year if it even lasted that long. So how could anyone ever fathom an AFL team getting within a first down of beating an NFL champion?

After reading with nostalgic enthusiasm a very well-written book titled '63: The Story of the 1963 World Champion Chicago Bears by Gary and Maury Youmans, I felt compelled to take the debate one step further. Although the Bears were indeed an excellent team with a superior defense and a competent and steady offense, I believed that the other side of the story also needed to be told; about how good a football team the AFL Champion San Diego Chargers were in 1963. I then wanted to take an extra step by staging a computer-simulated AFL vs. NFL Championship Game using as many detailed facts, figures, and researched offensive and defensive team tendencies that could be generated to play an objective and impartial game to see just how well each team would fare against each other. In essence, a Super Bowl I three years before it became a reality.

The 1963 San Diego Chargers hold a significant place in the history of the American Football League for having the first truly explosive and league-best offense, as well as a dynamic and top-ranked defense. This Charger team, I felt, deserved to be as recognized for their greatness in professional football history as much as any other league champion. San Diego was in no way any less of a champion from any lesser league, and in every way displayed the skill, talent, speed, creativity, and championship quality that all great teams exhibit. Led by head coach Sid Gillman, who has been called "the father of the modern passing game," they were an excellent team that was capable of scoring from anywhere on the field. The San Diego Chargers were a team ahead of their time offensively, as well as being an excellent defensive team, coached by the man who, as a head coach later in his career, put together one of the most daunting defensive teams in pro-football history. He did it by incorporating the Chargers defensive philosophy and style into his Pittsburgh Steelers team that won four Super Bowls.

This book is about a team that could hold its own offensively and defensively with the best teams any pro-football league had to offer in 1963. A team that over the years would draw accolades from coaches like Don Coryell, Bill Walsh, and others who would build their successes on—and model their passing games after—the same foundations and systems created by Sid Gillman. When his defensive coordinator, Chuck Noll, brought the Charger defensive schemes to Pittsburgh, he used it to construct the daunting "Steel Curtain" defense that helped put four rings on his players' hands.

In 1963, the San Diego Chargers won 11 of their 14 regular season games and then overpowered the Boston Patriots in the AFL Championship game, 51–10. After defeating Boston on January 5, 1964, Sid Gillman awarded his players championship rings that were inscribed "San Diego Chargers—1963—World Champions." Upon presenting the rings he announced that, "if anyone has a problem with that inscription, tell them to play us and we'll prove it!"

Offers from Gillman and AFL commissioner Joe Foss to Bears coach George Halas and NFL commissioner Pete Rozelle to play such a game were politely declined.

Were the Bears the best team in pro-football? Maybe. Were the Chargers? Possibly. Could the Chargers have beaten the Bears in a head-to-head battle for the championship? Perhaps. Were the Bears an excellent football team? Absolutely, but so were the San Diego Chargers, and it is long past time for them to be recognized as one of the best teams of the sixties. While the debate may continue among football aficionados who remember the time and teams, this book offers an in-depth look at the Chargers championship season and presents an entertaining simulation of the championship game between the Bears and Chargers that was never played. It might even create more fuel for the fire that still burns in those who remember, to debate and speculate again about what might have happened had this game been played more than fifty years ago.

FOREWORD BY LANCE ALWORTH

BRING ON THE DAMN BEARS!!!

I remember it well. We had just beaten the Boston Patriots in the 1963 AFL championship game and were begging for more competition. The Other League? The Mickey Mouse League? Well, we were the proud champions of the AFL and we were hoping, no, *praying* for a chance to play the Chicago Bears, who had wrapped up the NFL title just a week before. Sid Gillman proposed a game between our squad and the NFL champions, a "World Series" of professional football, as *Sports Illustrated* had called it. Sadly, the game never materialized, and we've been left to wonder for the last fifty years, who would have won?

We'd had a rough year in 1962. It seemed like we lost a player or two to injury every game. I hurt my thigh and was only able to play in four games. Our quarterback situation was unstable. Jack Kemp got hurt and ultimately went to Buffalo. John Hadl was injured as well. We brought in a few other guys, but there was no sense of continuity, and we ended up losing 10 games that season. Sid and the coaching staff worked hard that off-season. They brought in a few veteran players and put together an excellent draft class. We knew we had talent going into 1963, and our offensive strategies were unmatched. It was just a matter of coming together and playing as a team.

I grew up in the country, so I wasn't too upset when the Chargers opened training camp in Boulevard, California, in the summer of '63. It was hotter than Hades. There was no grass, but plenty of rattlesnakes, and the only source of entertainment was a small beer joint about seven miles down the road. But whether it was in spite of our meager surroundings or because of them, our team came together like none I've seen before or since. We had ballplayers from all over the country; blacks and whites, Northerners and Southerners, guys who built snowmen on the East Coast and others who grew up surfing in the Pacific Ocean. There were Jews, Catholics, Baptists, Methodists, Presbyterians, Lutherans, and even a Serbian Orthodox (Emil Karas). But I'll tell you what: When it came to football, the 1963 San Diego Chargers ate, drank, slept, breathed, passed, caught, blocked, and tackled together as a single unit.

I've been a member of some excellent football teams. I played in the Cotton and Sugar Bowls while at Arkansas. I was part of the 1971 Dallas Cowboys team that won Super Bowl VI. Those were great teams but, for my money, the 1963 San Diego Chargers were better.

We had talent at every position. Camaraderie is very important, but when you're lacking for ballplayers, there isn't a whole lot you can do. We were fortunate. We had some of the greatest offensive players in the league, and we had Sid Gillman, the Father of Modern Offensive Football, as our head coach. Sid was exceptionally bright. I feel he would have been a success at anything he may have done, but his passion was football and his game-planning was so far ahead of anyone else in the game that it was almost unfair.

History tends to remember that Chargers team for its offense, and perhaps rightfully so. But we were nothing without our defense. Ernie Ladd, Earl Faison, Bob Petrich, George Gross, Hank Schmidt, and Fred Moore made up our defensive line. That was probably the biggest and strongest line in professional football at the time. The pressure they put on opposing quarterbacks really helped our linebackers and defensive backs in coverage.

The other thing that we had going for us was something that I've never heard mentioned by the sports media, but played a major role. The entire American Football League felt that it had to prove itself every time a team stepped on the field. If we had been given a chance to play the Bears in 1963, we would have tried to whip them not only for ourselves and for Chargers fans, but for every owner, coach, player, and fan of the American Football League.

I've been asked about the proudest moment of my football career. I was fortunate to have many proud moments, but the one that meant the most didn't actually involve me. When Joe Namath and the Jets defeated the Baltimore Colts in Super Bowl III, it was a monumental success not only for the Jets, but for the entire AFL. We certainly tried to beat each other on the field, but the camaraderie was very strong among players. We were all fighting to make sure that the AFL was a success, so each time an AFL team did something well, it was a step in the right direction for us all. Having an AFL team win a world championship meant more to us than you could imagine back then. As a matter of fact, it still does today.

Those were great times. We were young and making a living by playing the game that we loved. The Chicago Bears? They may have been the Monsters of the Midway, but every one of the 1963 Chargers would have jumped at the opportunity to show them who we were. And you know what? We would have won.

BRING ON THE DAMN BEARS!!!

THE PATRIARCH: SID GILLMAN

He had a tan that rivaled George Hamilton's, donned sunglasses that were classic Hollywood, and wore bow ties that fashioned him more dapper than Dave Garroway. He was the epitome of class and panache, a visionary and an innovator, a believer in the power of team togetherness, and at times—especially as a general manager at contact time—a tightfisted ogre, all rolled into one. He even stepped outside his comfort zone occasionally to make cameo appearances on popular television shows like *The Rifleman*, *Adventure Showcase*, and *Alcoa Theatre*.

Beyond being recognized for his creative and innovative passing game, Sid Gillman was lauded by his peers and owners for showing the AFL how to go big league. When head coaches from different generations praise him for the influence he had on them, it exemplifies the caliber of his brilliance as a coach and offensive pioneer. Hugh "Bones" Taylor, who coached the Houston Oilers in the mid-sixties, credits Gillman, whom he was an assistant under, for being a master of organization. Don Coryell, who coached the Chargers from 1978 to 1986 and established the famous "Air Coryell" passing attack that consistently led the NFL in offense, passing, and passing yardage, regularly brought his San Diego State team to watch Gillman's Chargers practice so they could see how he ran an offense and learn his passing system. Bill Walsh, Hall of Fame coach of the San Francisco 49ers teams that won three Super Bowls in the eighties with his West Coast offense, credits Gillman as being its inventor. And Al Davis, a former offensive assistant for Gillman and the Chargers, who turned the Oakland Raiders from a 1–13 team into a 10–4 in one year and whose team played in five Super Bowls, called Gillman "the father of modern-day passing" for his innovations in the downfield vertical passing attack. His influence in the evolution of the game has stretched from the field to the film room, from college coaches to the pros. His tireless work ethic, nearly obsessive attention to detail, and practice repetition became the backdrop for every organization Gillman touched. A native of Minnesota, a young Gillman spurned offers from the Golden Gophers—the best team in the country at the time—to begin his college football education at Ohio State University, where we played end in the early thirties. He earned All-American status in 1932 and honorable mention in 1933, and even played in the first annual College Football All-Star game against the NFL Champion Chicago Bears. He then (with a touch of irony) played professionally in the renegade American Football League in 1936 for the Cleveland Rams. With the league's demise, he moved back to Ohio to begin a coaching career that would continue through six decades. He worked as an assistant at Denison University before heading back to Ohio State for three years and then on to the University of Miami (Ohio), where in 1944 he was named head coach. While at Miami and calling his own shots for the first time, Gillman began to craft his innovative passing system that opened up the running game and developed a wide open combination of ground and long range aerial assaults that confounded his opponent's defenses. In three years at Miami, Gillman and his offensive system earned accolades by leading the Redskins (now the RedHawks) to a 31–6–1 record, including an undefeated season in 1947, in great part because of his creative and ground-breaking passing attack.

From Miami, Gillman continued his football education as the offensive coach at Army under legendary coach Red Blaik, helping them to an undefeated season. He returned to Ohio a year later to take over the 3–6–1 Cincinnati Bearcat program in 1949. In six seasons at Cincinnati, his teams went 50–13–1 overall and a record of 35–4–1 in his last four seasons.

By 1955, Sid was a hot commodity. Although Cincinnati was not a nationally ranked team and was considered a small independent college, Gillman's system had caught the interest of other college coaches around the country and had him lecturing about his offensive philosophy at clinics. His theories on passing were being widely imitated by other programs and his notoriety was growing in the football ranks. Gillman's belief in forcing the defense to defend the entire field—both vertically and horizontally—opened up an exciting new way of playing offense. It was Gillman who starting to alternate special units on offense and defense, which was the introduction of the platoon system. But for all the attention his passing game was receiving, Sid was anything but a "one trick pony." He invented an option running game that he called the "ride" series, where the quarterback would have as his first option, giving or faking to his fullback powering up the middle. He would then run wide to sweep the end, where he could either pitch to a trailing halfback or keep the ball himself and run. The option kept the defense guessing and pursuing, opening the field horizontally before turning up vertically. In kind, it was the first type of Wishbone offense popularized in the seventies by Texas and Oklahoma. His blocking techniques were also unconventional in that he taught each player up front not to concentrate so much on the man across from him but to instead go for the nearest man. While on Blaik's Army staff as his offensive assistant, Gillman helped develop the concept of option blocking and realized the untapped potential and versatility of the tight end, whose primary role at the time was to block. Gillman saw the value of having the tight end be more involved as an offensive weapon and began the evolution of the position as a receiving option as well as a blocker.

Fred Arbanas, All-Time AFL Team tight end, Kansas City Chiefs

When I played for him [Gillman] in AFL All-Star games that he coached, I was always amazed at his technical understanding of the passing game. In Dallas and Kansas City, we were always a run-first team and Hank Stram had a simplistic passing game. With Sid, in our All-Star game meetings, he really got into it. His passing system was a lot different from ours. He spent a lot more time on it, with different routes, alternate routes, and ways of screening off linebackers and safeties to break the other guys free on patterns. He wouldn't just show us stuff on the blackboard, though. He would tell us all the reasons why they would work at different times in the game and when to work the screenings plays. In those days, the defensive backs could knock you around all over the place until the ball was in the air. Sid's screen patterns for his receivers helped break those guys away from you, especially for me because the middle backer would drop off and give you a shot to knock you off a pattern, but the way he set up those screens broke us free. I really learned a lot about passing in those All-Star game sessions just listening to Sid and his ideas about passing. He knew more about it than anyone I had ever been associated with.

Gillman also was innovating the way coaches scouted other teams. Raised by parents who ran a movie theater, Sid learned the film industry as a child while ushering for his father. Often times he would splice the football highlights out of the weekly newsreels and take them home to study. That was a skill that proved very helpful back in the 40s and 50s, since it was the coaches who normally did all the splicing and preparing of films. They even took their own movies at practice. With his background in the family business, Gillman was already ahead of the game.

In ten years as a college head coach, the "pass master" compiled an 81–19–2 record and, before he knew it, Hollywood (in the person of Los Angeles Rams president Dan Reeves) came calling. The Los Angeles Rams had finished first in the NFL's Western Conference from 1949 through 1952,[1] winning the league championship in 1951 but losing a tie-breaking playoff game to the Detroit Lions the next year and dropping to third and then fourth place finishes the following two seasons. Reeves was now on the lookout for a new head coach after their 6–5–1 season in '54. And although noted coaching icons like Oklahoma legend Bud Wilkinson, Navy head man Eddie Erdelatz, and Georgia Tech's Bobby Dodd, as well as the 49ers Buck Shaw and the Lions Buddy Parker were all said to be in line to take over the Rams job, Reeves went for and got the guy at Cincinnati. In another touch of irony, Gillman was returning to professional football as a head coach with the same team he made his professional debut with as a player, the Rams. But now they resided in Los Angeles after moving from Cleveland. Sid was recommended for the job by Wilkenson (who was up for the same job) and endorsed by Blaik, who called Sid "the wisest choice." Even Red Sanders, coach of UCLA, stepped in to call Gillman "the absolute tops."

Gillman was well aware that coaching in the pros was going to be much different from the college ranks, and made it his first goal to win over his players, showing both honesty and humility.

---

1   Was known as the National Conference starting in 1950.

Coming straight out of college to the pros, Sid knew he did not have all the answers and readily sought the opinions and ideas from his players. By showing respect for their professional knowledge and experience, and with team leaders Norm Van Brocklin, Elroy Hirsch, and Tom Fears giving him their stamp of approval, he earned the backing of the rest of the club. In 1955, the Rams returned to the top of the Western Conference by beating out the Chicago Bears by a half game, but came up on the short side of the NFL championship game to the Cleveland Browns (losing 38–14). From there the Rams fell to the middle of the West for three seasons until hitting rock-bottom in 1959 (when they went 2–10), Sid's last year with the Rams. But it would not be his last year in Los Angeles, nor his last year walking the sidelines of the LA Coliseum as a professional head coach.

Sid always found a way of landing on his feet, and when Barron Hilton of the Hilton Hotel family bought a franchise in the new American Football League to begin play in 1960, Gillman was the natural choice to be their head coach. Now forty-eight years old, Sid brought the new Los Angeles franchise immediate credibility, experience, and class, and was one of only two coaches of the original AFL eight to have professional football head coaching experience.[2] With still another touch of irony, Sid was back in the AFL, where his professional football career began.

It was obvious from the beginning that the upstart AFL was going to be different from the established NFL, and right away improvised on some of the traditional components of the game. They would offer teams the option of kicking an extra point,

---

2   The other being Frank Filchock of the Denver Broncos, who was a
     head coach in the CFL.

which would be worth one point, or trying for two points with either a run or pass. Another change was an idea Gillman suggested to bring the league and players a separate identity by putting names across the back of their uniforms. He also knew that to win over football fans for the new league, they would have to offer something different from the knockdown running style employed by the NFL. It would be the perfect venue for him to showcase his offensive program. Sid was always an offense–first coach, and especially liked an offense that could stretch the field north and south as well as east and west. He wanted to make things happen and wanted his teams to be able to strike from anywhere on the field . . . and that is how he was going to operate his appropriately named Los Angeles Chargers. Gillman himself often said, "The big play comes with the pass. God bless those runners because they get you the first down, give you ball control, and keep your defense off the field. But if you want to ring the cash register, you have to pass."

As his first order of business, Gillman had to create a coaching staff. Of the four assistants, three went on to become professional head coaches.[3] No matter what area of football Gillman needed to put his eye on (coaches, players, or scouts), he was one that could pick winners. And once he brought his staff together, he had such confidence in those he chose that he left them do their jobs with relatively little interference.

---

3   Defensive coordinator Jack Faulkner (Denver Broncos head coach from 1962–64), receiver and backs coach Al Davis (Oakland Raiders coach from 1963–65, but known more famously as the team's Hall of Fame owner), and linebacker and defensive backs coach Chuck Noll (Pittsburgh Steelers coach from 1969–91, winning four Super Bowls with the club and being elected into the Hall of Fame in 1993).

Coaches (l to r) Joe Madro, Chuck Noll, Al Davis, and Jack Faulkner kneel in front of Sid Gillman.

Al Davis once said that, "Being part of Sid's organization was like going to a laboratory for the highly developed science of professional football."

Chuck Noll noted that, "Sid was something of a rocket scientist when it came to offensive football and the passing game. He saw things other coaches hadn't seen. And he wasn't afraid to put his ideas into action. His offensive style helped put the AFL on the map."

Chuck Allen, Chargers middle linebacker
Chuck Noll was our defensive coordinator and called the defensive signals and I called them in the huddle. Our

defense was the top defense in the AFL in '63. Noll was a real good coach and Gillman left him alone, although he was always on him if things weren't going as planned. But for the most part, Noll developed his own system. When he became head coach in Pittsburgh, he traded for me his second year and we put in the Chargers system of defense for the Steelers to use. So it worked for us and it worked for Pittsburgh, too.

Sid always wanted the smartest people on his staff, and he was confident and comfortable with whom he recruited.

Faulkner had played for him at Miami and coached under him at Cincinnati and with the Rams, and was a loyal and competent disciple. When the Broncos went looking for a head coach after the 1961 season, Gillman recommended Faulkner for the position. His association with, and knowledge of, the Gillman way helped him create a new image and sense of professionalism the franchise had been missing. The Broncos, who were 3–11 in 1961 started the new season at 6–1 and had their best record of the decade in 1962.

Davis was even more successful. After taking command of the Oakland Raiders in 1963, he took a team that had won only 3 of its last 28 games to the brink of the Western Division title in his first season. When Davis left San Diego, he took Gillman's playbook and ideas with him.

Chris Burford, split end, Kansas City Chiefs

Al Davis was a schemer, always looking for an angle to get the edge of the other team. I remember when I played in the All-Star game in '61. The conference winner always coached the team, so Davis was part of the Chargers coaching staff for the game. He was working with the receivers at practice and was going around to all the guys and asking them what their favorite pass pattern was so they could run it during the game. He'd say something like "let me see your best move," or "what do you do against certain corner backs?" We all knew he was just trying to get an edge on us and take the information back to plan against us the next year, but he didn't hide anything. We'd run "sloppy" routes on purpose to disguise what we really wanted to do. When he went to Oakland, part of the reason they beat the Chargers twice in '63 was because he knew them better than anyone. He learned a lot of football from Gillman and getting the edge on the other guy was part of being educated by him. Gillman coached his coaches as well as his team.

As the Chargers were building their first team in 1960 and right before training camp was to begin, their general manager, Frank Leahy, resigned due to health reasons. With all the decisions that had to be made, it was not in Hilton's best interest to suddenly go out searching for a new GM, especially since Sid Gillman was right under his nose and interested in the position. He happily began his dual role and was now in charge of organizational decisions both on and off the field.

After establishing his staff and settling into his dual role before their inaugural training camp, the challenge that faced Gillman—and all the other teams in the new league—was to build a team from scratch. Every team experienced growing pains the first few years, but by 1963, Sid had put together an impressive arsenal of offensive talent to utilize in stretching the field he so passionately espoused. He was able to put in five-man passing routes to stretch the defense and attack zone coverages from all angles, both running and passing. His wide receivers, Lance Alworth, Don Norton, and Jerry Robinson, were the fastest group in the league. His tight ends, Dave Kocourek and Jacque MacKinnon, were not as much foot-speed fast as they were quick to the step and had great hands to go along with their large size needed to block linebackers. His backfield was exceptionally fast, with Paul Lowe leading the way. Running mate Keith Lincoln, by his own account a "garbage man," was described more accurately by Gillman as "the most versatile back in the AFL." He was able to skirt the ends, blast up the middle, block, catch both long and short passes, and even throw a few. His role players, Bob Jackson and Gerry McDougall,

complemented the two starters with tenacious and steady blocking, running, and sure hands. Now with the veteran Tobin Rote as his alter ego on the field, Gillman was ready to distance his team from the rest of the league.

John Hadl, Chargers quarterback

Sid was real smart, particularly in the passing game. He worked on it all the time, fifteen hours a day. We were doing the West Coast Offense before it had a name. Bill Walsh, who is given credit for it, will tell you that he learned it from Gillman. He taught me how to work and have a work ethic. I came from a college that rarely passed the ball, but he taught me so much about that part of the game. We worked on pre-snap reads and how to look at the defensive player's eyes for cues. Sid taught us that if a defender was looking at a back, he was most likely going to be in man-to-man coverage, and if he was looking at the quarterback, it was zone coverage. He taught us to how to work on coverages and pick up what the defense was going to do and make adjustments. We had adjustment routes based on what coverages they were in; different patterns for different coverages. We worked on being on the same page with one another all the time. If Alworth went to the line and saw a certain formation or a player in a certain spot, we'd look at each other and knew we both saw the same thing and make an adjustment to the play at the line. He also taught us to design our play calls on particular downs and their distance tendencies that Sid would prepare for from all the film he studied. He had a high percentage of correctness, too.

He had our receivers screening, like setting picks in basketball for each other to get space between the defender and our primary receiver or throw flairs to spots they vacated when they followed another guy over the middle. We'd send two backs out in a five-man route with each going in different directions. He even had Lincoln and Lowe run flairs in different directions to get isolated on a linebacker they could outrun.

We practiced so much repetition and watched so much film that I can still remember the plays we called. I played for the Rams, Packers, and Oilers after the Chargers and can't remember any of their plays. But the ones we ran in Sid's scheme were so drilled-in through repetition that I can still call them in my sleep.

He really taught me how to study and develop a game plan. The way he was, always so precise in his passing game, was so far ahead of his time. He kept notebooks of pass route descriptions, drawings of each pattern and what everyone else was doing. He was really a master at understanding the game and he wanted his quarterbacks to know it all.

Billy Joe, Denver Broncos fullback and 1963 AFL Rookie of the Year

I played against Sid's teams starting in 1963 as a rookie and he had a great sophisticated passing attack. His receivers just did things in precision. After I retired, I coached at Cheyney State College in Pennsylvania for a few years and then joined the Philadelphia Eagles coaching staff during their run to the Super Bowl. Sid was the passing consultant for Dick Vermeil and he'd come and talk to us about his theories of the passing game. He was still selling the same passing principles in the late seventies and early eighties that he'd developed in the early sixties with the Chargers and they still proved to be the best and

STUB SERIES

THE STUB SERIES IS A STRONGSIDE F3 PASSING SERIES FIRST AND SECOND
A SERIES THAT ALLOWS US TO LINE THE FB UP OUT OF THE BACKFIELD AND
RELEASE WITHOUT CONCERN FOR S.F.U. IT IS CALLED STUB TO ALERT THE
UNCOVERED LINEMAN TO DOUBLE PICK UP MAC TO STUB WHILE THE HB S.P.U
ON BUCK. THE QB READS B.L.S. TO SAM AND THE STRONG BUZZ SYSTEM.
BASIC THOUGHT IS "I'M PLAYING CATCH WITH THE FB"! HIS DROP IS 7 O:
7 & 2, BUT HE HAS TO BE PREPARED TO SET AT ANY TIME, DEPENDENT UPO:
WHEN THE FB COMES OPEN.

ALL RECEIVER ROUTES MAINTAIN THEIR ORIGINALLY ASSIGNED BREAKING
POINTS. THE SIGHT ADJUSTMENT PRINCIPLE IS ON AND Y CAN BE ASSIGNE:
A HOT READ ON MAC IF HE DOGS. WE CAN NOT PICK UP A SMACK DOG -
BOTH MAC & STUB DOGGING!

STUB CAN BE COMBINED WITH OTHER SERIES CALLS. EXAMPLE: STUB- FIRM
BACKS HOOK
THE BASIC PRINCIPLE OF WORKING TO THE FB IS:

    1. FB BREAKING OUT = X ON A 5 - Y ON A 40 - Z ON A 9
       (549)
    2. FB BREAKING IN = X ON A 5 - Y ON A 90 = Z ON A 5
       (595)

STUB PATTERNS CAN BE USED IN PLACE OF A NORTH PATTERN IF WE DON'T
WANT THE FB TO HAVE TO S.P.U.!
STUB PATTERNS:

1. STUB - 549 OPTION - OUT - HOOK - FIN - FLY - FLAG

2. STUB - 595 - ANGLE - IN - CHOICE - POLE

3. STUB - 444 BACKS FAN

4. STUB - 545 BACKS HOOK

5. STUB - 866 FAN/UNDER

6. STUB - 639 UNDER/LOOP OR FLAT

7. STUB - 272 FLAG/POLE

Sample of one of Gillman's passing schemes.

THE UNCROWNED CHAMPS

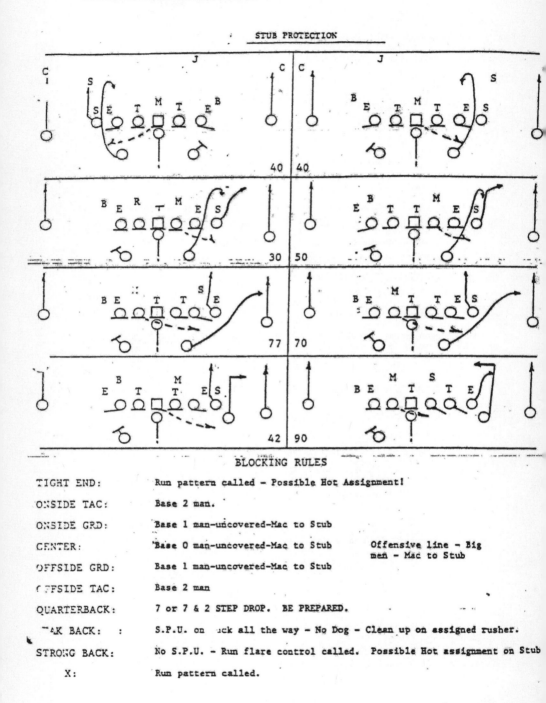

STUB PROTECTION

BLOCKING RULES

TIGHT END:	Run pattern called - Possible Hot Assignment!
ONSIDE TAC:	Base 2 man.
ONSIDE GRD:	Base 1 man-uncovered-Mac to Stub
CENTER:	Base 0 man-uncovered-Mac to Stub Offensive line - Big men - Mac to Stub
OFFSIDE GRD:	Base 1 man-uncovered-Mac to Stub
OFFSIDE TAC:	Base 2 man
QUARTERBACK:	7 or 7 & 2 STEP DROP. BE PREPARED.
WEAK BACK:	S.P.U. on uck all the way - No Dog - Clean up on assigned rusher.
STRONG BACK:	No S.P.U. - Run flare control called. Possible Hot assignment on Stub
X:	Run pattern called.

16

X and Z SHORT ROUTES

QUICK and DRIVE

1) Sprint up the field 4 yards. Set down and take fake of the QB. Drive at 45° Angle to inside.

2) QB foot 1-2 - Pump and reload. Lay the ball in the air.

3) This is a companion to the Quick.

QUICK OUT and DRIVE

1) Run a quick out - 4 yards. Take 2 strides to the outside. Plant on outside foot and drive to the inside at 45° angle.

2) QB footwork 1-2. Pump the ball on Quick Out. Reload and lay it in the air on start of drive.

3) This is a companion to the Quick Out.

DOUBLE QUICK

1) Run a 4 yard Quick. Set down and take the fake of the QB. Pivot to the outside, drive up the field 4 yards and set down.

2) QB footwork 1-2. Pump at Quick route, reload and drill the ball at end of 2nd Quick.

3) This is a companion to the Quick.

WRINKLE IN

1) Drive up the 4 yard or half the distance if Tight Coverage. Break parallel to the inside. Make hitch move as though you were going to pivot to the outside.

2) This is a companion to the Pivot Out.

3) QB footwork is 1-2. Pump at Hitch Move. Reload and semi drill the ball.

SLANT CORNER

1) This is an abbreviated corner. Drive up the field ½ the distance of the coverage. Take corner man well to the inside - get him going, then break sharply to the corner. Break off flat if the coverage is Tight.

2) QB footwork is 1-2. Pump on In Move. Lay the ball in the air on corner.

3) This Route is a companion to Slant.

GLANCE

1) Good 20 yard line route. Need inside room. Route is run like Slant. UP move is 8 yards. Put on shake or head and shoulder fake as you break to the inside.

2) QB footwork 3 or 3-2 and lay the ball in the air on the break.

3) This is a Short Post Route.

Series & Protection: __STUB__   Pattern: __549 (ABLE 75)__ Flare: __HOOK__ / __OPTION__

Cov. 6 | Cov. 6

Quarterback

P.S.L. __SAFETIES-JACK__   Read: __B.L.S. to SAM to BUZZ SYS. STG__ Drop: __7 & 2__

Pattern Progression Wk.: __HB to X__   Progression Stg: __FB to Y to HB to X__

Blitz/Dog Principle: REC's S.A. SAFETY BLITZES: HOT CALL = FB HOT VS. STUB DOG
                                                           Y HOT BY G.P. ON MAC DOG!
Rec. Adjs. Vs. Cleo = X/Q: __BURST__   Y/Slot: __NONE__   Z: __FADE__   HB: __NONE__

FB: __STOP__   Adj. Vs. Cov. 2 & 8 = Y/Slot: __R & B__

Rec. Adjs. Vs. Coverage: B & G COVER 3 & 5!

Formation Variations: 1. GREEN/GREEN SLOT   2. ACE STRONG
3. BLUE   4. SLOT/TWIN SPLIT   5. ACE SLOT STRONG!
6. "D" FORMATIONS   7.   8.

Series Variations: 1. __STUB HOT__   2. __NORTH HOT__   3. __SOUTH HOT__

Rec Variations: X/Q: __- /   /__   Y/S: __19 /   /__   Z: __- /   /__

FB Flare Variations: __OUT/HOOK/FIN/FLAG__

Use of Movement: ZOOM/ZIN/ZOT/TIM/TOM

QB Coaching Points FOR STUB WITH FB BREAKING OUTSIDE!

1. Stride for 7 steps and settle in 2 steps! (Drop Option)
2. Sam is used as a coverage indicator for strong or weak coverage!
3. Strong coverage read Sam to strongside buzz system!
4. Concentrate on getting the ball to the SB! Know who can take it away & read 'em!
5. FB covered, think Y to weakside combination! Alert for Cov. 3 or 5!
6. Stub 1 on 1 man on SB, SB will beat on an 8 yd. out!
7. Stub buzzes wide area, SB will Stop at 8 yds.! Alert Sam buster! Cleo, SB will Stop!!
8. Hot call, SB will be hot vs. a Stub dog! You are not picked up vs. a Smack dog!
9. FIN CALL: Change Y to a 19 Combo! FB will release inside Y & hit the crease with Fin!
10. Read the same, but be very alert to study stg. corner coverage on Z 9! Can fall off!
11. Basic rule for SB breaking outside, put Y or Slot & Z on a 49 Combo!
12. You may have to shorten your 7 & 2 drop if the SB comes open earlier!
13. Be alert for multiple LB'er defenses and forms of nickel!
14. 90 front. Read the same with more awareness of how Sam plays!

most sound ideas about how to throw the football. It just shows his genius in the passing game and how far ahead of the pack he was back in the early sixties.

Sid loved timing patterns. He basically invented them and had his quarterback drops timed with his receiver's routes. He had his quarterbacks throw based on steps and distance, throwing the pass to an area where the receiver was supposed to be. If the first option wasn't open, the secondary receiver was cutting to his spot a step later, that way both pass catchers would be cutting into the pass before the defender could react.

According to former NFL quarterback and football analyst Ron Jaworski, Gillman more than any other coach understood the geometry of the game and designed his passing routes to be different. Jaws said that every passing concept today stems from Gillman's understanding of timing, rhythm, and anticipation. Sid was totally immersed in the concept and was so intent on getting it right that he even kept a math professor on call to make sure his passing angles were right and made sense. He paid more attention to detail than anyone else in the game.

But sometimes, as they say, "the devil is in the details." At times, those details included dollar signs. As great a coach as Gillman was, his role as the GM often became a wedge between him and his players.

John Hadl

I had a great relationship with him [Gillman]. Heck, we spent so much time together at practice and after practice going over things and watching hours of film together, but contracts were tough with him. One year he sent me a contract that included a note that read, "Sign this contract and take this money or don't come back." I called him up and asked him if he wrote the note and he said he did. So I told him "Fine, I'm not coming back!" A few seconds later he said, "Okay, come in and we'll talk." I think sometimes he was just trying to save Hilton some money or thought he'd get a bonus if he came in under budget with salaries.

Dick Westmoreland, Chargers cornerback

I had a good year in '63 and he knew everyone had a lot of confidence in me, but he was tough to deal with on contracts. We had no attorneys or agents back then. My first contact negotiation was at the start of my second year. He sent it in the mail. I wanted a raise of a couple thousand dollars and remembered how he used to rave about me during the season. I was a walk-on starter as a rookie and second in the rookie-of-the-year voting. When I went in to meet with him, he said "well, you know you had a piss-poor year last year, don't you." I was so mad I couldn't talk to him. I turned around and just left his office. I think he wanted to rattle me. So two weeks went by and I was still mad at him and he knew it because I was having some bad practices. He finally came over after practice one day and told me to come back to his office after practice and sign for what I wanted. "We gotta have you at your best," he told me. I was young and naive, and just wanted to deal with people up front and honestly, no games. I didn't like that part of dealing with him.

Dick Harris, Chargers cornerback

Sid was a great family guy and big on togetherness. In '63, that time we spent at our summer training camp in the middle of the desert at Rough Acres Ranch in Boulevard, California, really built the foundation for our success that season. There was no offense or defense, black or white, just the team. But he was also a no-nonsense guy. I was always being fined for stupid stuff like coming into meetings late, stuff like that and always losing money. But dealing with him at contract time was the worst. I made all-league one year and he offered me something like a $50 raise. I think in the long run it hurt the team with Sid coaching and negotiating because a lot of guys carried it over onto the field. I think Sid did a little bit, too. It created some bitterness over time.

Lance Alworth, Chargers Hall of Fame flanker

I was negotiating a contract with Gillman and wanted a raise to about $30,000 a year. Gillman would not budge and we weren't talking. Then one day I got a call from Al Davis of the Raiders and he told me to go see Gillman and to take my play book with me because he just traded me for wide receiver Art Powell. Apparently, Gillman called Davis, whom he respected for his opinion, to see what Davis thought about my raise request. Davis told Gillman that if he didn't want to pay me that he'd take me off his hands. Once he knew how Davis felt, he changed his mind. When I went to see Gillman he asked me what I wanted for a contract and just said "okay," and that was it. He just wanted to see how Davis would react and once he knew Davis wanted me Gillman gave me what I wanted.

Another time I hurt my wrist and it had to be fused together and put in a cast when it was broken in an exhibition game. We couldn't wear casts in games back then, so if I played it would have to come off. Gillman told me he needed me to play so I would take the pressure off Lincoln and Lowe, but told me that I shouldn't hit anyone or block anyone. Basically, I was to be just a decoy to open up the rest of the offense and make the defense concentrate on me because they didn't know I was hurt. So I had to take the cast off because he wanted me out there but he didn't want to take the chance that I'd hurt the wrist any more. Well, I had a great game, but later on when the team was watching the film Gillman said to the team, "I want you all to look at this film." It was of me jumping out of the way and not blocking anyone, just like he told me to do. The son-of-gun spliced the film up to embarrass me. I was so mad I walked out of the room and Hadl and Gillman came running after me. Gillman said he didn't mean anything by it and it was just for a joke. He did it just so he wouldn't have to pay me.

Ernie Ladd, who had as good a relationship with Sid as anybody in the early years, also felt that Sid's role as GM affected some of his on-field decisions. He negotiated hard and the players resented that. It almost seemed contradictory to his team togetherness philosophy. Ladd always felt that Gillman should have just been the coach. That's where his real gift was: analyzing, creating, planning, and teaching. In an interview with *Sport* magazine, Ladd told Bill Libby that he loved San Diego and his teammates and coach Gillman and thought he was the premier coach in football. But he didn't like his general manager Sid Gillman because he was too tough a businessman. Years later, many of the players felt that his cross-over role as GM caused him to make some personnel decisions that led to the Chargers losing players. But then there was his genial side, which usually surfaced through it all. Ladd also knew how to yank Gillman's chain and would call Sid at peculiar times and complain about trivial things just to get him going—things like not liking the team meals or his room situation in a hotel. He would threaten Gillman that if his complaints weren't fixed right away, he would not show up to play or practice. Gillman usually came through for his star defensive player, who could be moody to a fault. Gillman would usually give in rather than fight with him.

Sid Gillman was the epitome of class and panache, a visionary and an innovator, a believer in the power of team togetherness, an actor and, at times—especially as a general manager at contact time—a tightfisted ogre all rolled into one. But he was a masterful one.

The American Football League operated successfully from 1960 to 1969, and Gillman is one of only two men to coach the same team all ten years.[4] His teams appeared in five of the first six AFL championship games, and were strong challengers in two of the last four years. In 1963, Gillman's San Diego Chargers were the AFL Champions.

---

4   The other being Hank Stram, who coached the Texans/Chiefs.

THE UNCROWNED CHAMPS

2

CHARGERS HISTORY, 1960–1962

Beginning as the Los Angeles Chargers—the sixth team admitted to the upstart American Football League in 1960—the now San Diego Chargers quickly established themselves as the elite team in the Western Division and one of the top two in the AFL.

Gillman was hired to lead the team on the field as its first head coach in January of 1960 after successes at the college and professional levels while leading Miami of Ohio, Cincinnati, and the Los Angeles Rams. Working closely with General Manager Frank Leahy, the legendary Notre Dame player and coach, they assembled a squad by holding open tryouts for every bartender, school teacher, and electrician who answered the call, some 300 aspiring candidates including those drafted out of college.

Things changed shortly before the LA franchise opened their doors for its first training camp. Hired on October 14, 1959, Leahy laid the foundation for the organization with Gillman throughout the winter months. Then on July 1, 1960, Leahy was forced to relinquish his position due to health problems. With their camp starting in only a few days, owner Barron Hilton filled his GM void by designating Gillman for the dual role of coach and GM on July 9.

Gillman's opening day squad started slowly as the AFL began play and won only two of their first five games. Over their last nine games they hit their stride and ran off four-straight wins twice, surrounding only one other setback. Their 10–4 record placed them at the top of the Western Division and an invitation to play in the first AFL championship game against the Houston Oilers. In that game, the Chargers trailed 10–9 at half time and 17–16 at the end of the third quarter. After falling behind in the fourth by eight points, they put on a last-ditch effort to tie the game by mounting one last drive in the closing minutes, but ran out of gas and downs in Houston territory to end their first season with a 24–16 loss.

When the AFL's first season ended, Hilton's Chargers had averaged less than 16,000 fans for their seven home games and filled less than 10 percent of the Los Angeles Coliseum's seats for their final regular season home game. The season left nearly 90,000 seats empty and the franchise's bank account nearly one million dollars lighter. Not only were the Chargers outdrawn at the Coliseum nearly 6 to 1 by the NFL's Rams, as well as the USC and UCLA football teams, they also drew smaller average crowds than their baseball counterpart Los Angeles Dodgers, who opened the Coliseum gates seventy-eight times.

Hilton naturally began looking for a way to reduce his monetary losses and also bring in more paying customers (he passed out nearly 4,000 complimentary tickets for each game) when civic leaders from San Diego began courting him. On February 10,

1961, the Chargers were given permission by the league to move 100 miles down the coast to the "City in Motion."

Making their new home in ancient Balboa Stadium, the new San Diego Chargers became one of the strongest teams in AFL history by winning their first 11 games and again winning the West with a 12–2 record. As the favored team in the second AFL championship game and playing in their home stadium, the Chargers came up short to the Oilers for the second straight year, this time 10–3. They were one point closer, but still without a title. On January 7, the Chargers and Balboa Stadium hosted the first AFL All-Star game.

With hopes of finally jumping the hurdle to the top of the league the 1962, it seemed like the football gods were sending the Chargers a pre-emptive message of doom. In February, news came out that linebacker Bob Laraba was killed in a car accident. As the weeks moved forward and the regular season neared, the number of team injuries was becoming a cause of great concern. The first to be lost was leading rusher Paul Lowe, who broke his arm on his first run from scrimmage in the team's first exhibition game. He was lost for the season.

The next big loss occurred when quarterback Jack Kemp ruptured a finger on his throwing hand in the second game of the season and was placed on the injury list. Adding insult to his injury, a clerical error in not listing Kemp on the weekly injured reserve list correctly caused Kemp to become available to any team immediately for the bargain price of $100. The Buffalo Bills, who had trouble keeping pace offensively with the rest of the league—due mostly to inept quarterbacking—jumped at the opportunity and without warning claimed the Chargers team leader. Still, the Chargers were only one game behind Denver, the leader in the West, five games into the season, but the injuries continued to mount.

Rookie sensation Lance Alworth caught 10 passes in his first four games but then missed the rest of the season with a leg injury. Center Wayne Frazier also missed half the season due to an injury. Guard Pat Shea played only five games. Defensive end Earl Faison, the 1961 Rookie of the Year and one of the more ferocious members of the front line, missed six games. Cornerback Charlie McNeil, the team's leading pass interceptor, missed ten and Ernie Ladd played hurt all season with nagging injuries including a separated shoulder. Middle linebacker Chuck Allen also saw time on the injured list. In all there were twenty-three Chargers from the thirty-three-man roster who missed at least two games, including the seven starters who missed more than half the season. As the injuries mounted, so did the losses—10 in all—which buried the team in third place ahead of only the 1–13 Raiders. For Sid Gillman and his two-time Western Division champions, 1963 was in need of some revisions to their usually successful script to get back on track.

The Chargers immediately began making plans to rectify their injury-plagued team by looking to make some roster changes. One of their first moves was a look up north to the Canadian Football League, where Gillman hired the services of Toronto Argonauts fullback Gerry McDougall for the last month of the '62 season. Then, using the connections McDougall had with his old team, he contacted his teammate and leading CFL passer Tobin Rote, who was contemplating retirement. When the possibility of signing the veteran quarterback who led the NFL's Detroit Lions to the 1957 championship became a real possibility, Gillman put in a claim with the league office to pursue acquiring him. Rote, however, was considered to be territorial property of the closest AFL team to Toronto, which was the Buffalo Bills. Since the Bills no longer needed the services of an experienced quarterback after poaching Kemp from the Chargers, the Bills agreed to trade his rights to whoever pursued him. As the league put out word of the agreement and essentially created an open market for Rote, Jack Faulkner and the Denver Broncos also put in a claim for the quarterback.

Having two claims on the free agent now created a dilemma for Commissioner Joe Foss. Should he let each team wage a bidding war for the thirty-five-year-old quarterback, or could there be another resolution that he could engineer to solve the dilemma? Through the suggestion from Bills owner Ralph Wilson, Foss, Gillman, and Faulkner agreed to meet in the San Diego Hilton Hotel in February to determine who would claim the veteran passer by virtue of a simple coin flip. Although no one can remember who made the call, the nickel tossed by Foss turned up in the Chargers favor, and Tobin Rote became the official property of the San Diego Chargers, immediately making them the division favorite for 1963.

Other changes were also in store. In 1961, the Chargers were the top overall defensive team (first in passing defense and second in rushing defense), but had slipped in 1962 to the second worst in team defense (fourth against the pass and sixth of eight in rushing defense). Offensively in 1962 they were ranked fifth in total offense, sixth in passing offense, and fifth in rushing offense after finishing 1961 as the third best offensive team with the second best in passing offense. Offensively Gillman talked guard Sam DeLuca back for the '63 season after a year in retirement and teaching high school. Back too would be offensive stalwarts

Paul Lowe and Lance Alworth. The addition of Rote to take over as the offensive leader gave Gillman the experience he missed with the injury and loss of Kemp, even though rookie John Hadl, who lacked the leadership and passing skill-set needed to lead a pro offense, had played valiantly in Kemp's absence. The elder Rote would also be responsible for mentoring Hadl and grooming him to step in when he moved on. At thirty-five, Rote was not expected to be a long-term investment. But for this year, the expectation was to have him lead the Chargers to playing in a championship game.

The changes on defense would be more subtle with the signing of college stars Walt Sweeney, Bob Petrich, George Gross, and Dick Westmoreland to push the veterans who were unable to make it through 1962 at full fitness. All but Sweeney would be starters by September.

One other change that needed to be made was one that Gillman would rather not have had to address. For the second year in a row, one of his top assistants would be taking over as a head coach of a division rival. Last year defensive coordinator Jack Faulkner took over the Broncos and led them to their best season. Now Al Davis was moving to Oakland for the same position. Faulkner's loss was compensated for with the promotion of Chuck Noll, but this time Gillman went outside the organization and hired Hugh "Bones" Taylor, a former Washington Redskins All-Star to assume the role vacated by Davis.

. . . and then came Rough Acres Ranch.

3

ROUGH ACRES RANCH

Injuries saw seven starters miss half the season and a total of twenty-three different players miss at least two games, leading the 1962 Chargers to a 4–10 record. That was cause enough for Sid Gillman to reevaluate his methods for getting his players ready and keeping them healthy for the regular season's 16-week grind.

Until now, the Chargers had been training at the University of San Diego and its cool and elevated campus. The location was hospitable to the players who were able to drive to and from the training ground daily as well as visit the beach or even Tijuana, Mexico, which was a short half-hour drive away to explore the nightlife after practice. It was precisely because of those comfortable accommodations which made Gillman decided that perhaps they created too soft an environment and may have influenced a good number of those injuries the previous year.

Gillman not only sought to toughen up his team and make them stronger, but he also felt that because of all the injuries, the team had no degree of unity. For those reasons he decided to move the preseason training camp to a location 66 miles east of San Diego, down highway 80 in Boulevard, California (a town with a population of fifty), known as Rough Acres Ranch. The location was so remote that the last five miles leading up to the site were on a simple dirt road. The ranch had just been purchased by a physician, who hoped to turn it into a dude ranch after it had been abandoned for a number of years. As expected, the compound needed a lot of TLC, but for the next seven weeks it would be called home—as well as several other names—for the Chargers.

The veterans were to report on July 17, with the first official practice scheduled for the following day. Many players who lived in the area all-year-round carpooled in station wagons packed as if they were going on a family vacation. Shorts and T-shirts would be the formal wear for camp, so plenty were packed, along with the rest of training camp essentials like toiletries, shower shoes, a few summer shirts for evening adventures, and some light reading material. (Sid Gillman would provide the heavier stuff that the Chargers would meet nightly to discuss and memorize.)

Dick Harris

I remember there was just nothing there. The property was in need of a lot of work and it was pretty much abandoned when we got there. I have no idea how Gillman found it but I'm sure he thought it would do us good to get out of the city and isolate us to concentrate on just football. Well, I think he accomplished that because after practices there was nothing to do but talk to each other and play cards or something with your teammates. But the place was unbelievable and something I'll never forget.

What greeted them at the Rough Acres Ranch in the middle of the desert was sunshine, enough to reap 100 degrees of intense heat and humidity on the two-a-day practice sessions, rocky hills and mountains, and plenty of dust and tumbleweeds. The cabins that were called ponderosas were set up in a horseshoe and looked out at the main dining hall across the camp, which was the hub of the ranch. The ponderosas were made of stone and shaped like diamonds (yes, in the Rough), with two bedrooms and a small sitting room. It was Gillman's plan to totally integrate his team by making room assignments by position no matter what the age, race, or experience of the players. Most of the cabins had windows but few worked, and there were no screens or air-conditioning to deter the insects and bats that were so plentiful that it seemed as if they had taken up residence long before the Chargers arrived.

Earl Faison, Chargers defensive end
All we could do was concentrate on football. The showers were outdoors and they had no roof on them. And there was rarely anything but cold water. The cabin rooms—some had windows that didn't open and some didn't close at all. There were no screens on the windows so bugs and what-not were always flying around. One morning I woke up to a cow mooing, and when I opened my eyes there was a giant head of a cow looking in my room window.

Chuck Allen
Every room had bugs in them and they were so hot out there in the desert. Nobody had fans or anything. I remember opening the medicine cabinet with bugs in

Ponderosas at Rough Acres Ranch.

them and occasional bats flying around the room. Sam DeLuca once reached for his toothpaste and was bitten by a spider.

Gillman had many reasons for moving the preseason camp away from the University of San Diego. He felt that getting them into top shape that would last through the twenty-two-week season (which included five exhibition games) and back to their title contending form was his first priority. And to that end he was unrelenting. He also wanted his players to be more cohesive; to develop a feeling of esprit de corps that knew no borders.

Hank Schmidt, Chargers defensive lineman

I remember being together in the Marines. You sat around and talked to each other a lot. You got to know the people who were in your unit really well. I thought that going to Rough Acres and becoming so tight with our teammates was great. Sid wanted to get us away because of the horrible year we had in '62. He wanted a unified, synchronized team and I think he accomplished that. But we sure were happy when those seven weeks were over.

The practice field had very little grass, causing the Chargers team managers to attempt to soften the player's falls by spreading sawdust around the training grounds daily. Often the hot desert winds at night would relocate the sawdust everywhere in camp but the field. But the show continue to go on day-after-day with much the same results; a dirt field with little cushioning and a lot of dust.

Bob Petrich, Chargers defensive end
It wasn't what I expected but . . . well . . . this is what it is. I was just a rookie trying to make the team so I didn't pay much attention to the conditions. Being from West Texas where it was just as hot, it really didn't bother me. Like I said, I was there to make the team and that was enough. I did notice that the grass was really thin and needed a lot of care, which it was not going to get. We played on wood shavings some days and our cleats barely went in.

At most meals they spent half the time swatting insects away from their food. Many times they would go to the dining hall for dinner which wasn't yet ready, so they'd have to sit around and fraternize. Some wondered if that was another scheme dreamt up by Gillman to bring the team closer together. At any rate, what-

(l to r) Bud Whitehead, George Blair, and Chuck Allen having breakfast at Rough Acres.

ever the reason for the delay, it worked. Upon finishing dinner they would hang out with each other and play pool, ping-pong, or cards, and when they went back to their rooms and turned on the lights, many times they would be greeted by bats flying around or even tarantulas crawling around the floor.

Chuck Allen

One night I walked back to my cabin and I saw DeLuca throwing rocks at the roof. He said he was going to get the bats out before he went in.

They would all joke that just being able to make it through the night would make them tougher.

Lance Alworth
It was so dark and had so many critters roaming around that some players would not go back to their cabins at night unless they were in pairs and with a flashlight.

But the coaches loved it out there. They had a captive audience and its undivided attention. With the distractions eliminated there were only three things to do: play football, study football, and have meetings about football. The result was a closely knit team of brothers that became strong both physically and mentally because of the nearly two months they spent together in the middle of nowhere.

Another unexpected benefit that helped Sid's boys play together was the fact that after practice there was nowhere to go except to a small gas station about three miles down the road, where they had a soda machine and beer. Often times the players would pile into someone's car for the short road trip where they could relax away from the compound.

Bob Petrich
Tobin Rote gained a lot of respect and influence right away because as the old veteran of the team he used to drive us down there and teach us drinking games. He said that if we didn't drink together we wouldn't make the team. We all made sure we made the team.

For those who chose to hang around back at the ranch, they soon found out that going back to their rooms for a "nooner" between practices usually ended up boiling them in their own sweat. The rooms were so hot in the middle of the day that many took showers after a short nap to feel refreshed.

Dick Westmoreland

I was a rookie so I didn't know any better. I thought that was how all teams practiced in preseason. That was my first look at California after growing up in Charlotte and going to college in Greensboro, North Carolina. I had no idea what California was supposed to look like so I thought, 'Okay, this is it. Let's start practicing.' And that is what we did because there was nothing else to do. We'd practice, eat, hang-out, and sleep. Then we'd wake up and do it again.

At their first practice, Gillman informed the team that they would have two-a-day practice sessions as well as an added weight training session. Leaving no stone unturned this season, Gillman employed a strength coach to work with the team on building more muscle mass. A few other teams in pro-football were also starting similar programs, but it was believed that the Chargers were the only AFL team to incorporate weight lifting into their workouts with a designated coach.

Overseeing the training was former USA Olympic strength coach Alvin Roy, who was considered one of the more outstanding men in the relatively new field. Roy was also a big believer in supplements—mostly vitamins—but there was also a different pill that Roy was encouraging the players to take. It was pink in color and was said to be a magic pill that would help the players get stronger faster and gain more bulk weight

without sacrificing any speed or agility. Many players balked at the pink pill that they were supposed to take three times a day. Some took only a few and some followed the orders they were given. Gillman even levied fines if the players were caught not taking the supplements.

Dick Harris

Alvin Roy came in with a reputation for making athletes bigger, stronger, and faster. He worked down at LSU for Paul Deitzel and with Billy Cannon the Heisman

Alvin Roy in his USA Olympic sweater at the training camp weight lifting station.

Trophy winner and I think even other LSU players who were in the NFL. I decided I was not going to take the stuff and made the mistake of announcing it at my dinner table one night. I think either Roy or Gillman heard it and I soon found myself in front of Gillman, who was telling me I would be fined if I didn't follow the program. Well, after the first exhibition game Sid told me I was not going to be paid for the game (I think we got about $60 for the exhibition games) because I was not taking my pills. I had never lifted weights in my life and certainly didn't want to take those damn pills, especially those pink ones that became the talk of the camp. I'll never understand why we had to lift weights before we scrimmaged. In my mind, we were breaking down our muscles right before they wanted us to use them. That seemed crazy to me.

Len Dawson, quarterback, Kansas City Chiefs

I remember when Alvin Roy came to Kansas City to talk with Hank Stram about his strength-training program. He sold barbells and other weight-lifting sets. No one had them in the early sixties and he talked to Hank about the advantages of lifting. Well, if there was a way to get an advantage on someone, Hank was interested. Then Roy walked over and sized Stram up and said, "Coach, if I'd have had you in my training program when you were younger you would have been a champion weight lifter." Stram was beaming, and Roy sold him a full set of weights right then for the Chiefs. Alvin Roy was quite a salesman.

The pink pill that was creating all the doubt was Dianabol, an anabolic steroid that Roy became familiar with while traveling with the US Olympic team in Russia. The Russian weight lifters used them and Roy started using the program in the States with success. It hadn't been around too long and was a legal supplement that wasn't banned anywhere. No one really knew about the side effects at the time but they did like what the results were showing. Still, many players eyed the pill with apprehension and resistance.

Dick Harris

Each dining table had a plate of pills on it. They didn't tell us what each one was, but he [Roy] would come around with them without telling us much about what it was other than it would help assimilate protein, help us recover, and make us stronger.

Dinner time at Rough Acres. Note the bowl with "Vitamins" on the table in the foreground.

Chuck Allen

Most of us threw the pills under the table or out the window. Few of us kept one in our mouth.

Bob Petrich

Nobody even bothered with it too much. They told us it was to gain weight and to take three a day. There was nothing that people thought about. They told you what to do so I thought they knew what was best. We just didn't know enough. Some of the players were just putting it in their mouth and then tossing it when they left the hall.

Using steroids to supplement training in the sixties was still relatively new, unstudied, and not very common. And with the players already hearing about Roy and his program's success in the college football ranks and other sports, it wasn't something that was being hidden anywhere either. There was very little if any understanding of it in the private sector and almost no information around for someone to educate themselves about it. So it was all done out in the open and unshrouded, but it was not without its doubters. Then, prior to the start of the season, several players raised concerns and objections about the pills and they stopped being mandatory. Many researchers doubted that taking the pills could have affected the player's performances beyond Rough Acres for the short amount of time they were available.

Dick Westmoreland

In those days when they told you to do something, you did it. I was a rookie and I worked my whole life with the goal of being a professional football player. I was raised to do what I was told to do. If they told me to get a haircut, I went and got a haircut. It was just blind respect and, as a rookie, that's all I could do because I wasn't going to let anything get in my way of making the team.

After a while I could tell the difference when we lifted weights and I saw that I got bigger and stronger but didn't lose speed. My neck was getting bigger and everything. It wasn't illegal then and no one knew it would be; it was just a supplement to the weights. We were the first to do that. All teams at that time were giving players bennies and we didn't know it. They just said I'd play better. As a corner back I was going to be out there alone and I had to be able to react. That was my game and you needed to be ready to play the next day.

Dick Harris

We'd go around to these different stations as groups and lift. Each station worked different muscles. Hell, nobody back then was doing any weight lifting or off-season training because we all had to get full-time jobs.

Alvin Roy with Emil Karas squatting (l to r), Ron Mix, Ernie Wright, Earl Faison, and Jacque MacKinnon.

One coach who especially embraced the weight training was offensive line coach Joe Madro.

His men had been particularly targeted as the Chargers weak link in 1962's breakdown, recalling the insults given to them by the Oilers in referring to his men as soft.

The competition for roster spots would be especially intense this year, and Gillman loved to keep his players on edge. After winning only four games the previous year, he made it very clear that no position was a lock and that everyone had a chance to jump into a starting spot. That sounded good to the coaching staff and was probably true in some cases, but the players knew that at this point, Earl Faison and Ernie Ladd had little to worry about on defense. And barring a total implosion on the offensive line, Ron Mix and Ernie Wright were already penciled into starting roles. But Gillman's words did leave several incumbents feeling a bit insecure. Ron Nery, the right defensive end, and reserve Hank Schmidt were being pressed by a few rookies who came to camp who were bigger and faster than the two incumbents. And everyone knew that Gillman had allegiance to only one thing: winning. Nery was in need of more speed to pursue sweeps to his side, and Bill Hudson, the other starter on the front four, had already been passed along to Buffalo as part of the compensation for signing Rote. Both Nery and Schmidt knew they would be fighting for roster spots this year. George Gross, a defensive tackle from Auburn; Fred Moore, a defensive end from Memphis State; and Bob Petrich from West Texas State were drafted rookies who all came in with high expectations of making the team, and it was still unclear what side of the ball Syracuse hot-shot end Walt Sweeney was going to be tried on.

The linebacking corps of Chuck Allen, Emil Karas, Frank Buncom, and Paul Maguire, who was also the team punter, were being pressed by youngsters Bob Mitinger from Penn State and Rufus Guthie of Georgia Tech, as well as Ron Carpenter from Texas A&M. And the fly hawks in the defensive backfield were on edge as well, just as Gillman wanted them to be. Claude Gibson, who led the team in interceptions the previous season, had been picked by Oakland in the supplemental stocking draft, leaving one starting spot officially open. Charlie McNeil, coming back after missing 10 games the previous season, and Dick Harris, both holdovers from the 1961 record setting *Seven Pirates*, may have had a slight advantage in experience, but they certainly did not appear to know it. Bud Whitehead and George Blair, who doubled as the team's place kicker, and Bobby Bethune all saw action as starters in '62 but were well aware that not everyone was going to be back. They also knew that the rookies in camp wanted their jobs just as much as they did. Keith Kinderman from Florida State came in with impressive credentials, but by the end of the first week of practice, the rookie who was catching everyone's eye for his high degree of energy, enthusiasm, and desire to learn was Dick Westmoreland, an undrafted cornerback out of North Carolina A&T.

Dick Westmoreland

When I came out to California, that was my shot; I wanted to be a football player. I got hurt my senior year in college. I was getting calls from NFL teams. The Lions called a lot, but then I hurt my knee and they stopped calling. Then the Chargers called and I signed. The coach was looking for the best people and I took it one practice at a time and worked as hard as I could. Coach Noll was a great coach for me. He was always talking to me, being optimistic and telling me I was doing well even if I thought I wasn't. He just never let me get down on myself and that really kept me going.

He saw something in me. As an unknown rookie coming in to camp I did everything I could to make the team. I didn't want to go back home and tell people I didn't make it. This was all I wanted to do since I was a kid, so I just went after it as hard as I could. I guess I did okay, 'cause at the end of camp I was a starter and was the league's best defensive rookie at the end of year.

The offensive line was another area where Gillman had a log jam and would need to make a few decisions. Guard Sam Deluca was talked back after a year in retirement and Pat Shea, who spent a lot of quality time chasing down kick returners the previous year, had earned a chance to become a starter at guard. Sam Gruneisen raised many eyebrows for his size and play the previous season and would also be vying for a starting spot at guard. Ron Mix filled in for the many line injuries at guard the year before and was All-AFL at that position. He was returning to his right tackle spot this year, where he was the best in the league. Starter Sherman Plunkett, a fine pass blocker at tackle, weighed in at 300 lbs. and irked Gillman who liked to use his tackles to pull on sweeps. By not controlling his weight, he was now in Gillman's dog house. With Mix's move, Plunkett was now the odd man out, since tackle Ernie Wright looked like a lock on the left side. And if Gillman decided to give rookie Walt Sweeney a try on offensive instead of defensive; the battle of interior line spots could be quite fierce and might finally put a smile on coach Madro's face. The fight for the center position would also be interesting, where former starter Wayne Frazier returned from injury to duke it out with veteran Don Rogers. Both had all-star potential.

The receivers and backs seemed to have things pretty well figured out in camp. Lance Alworth was coming back after missing 10 games as a rookie, and everyone knew he was going to be the flanker. Dave Kocourek was also a sure thing at tight end. He was considered one of the top players at his position in all of pro football. Second-year man Jacque MacKinnon, who split his time on the line and in the backfield was listed at the team's backup. Reg Carolan had an inside chance to make the squad at tight end as well. All were very large targets and liked to block. Don Norton and Jerry Robinson returned as split ends and there was little doubt that Paul Lowe would not return to his daring, breakaway form. Keith Lincoln, who filled in for Lowe in '62, Bob Jackson, the returning starting fullback, and Gerry McDougall all appeared set as running backs. The only question was whether Lincoln would switch to fullback, where he thought he was too small to play, or if Jackson would continue in that spot. McDougall seemed to accept his role as a backup off the bench. Bert Coan, a 6'4" speedster with dangerous potential, was another player who missed 10 games in '62 and was hopeful of finding a running back or flanker spot in '63. Although it was doubtful that Coan would be around in September.

The quarterback position was a foregone conclusion. John Hadl would back up Tobin Rote and Don Breaux would wait in the wings.

Bob Petrich

At our first practice, my roommate and I came out of our cabin and the first person we see is Earl Faison. My roommate shouts "Oh my god, look at how big that guy is." Faison was 6' 6" and 260 lbs. with a 38-inch waist and no appearance of any body fat. Then Ernie Ladd appeared and he was even bigger at 6'9" and 300 lbs. and no gut. Even though I'm from West Texas and was taught to fear no one and hit harder than everyone, I was really happy to be playing on the same defensive side of the line as them.

Ernie Ladd (71) and center Don Rogers (52).

THE UNCROWNED CHAMPS

During the first official day of camp, the players did all the housekeeping things like getting fitted for uniforms and pads, meeting with their offensive or defensive groups, and fidgeting through lectures about rules, fines, and other incidentals that all teams have to muddle through before the bell rings. By the third day at Rough Acres, the hitting finally started . . . first against the blocking machines and then against each other. Players hated the one-on-one head-banging drills but knew the coaches needed to see them in isolated action to determine who fit where and what level of toughness they brought along.

As the training and practice regiment quickly became routine, each day started with a team meeting in the dining hall after breakfast and then moved outside for weight lifting.

Hank Schmidt

We'd go to breakfast then have a short meeting then go the lifting stations. It was hot as hell but it was the same for everyone so you just did it and didn't complain. Complaining wouldn't do anything anyway because we were going to be here a long time, so we just made the best of it.

As the second week began, so did the scrimmages; a welcomed but difficult exercise for both sides of the ball. The players had been spending mornings together at breakfast, lifting and practicing in their special units except for the one-on-one drills. Then meeting again for lunch, then the second practice session, dinner, offensive and defensive meetings, and then sitting around with each other playing assorted games. Calling home offered little distraction, as there was only one public telephone at the ranch.

Now with the scrimmages starting, the competition for jobs was cranked up a notch. The tension could be felt in the locker room, as the usual sounds of team banter had given way to a nervous and concentrated silence.

Scrimmaging at Rough Acres Ranch.

Bob Petrich

When I was in camp I had to go against Ron Mix in scrimmages. The first time I faced him I was watching the ball and Mix nailed me before I got out of my stance. I never had anybody that quick hit me before. That was the big difference with the pros, and Mix was the best around, so I had to make an adjustment quickly. The next time my left hand got caught under his pads so he pulled back. When he did that he pulled me along with him and I sprung loose and got around him. It looked good but nobody realized what had just happened. It looked like I beat him with quickness and that impressed people who were watching, but it was more of an accident than anything else. Another time I was on the right side and Pat Shea, one of our guards, was pulling on a sweep and as he came across I knocked him on his back. Sid saw it and went berserk, calling it unacceptable for his guard to be taken out so quickly and made the team run it over again. Shea was a training maniac, always lifting and doing strength training. The next time I drove him back again and then again. One of my linebackers called me out and told me to let him beat me or we'll never move on. Well, on the next play Shea knocked me down and on his way back to the huddle he stomped on me. I figured that I'd be cut after that, but I must have made an impression on someone, 'cause I made the team and Sid traded Ron Nery to Houston.

Two weeks into camp and it was time for some R&R before the players went stir crazy. Even Gillman knew that grown men—especially professional athletes—would only endure so much confinement before there was a mutiny. All that heat, lousy food, dusty rooms where tarantulas, bats, spiders, and rattlesnakes roamed freely—as well as complete isolation from the outside world—needed some reward. And on July 22, Gillman had another great idea. He was going to take the team to town to watch a heavyweight championship fight.

Dick Westmoreland

We really got jailed as a team at Rough Acres. We actually looked forward to practice and scrimmaging because it was something to do. It was monotonous there.

Hank Schmidt

We all hopped on a bus that Sid got for us and went to this town, El Centro I think, to watch Sonny Liston fight [Floyd] Patterson [in a theatre]. When we got there we piled out and sat down to watch the fight and BAM! Liston knocked him out in the first round. I think even in the first minute or two. We all got up, piled back on the bus, and drove back to camp. That was our fun . . . that and the gas station.

With the addition of their new weight-lifting regime and evening team meetings, the players had time only to eat and sleep during the first three weeks of camp. And by that point they were on a first-name basis with the staff at the gas station down the road, which became their watering hole.

Dick Harris

I don't remember much grass to practice on, but there were lots of rattlesnakes. A bunch of us would always sneak down to the gas station three or four miles from the site. One day we jumped into Tobin's car and drove down after practice. We were just hanging out, drinking and chewing the fat and realized we needed to get back for evening curfew. On the way back I saw this snake on the side of the road and told Tobin to stop the car. I hopped out and got a stick and started dueling with the rattler like a Robin Hood sword fight and literally knocked it out with the stick I had in my hand. The guys in the car were going nuts, like I had just won a prize fight. I grabbed it and stuck it across the hood of Rote's car and we drove back to camp with it just lying there. Well, you have to know that Sid and I were always going back and forth. I liked Sid but I was always pushing his buttons. I was kind of a free spirit and Sid was always trying to reel me in and fining me, so I kind of knew what his reaction was going to be when we got back with this snake on the car. But that didn't stop me when we arrived. Sure enough when I got out of the car Gillman came rushing at me going crazy and yelling. Then Rote got out of the car and said "Hey, Sid, how do you like the snake I killed?" Sid just stopped cold in his tracks and started congratulating Tobin for his new trophy. I'll never forget that. Tobin was his guy. He saved my ass. But most times I deserved his chewing me out. Rote knew that and saved my ass from being reamed out and maybe even fined again. He was just a good guy and became our team leader from the day he arrived. He even had one of the two air conditioners in the whole compound. Gillman had the other.

Chuck Allen

That gas station down the road was very popular, as they were the only place that sold beer. That was our watering hole and I believe that because of those little trips down there, the team really became close to each other. Gillman, the staff, and the players, we all got along. We were all color blind, just bonded with the whole team: offense with defense, black with white, old with young. We were like in a boy's summer camp, only we were grown men. And we all made the best of the situation. Looking back now makes for great memories fifty years later.

As August staggered in, the Chargers were into their third week at the ranch and looking forward to their first exhibition game back in San Diego against the AFL Champions that had recently relocated to become the Kansas City Chiefs. It would be the first chance for the coaches to see if there were any early results to bank on from their lifting program. August 3 couldn't come fast enough.

Bob Petrich

We scrimmaged twice a day, six days a week, on sawdust and wood shavings because there was no grass in the middle of the desert. It was unbelievable and even hotter than Texas. By the time we got to the preseason games it was like being on a break. We worked so long and so hard in camp that playing the games was the easy part.

Back at Balboa Stadium in front of 25,000 fans for their first taste of competition outside of knocking heads with their own squad, Sid reminded his men to stay relaxed and have fun and that the rest would fall into place. It was a comforting jest coming from the head coach, but for those who were on the roster bubble there would be no comfort. The game also took on some extra meaning beyond winning jobs. Since the league had begun play, the Chargers had played twelve exhibition games and won them all, so they were looking to make number thirteen a lucky one by keeping the streak alive.

Kansas City would offer a good test for the recovering Chargers as they were the league champions and had a muscular front four of veterans. They were also trying out two hungry rookies that were pressuring their veterans. All-Americans Buck Buchanan and Bobby Bell added size and aggressive and would be offering the first assessment of the Charger line's weight-training progress. Gillman was anxious to turn his new backfield loose as well. Despite a protest from Keith Lincoln, he was used as the fullback after filling in at halfback the previous season. For Paul Lowe it would be his third running mate in as many seasons, starting first with Howie Ferguson then Charlie Flowers and now Lincoln. Lincoln's protest was that he felt undersized for the fullback position that was used primarily for plunges up the middle and blocking big linebackers and linemen on passing plays. Gillman, always a salesman, explained his usage of the two as tandem halfbacks instead of having a defined fullback. Both would be blocking backs, inside and outside runners, and pass catchers. The difficult part would be keeping both of them happy with a balanced workload.

John Hadl

The hardest thing about having Lincoln and Lowe in the backfield for me was making sure they always carried the ball close to the same amount each game. They both wanted the ball and didn't especially like blocking. But they knew they'd have to or they wouldn't be getting the ball as much. If I didn't balance their carries I would hear a lot of moaning in the huddle.

His backfield experiment would also give Sid an indication as to what his new guards were capable of. Deluca, Gruneisen, Shea, and Sweeney were all vying for a job and all hoped to impress Sir Sid against the Chiefs.

The 26–14 tally at the end of the evening told Sid that the night was a success. The hard work and weight lifting was not only building the team's physical stature, but its mental toughness as well. On the sidelines, everyone was focused and encouraging each other, watching every play closely. After giving up an interception on their third possession, the Chargers recovered

Paul Lowe scores on a 65-yard run.

a Kansas City fumble on the 23-yard line and scored four plays later for their first touchdown. For the most part the game was uneventful, with an offensive spark here and there. Dave Kocourek caught three passes, each for 20 or more yards, and Keith Lincoln broke the line for 13- and 18-yard runs. But the play of the night occurred on a broken play when Paul Lowe was pinned in on his own 35-yard line, then circled back to the 20 before finding a lane up the sideline and ran for a 65-yard touchdown. Together Lincoln and Lowe picked up 163 yards with Lowe accounting for 98 of them. John Hadl played most of the game behind center after Rote played only three snaps. Hadl completed 15 of his 23 passes for 172 yards.

In the locker room after the game, the players agreed that there was a different feel to the atmosphere; a feeling that their days at

Ernie Wright (75) and Lance Alworth (24) head to practice.

Rough Acres had benefited the team as a whole. And there was a quiet feeling of satisfaction among the entire team for extending their winning streak to thirteen games.

Despite the encouraging victory over the defending champions, there was some uneasiness in the locker room. On the Chargers first set of downs, Tobin Rote was sacked for a 12-yard loss and had to leave the game. After being taken to the hospital for x-rays, it was determined that Rote had an injured rib cage and would be sidelined for a few weeks. Gillman may have come away with a satisfying win, but he also left with a feeling of "here we go again."

Meanwhile, back at the ranch it was business as usual; breakfast, lifting, practice, lunch, practice, dinner, pool/cards/ping-pong/gas station, until they returned to San Diego for a Saturday night game against Boston, who had defeated the Chargers in their last three regular season meetings.

Bob Petrich

I thought I had a bad game against Kansas City, so when we got to Rough Acres I was called to Gillman's office. I thought he was going to cut me. He said "I really want you to work hard now that you have a game under your belt." I looked at him kind of funny and said, "you mean I made the team?" Gillman blew up at me, yelling "I'm not wasting my time on you talking, why do you think you're here? Of course you made the team, now get out of here!" My first year salary was $11,000 with a $1,000 advance.

Met by an overcast sky and a breezy 66 degrees, the Chargers would again be challenged by one of the best defensive front lines in the league. The Patriots were the hardest team to run on the last two years, so the Lincoln/Lowe tandem and the offensive line would be tested. John Hadl got the start at quarterback as Tobin Rote continued to sit out with a sternum injury. He was replaced by rookie Don Breaux. The offense appeared out of sync early and a few mix-ups in the back field thwarted a few drives. When Hadl and Alworth hooked up on two consecutive completions for 18 and 56 yards and Paul Lowe finished the drive off with a 9-yard touchdown on a pitch out, things finally got rolling. Two more touchdowns in the second quarter gave the Chargers a 24–7 lead, and it only got better from there. Everyone got into the act in the 50–17 victory including Charlie McNeil who returned one of the four San Diego interceptions 44 yards for a touchdown. The win extended their exhibition season win streak to 14 games. Gillman was especially happy with the play of the kick return team, with Paul Lowe returning the Patriots first punt 52 yards to set up a George Blair field goal and Lance Alworth returning another 57 yards that set up a 32-yard touchdown pass from Hadl to Norton on the next play. Keith Lincoln also returned a kickoff 57 yards to set up another touchdown drive. On the night, the Chargers piled up 424 total yards against the Patriots 232.

There were still three more weeks of training to make it through in the desert and three more exhibition games to play before the Chargers would open the season at home against Buffalo. And there were still more cuts to be made until the roster was trimmed to satisfy the league limit of 33. Now there was a new critter at Rough Acres to contend with and more dangerous for some players than the bats and rattle snakes. It was known as "The Turk." It was that dreaded knock on his cabin door informing a player that his presence was requested in Coach Gillman's office, and to bring his playbook along with him.

Keith Lincoln is brought down after a 57-yard kickoff return.

A trip to Denver followed. Playing the Broncos in the mile-high city presented a match-up that always gave the Chargers trouble. It may have been the thin air or the team's familiarity and respect for their former defensive coordinator Jack Faulkner, but the Broncos always seemed to give the Chargers fits at home. While the outcomes of the games were usually favorable for the Chargers, they always seemed to need to hold off a last period rush—or create one themselves—to get away with a win. In three previous visits they won by 4 (23–19 in 1960), by 3 (19–16 in 1961), and lost by 9 (30–21 in 1962). Now in a game that took them to the mid-way point of their training camp, they lost again, 31–25. There were too many defensive lapses that led to three long touchdowns, starting with Denver rookie fullback Billy Joe busting through the middle for a 27-yard touchdown. That was followed by long passes that scored from 75 and 60 yards, adding significantly to the Broncos 338 total yards on the night. The four-year winning streak had come to an end after 14-straight, and it was clear that there was still much work to be done.

For their fourth exhibition game, the Chargers traveled to Houston's Jeppesen Stadium on August 22 to play the Oilers in what could best be described as the team being *outgained but not out-gunned*. While the offense struggled and was still without Tobin Rote, the defense turned in its best performance to date, even though in the first two quarters Houston ran 46 plays to San Diego's 15. The Chargers led 7–3 at the half due in large part to the ability of the defense completely shutting down the Oilers scoring. In their first four possessions, Houston fumbled, were held on fourth down and goal at the 2-yard line, and were intercepted twice. And it took until their sixth possession with only 41 seconds left in the half for them to score their only points on a field goal. The Chargers defensive second half was even more dominating. In order, the Oilers' seven possessions ended with a missed field goal, a punt, a 19-yard sack by Faison, an interception by Maguire, a 10-yard sack by Petrich, and two interceptions by McNeil. And even though they allowed 138 yards rushing and 150 passing yards, San Diego won 21–3.

The defensive play of three rookies was turning heads, which offered them more and more opportunities on the field. Front four mates Bob Petrich and George Gross seemed to be inching closer to becoming starters along with the defensive surprise of training camp, cornerback Dick Westmoreland (who had already sealed a starting spot).

One game remained before the squad would need to reach its maximum roster limit and then bid farewell to Rough Acres Ranch. The game would return the team to San Diego to play the new and improved Oakland Raiders under the direction of popular coach and former Charger assistant, Al Davis. It would also return Tobin Rote to the field where he had missed all but three plays of the exhibition season. The plan called for him to go from start to finish and give him as much time with his new offense as he could get before the season's opener.

The last tune-up was played under clear skies on the last day of August before a crowd of 17,000, with the Chargers dressed in their visiting white uniforms, probably to give the fans a different look for the last game. Both teams sported a 3–1 preseason record, which for the Raiders was two more wins than they experienced last year, and even though they did not count in the standings, it was a totally new feeling for the team to build upon.

The defense was again dominating, and started the game as they had in Houston recovering a fumble on their first series— this time on the first play— which led to a field goal. Four more interceptions against the Raiders gave the Chargers 12 in their last three games, and complemented their three fumble recoveries and a blocked field goal. They had also now allowed only 3 points to reach the scoreboard for the second straight game. Tobin Rote was a bit rusty in his first outing, throwing four interceptions and fumbling three times. The offense sputtered too, scoring just one touchdown, surrounded by two field goals that outscored Oakland 13–3. The Chargers preseason ended with a 4–1 record. The next time they would be on the field would be the first step on the road they hoped would take them back to the top of the Western Division.

Their preseason record and stellar defensive performance the last two weeks were an indication that surviving Rough Acres was great preparation for the team in beginning their comeback season. For the players, the enduring experience and torturous regiment of the infamous seven-week camp would be bittersweet. They survived a truly unique and in many ways groundbreaking test that some felt was the key ingredient which led to their most rewarding season to date.

Hank Schmidt

I liked it there. I was in the Marine Corps and when you are trained by the Marines you just do what you are told and do it well. I liked the desert, too, and I was always a weight lifter so for me it was just another camp. I remember being in the military where you did everything together. You got to know each other. For me, I think it was one of the best ideas Gillman ever had. He wanted us to get away and focus only on football and our team. And that's what we did. That's what we had to do because there was nothing else we could do! We came away from camp as a unified, synchronized team. When we first heard we were going there, we all had the same reaction: "Where the hell is Rough Acres Ranch?" But when we broke camp to start the season we were all happy. I guess you'd have to be after going through what we did.

As the Chargers turned out the lights and closed the doors at Rough Acres, it was doubtful that anyone would miss that god-forsaken place. But what would be missed were the many bizarre memories and frequent road trips to the gas station they shared while sequestered in the desert. The daily ping-pong battles between Keith Lincoln and Ernie Ladd, complete with arguments over who won points and each other's skill level would be talked about for years, and the card games that everyone joined in on would be at the forefront of those memories as well as all the crazy experiences they had at the ranch. Over the years many stories and memories about this experience would be told and retold, embellished and adored, and create a bond that would last a lifetime.

Stories like Earl Faison finding what he thought was an Indian bracelet, only to realize it was a baby rattlesnake when he bent over to pick it up. Or players waking up in the middle of the night to capture a bat circling the room, or finding tarantulas parading around the floors and spiders scattering to every corner of the room the second the lights went on. The comradery that was built, the memories that were made, and the esprit de corps that developed were the things the players would take away from that summer of hellish temperatures and ungodly conditions in Boulevard, California. It was the foundation to the season, their renewal of the team's direction and commitment to their willingness to move beyond what had already been achieved in order to establish a framework for greater success. The Chargers had just made it through the most difficult part of their season, and they had not yet played a regular season game. Throughout the training camp experience, Gillman kept preaching that making it through the adverse conditions and grueling heat Rough Acres presented would bring them closer together and make getting through the season that much easier.

(l to r) Dave Kocourek, Tobin Rote, Paul Maguire, and Emil Karas playing cards after practice.

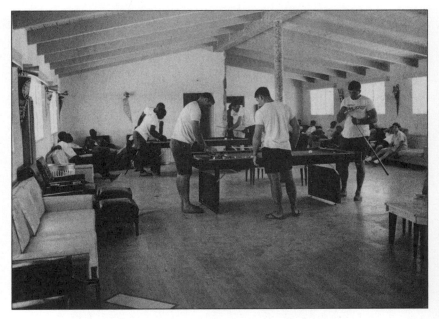

Keith Lincoln and teammates prepare for a game of pool.

Dick Westmoreland

Race was something that was never an issue with the Chargers. We had about ten or twelve African Americans. Most NFL teams only had four or five back then, but the AFL had a lot. We all hung out together like a big family. If we went somewhere together and the place said they didn't serve colored, well, the whole team left. That really made us feel like we all had each other's backs. I don't think it would have worked out as well as it did without those weeks at Rough Acres.

Gillman had good reason to believe his choice of training facilities and methods had the team headed in the right direction. He surely knew how to pick winners, all the way from training sites to coaches, and especially the talented players he selected to teach and develop. As the desert camp came to a close and the players returned home to prepare for the Bills in week one, San Diego's final 1963 roster of 33 (plus 5 reserves) included 11 original Chargers: Ron Mix, Sam DeLuca, Dick Harris, Emil Karas, Dave Kocourek, Paul Lowe, Paul Maguire, Charlie McNeil, Don Norton, Don Rogers, and Ernie Wright would all be together again for another year.

In the words of Sid Gillman, "We are looking ahead to a bright future. The past is behind us."

It was finally time for the 1963 season to begin, and for the team to take that first step back to the championship game!

THE UNCROWNED CHAMPS

1963 San Diego Chargers Roster			
#	Name	Position	Age
50	Chuck Allen	MLB	24
19	Lance Alworth	FL	23
39	George Blair	K-LS	25
55	Frank Buncom	OLB	24
89	Reg Carolan	TE	24
60	Sam DeLuca	LG	27
86	Earl Faison	LDE	24
43	Gary Glick	DB	33
79	George Gross	DT	22
65	Sam Gruneisen	G	22
21	John Hadl	QB	23
36	Dick Harris	CB	26
40	Bob Jackson	FB	23
56	Emil Karas	LLB	30
24	Keith Kinderman	DB	23
83	Dave Kocourek	TE	26
77	Ernie Ladd	DT	25
57	Bob Lane	OLB	24
22	Keith Lincoln	FB	24
23	Paul Lowe	HB	27
38	Jacque MacKinnon	TE-FB	25
84	Paul Maguire	P-RLB	25
20	Gerry McDougall	HB	28
27	Charlie McNeil	RS	27
82	Bob Mitinger	LB	23

74	Ron Mix	RT	25
88	Don Norton	SE	25
61	Ernie Park	G	23
85	Bob Petrich	RDE	22
29	Jerry Robinson	SE	24
52	Don Rogers	C	27
18	Tobin Rote	QB	35
76	Hank Schmidt	DT-DE	28
64	Pat Shea	RG	24
78	Walt Sweeney	G	22
25	Dick Westmoreland	RCB	22
47	Bud Whitehead	CB-S	24
75	Ernie Wright	LT	24[4]

4   The 1963 Chargers were the second-youngest team in the AFL (average age of 25.1), and the average team age in the AFL was almost a full year younger (25.525) than those in the NFL (26.47). Interesting enough, the average age of the 2014 San Diego Chargers was 25.9.

4

THE 1963 SEASON

Game 1: The First Step
Buffalo Bills
Sunday, September 8, 1963, at San Diego
Balboa Stadium
Attendance: 22,344

By the time the Chargers trotted onto the turf of Balboa Stadium on that first Sunday afternoon, they were well aware that the defending champion Kansas City Chiefs had torched their closest competitors of a year ago, the Denver Broncos (in Denver), 59–7, which set a league record for most points scored in a game.

Now it was the Chargers' turn to start their journey for the title. Emotions and expectations always run a little higher on opening day, and on September 8, the crowd of over 22,000 awaited with anticipation to see if the team that fell from 12–2 in '61 to 4–10 in '62 would be able to return to their title-contending form.

Another reason for the crowd to be excited was the homecoming (of sorts) for Buffalo signal caller Jack Kemp. Kemp had not returned to San Diego since being claimed from the injury list last season. After spending eight weeks in recovery, he was activated with four games left and gave everyone in Buffalo a taste of what the future would hold by leading the Bills to a 3–1 finish. Both teams were considered to be challengers in their divisions, and for the Bills it was the first time they felt as though their team had enough tools to make them a contender.

Historically a slow starter, the Bills had yet to win a season opening game and, in fact, had made a habit of not winning more than one of their first four games in any season. The worst of those starts came the previous year, when it took them six games before they could register a victory. Under their first coach, Buster Ramsey, the Bills forte had always been defense, and the team was consistently ranked among the top in those categories. They continued to build on that reputation when Lou Saban replaced Ramsey in 1962, but just as before they never challenged for the division lead—most likely due to their slow starts and lack of offensive weaponry, especially consistent passing. Near the bottom of the league in most offensive categories, they were also the worst passing team over the league's first three years.

Things did start to change for the better with the addition of fullback Cookie Gilchrist from Toronto the previous year, which propelled the Bills to the top of the list in running by leading the league with 1,096 yards. Their offensive line was led by tackle Stew Barber, guard Billy Shaw, and center Al Bemiller. Now with Kemp taking over as quarterback for the entire season, the Bills believed they had put enough together to challenge the Oilers, who had finished first in the East every year. The defense was still the cornerstone of the franchise, with a front four anchored by All-Star Mack Yoho, 2nd Team All-Pro Sid Youngelman, and standout All-Star Tom Sestak. They also had an aggressive group of linebackers with the heavy-hitting Mike Stratton and the experienced and energetic Marv Matuszak, as well as a young and aggressive secondary of Willie West, Booker Edgerson, Ray Abruzzese, and Carl Charon.[5] It looked to many like Buffalo was primed to take control.

One of the questions proposed by San Diego newspapers leading up to the season was whether the team's 4–1 preseason record was for real. And with Kansas City looking unbeatable against Denver, the Chargers needed no more incentive to get out of the gate quickly. Another question that needed to be answered was how ready and healthy Tobin Rote would be with only one exhibition game under his belt. As a warm wind and 74-degree temperature moved through the stadium at kickoff time, George Blair huddled with his Chargers at the 40-yard line to get the season started.

---

5   The secondary totaled 22 interceptions, while the linebacking core pulled down an additional 12 in '62.

The Bills started at their own 23 with Kemp appearing as calm as a hometown favorite. The Chargers started a front four of Earl Faison, Hank Schmidt, Ernie Ladd, and rookie Bob Petrich; with Chuck Allen, Paul Maguire, and Emil Karas as the linebackers. Bud Whitehead was at left corner and rookie Dick Westmoreland started on the right side. George Blair and Charlie McNeil were at the safety spots.

Gillman and Noll knew that Buffalo had relied heavily on their running game in the past and that they would need to contain the league's strongest runner. Before Gilchirst's arrival, the Bills ran as much as they passed, but that changed with Cookie's arrival, as they ran 150 times more than they threw a year ago.

In his few starts with Buffalo, Kemp used the ground game to set up more passing opportunities, and by the looks of the 3–1 record, it seemed to be a formula for success. The Chargers plan was to first stop Gilchrist—which would not be an easy task— and to force Kemp into catch-up play calling. The front four would be the key to setting the stage.

On their opening series, Kemp went right to the air, first tossing incomplete to split end Bill Miller and then a completed look-in to halfback Wray Carlton for 9 yards. On 3rd and 1 he sent Gilchrist wide left, hoping his veteran tackle Stew Barber could handle the inexperienced Petrich, but the fullback was pulled down for a 1-yard loss, bringing Wayne Crow and the punt team onto the field. Rote brought out the Chargers with an offensive line off Ernie Wright and Sam Gruneisen on the left, Don Rogers at center, and Pat Shea and Ron Mix on the right. Dave Kocourek and Jerry Robinson, filling for the injured Don Norton, were the ends with Lance Alworth at flanker. Behind Rote was a little surprise as Bob Jackson lined up aside of Keith

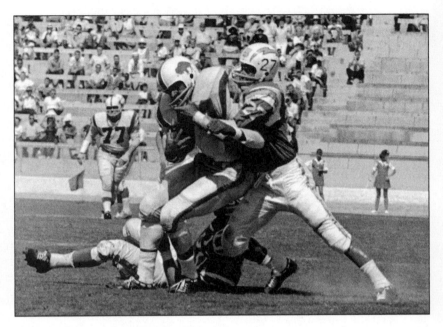

Charlie McNeil stops Cookie Gilchrist.

Lincoln on the first series that began on the team's own 30-yard line. Two runs—one by Jackson and then Lincoln followed by a swing pass to Jackson—got Rote a first down and then, avoiding a blitz, hit Jackson again for 14 more yards. Lincoln added an additional 12 on a catch and run, but the first drive of the year stalled at the Buffalo 10-yard line. George Blair came in to attempt a 17-yard field goal but missed wide, leaving the Chargers with an impressive drive but no points.

The Chargers caught an unexpected break when Cookie Gilchrist, who was still nursing injured ribs suffered in the preseason, left the game after picking up 5 yards on his second carry and would not return for the rest of the day. Without him, halfback Wray Carlton, the league's tenth-best rusher in '62, would now be teamed with rookie George Saimes in the Bills' backfield.

Buffalo started the second quarter at the 22-yard line after a fair catch of Maguire's punt and picked up a quick first down, but on the next play Bob Mitinger gave the Chargers their second interception at the 48-yard line (with the first being made by Bud Whitehead) where Tobin Rote started his first scoring drive for his new team. The biggest play of the drive came on a 31-yard completion to Kocourek that put the ball on the 1. Bob Jackson, San Diego's designated battering ram, powered in for the game's first score and put the Chargers ahead, 7–0.

The scoring drive saw Paul Lowe pick up the first 14 yards and then Rote completed a pass to Jackson for 26 yards. Gerry McDougall caught another pass for 14 and then Rote connected with Kocourek to set-up the score.

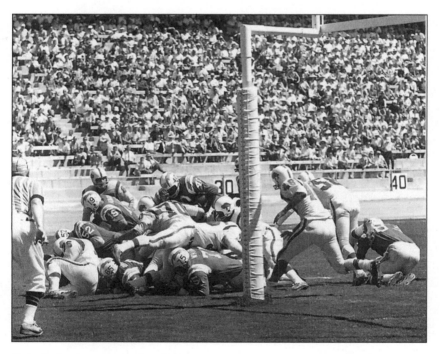

Bob Jackson scores a touchdown.

For anyone who wondered how the Chargers new quarterback would fare in only his second game, their questions were answered by looking at his halftime totals of 13 completions on 19 attempts for 201 yards. And for those who wondered where the Lincoln and Lowe combination was, they only needed to point to the production of fullback Bob Jackson's 4 catches for 48 yards for the answer. Splitting his time with Lincoln, Paul Lowe ran the ball only twice, sweeping for 7 and 11 yards. Lincoln also had two carries, his for a total of 9 yards. Gillman was playing his hand cautiously at first, passing twice as many times as his team ran and using the pass to try and open up the run. One area that did hurt the Chargers in the first half was their carelessness, which got them penalized seven times for 100 yards. (Although 45 of those yards came on one play.) The six others, however, were drive killers.

To open the second half, Jack Kemp was able to muster a couple of first downs and move the Bills to the San Diego 40, until he was faced with a 4th and 1. Looking to the sidelines, Kemp got the signal from Lou Saban to go for it, and sent George Saimes into the heart of the Charger defense where he was stopped cold by Ernie Ladd, who popped the ball loose and into the hands of safety Charlie McNeil. After recovering the ball, the Chargers started their drive through the air as Rote threw a 41-yard completion to Robinson, who made a leaping catch over Booker Edgerson as he tried for the interception. And then the ball advanced to the Buffalo 2 and the Chargers also faced a 4th down. And now it was Gillman's turn to signal his quarterback to go for it. Rote sent Jackson up the middle as he did for his second quarter touchdown, but his time the Bills stood him up and held the line, taking possession at their own 3.

In his first game in over a year, Paul Lowe had a knack for running wide—as he did back in '61— carrying three end runs on the next series. Then, as he often did in past years, he suddenly took a quick pitch to his right, cut back across the field, and was off on a 48-yard sprint to the end zone. It was Lowe's seventh carry of the day around end and put San Diego up, 14–3.

With 6:33 left in the game, Buffalo was able to close the gap to 14–10 when Jack Kemp, scrambling inside the Chargers 10-yard line, lateraled to his halfback Fred Brown at the 4. Brown punched the ball in for a touchdown. And when the Chargers wound the clock down to the three-minute mark and had to punt, Kemp and company got another chance to take the lead from their own 35. Needing to squelch Kemp's attempt to pull out a last-minute win, the Chargers defense came up with their best series of the afternoon. On first down, Faison knocked Kemp's pass out of the air. On second down, Ernie Ladd did the same thing. And on third down, Bob Petrich corralled Kemp and threw him down for a 12-yard loss with two minutes left in the contest.

The Chargers could now put the game on ice with a couple of first downs to run out the clock, but were forced to punt one more time, which gave the Bills one last chance with 90 seconds left. While they were hoping to pull off a big play to move the ball 90 yards to the end zone, a holding penalty on first down drove the last nail in their coffin. San Diego escaped with a 14–10 victory, handing Buffalo another opening season loss, and stepping into a first-play tie with the Chiefs.

The high-powered San Diego offense never really got rolling in their first outing, and thankfully the defense came up big when needed. Three interceptions, a fumble recovery, and four sacks totaling 28 yards where the main reason the team

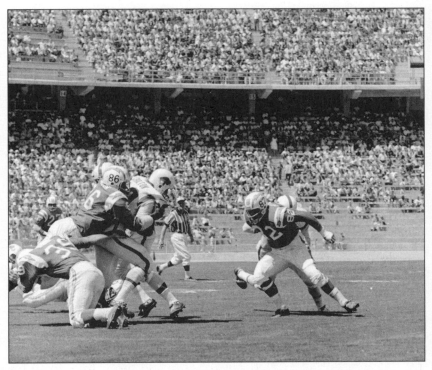

Earl Faison (86) and George Blair (39) tackle Buffalo's Wray Carlton.

walked away with a victory, and with Gilchrist out for all but two carries, the Chargers were fortunate to avoid his wrath. Gilchrist's injury definitely restructured the Bills offense, and even though the Chargers gave up 116 rushing yards, they were mostly short gains, with the longest run going for only 10 yards. With the injury to their leading rusher, the defense made sure to keep Kemp in check, holding him to 17 completions on 33 attempts with three interceptions.

Offensively, the Chargers were fortunate to break off some big plays with five pass completions picking up over 20 yards, and Paul Lowe netting 48 of his 96 yards on his touchdown run. After completing 13 of 19 in the first half, Rote toned down the passing game and completed only 5 of 10 for 59 yards (41 on one play to Robinson) in the second half.

Gillman was extremely pleased with his team's first official performance and called it one of the best and sweetest victories in a long time. Without singling out any one player, he stated that they all played well and would not award a game ball but instead give the team Monday off.

Buffalo Bills	0	3	0	7	-	10
San Diego Chargers	0	7	7	0	-	14

SD-Jackson, 1 run (Blair kick)
Buf-FG, Yoho 17
SD-Lowe, 48 run (Blair kick)
Buf-Brown, 4 run (Yoho kick)

Charger Statistics:

Player	Rush Att	Yds	Avg	TD	Long	
Bob Jackson	8	15	1.9	1	4	
Keith Lincoln	3	9	3	0	5	
Paul Lowe	10	96	9.6	1	48	
Gerry McDougall	1	6	6	0	6	
	Pass Att	Cmp	Yds	TD	Int	Long
Tobin Rote	29	18	260	0	1	41
	Rec	Yds	TD	Long		
Bob Jackson	6	56	0	26		
Keith Lincoln	2	38	0	32		
Dave Kocourek	2	60	0	31		
Lance Alworth	2	35	0	27		
Paul Lowe	2	13	0	7		
Gerry McDougall	2	13	0	15		
Jerry Robinson	2	45	0	41		

Interceptions: Whitehead, Mitinger, Maguire
Fumble recoveries: McNeil
Tackles: Allen 7, Faison 7, Petrich 6, McNeil 5, Gross 5, Maguire 5, Ladd 5

Around the AFL: On opening day the Oakland Raiders, winless until the last game of the season the previous year, shocked the Oilers in Houston by scoring 24 points in the second half to defeat the defending East champions, 24–13. In Boston, the Patriots knocked off the New York Jets, 38–14, after being tied 14–14 at the half. Boston would visit Balboa Stadium the following Saturday.

Tobin Rote

From the moment he walked into the Chargers' locker room, Tobin Rote was the leader of the team. He brought with him thirteen years of professional football experience, several league-leading statistics, and something every mesmerized

Charger was looking to have: a championship. It would be his experience, wisdom, and aging throwing arm that they would rely on for their winning formula . . . and Rote would have it no other way.

Wherever he went as a pro, Rote was looked at in the same way. Drafted and signed by Green Bay in 1950 out of Rice University, he quarterbacked the Packers through the lean years until he found himself as the odd man out, even though he had better credentials than Babe Parilli, Bart Starr, and Paul Hornung—the young guns of their youth movement. He led the NFL in passes attempted and completed passes in 1954 and 1956, passing yardage in '56, and touchdown passes in '55 and '56. He also led all quarterbacks in rushing six times. His 523 yards in 1951 was an NFL record that lasted twenty years. In three of his seven years with the Packers, he was also the team's leading rusher. So at a time when Green Bay was looking to the future and he became expendable, the Detroit Lions were looking for another championship. Needing an experienced and reliable backup for Bobby Layne in 1957, the Lions jumped at the chance to take Rote off the Packers hands and, in return, Rote quarterbacked the Motor City team to a 31–27 division playoff win against San Francisco after trailing 24–7 at halftime and an NFL championship a week later, defeating the Cleveland Browns, 59–14.

He left Detroit for the CFL after the 1959 season, and led the league in passing while taking his Toronto Argonauts, who had been 4–10 for three straight seasons, to a 10–4 record and the CFL playoffs. When it was time to come back to the States, he was claimed by San Diego by virtue of a coin flip. Again, Rote would be called upon to lead a team on the cusp of a championship, to the top.

Rote was now thirty-five years old and one of only three Chargers in their thirties. He was at least ten years older than most of the team, so it was natural that the young Chargers would take their cues from him. The consensus of everyone on the team was that Rote was the most respected player on the roster.

Hank Schmidt

Tobin was a good leader, the way he carried himself and liked everybody. The day he walked into Rough Acres, they [the players] turned their heads and watched. In the first couple days you already started to get to know people and he just was given so much respect for what he had already accomplished. You could tell he was confident but also a good conversationalist with everyone. The players liked that he talked to everybody. And later on, when the season got closer, he was really good at pep talks.

Dick Westmoreland

Tobin talked to me on the sidelines all the time from Rough Acres and all during the season. He encouraged me and was interested in me doing well. Maybe he wanted me to keep points off the scoreboard, but I didn't care. He was a team leader and was already a champion. He was just a real nice guy.

By the time he came to San Diego, Rote was no longer a running quarterback and hampered by persistent bursitis in his throwing arm. But his leadership and intelligence on the field and his ability to adjust to game situations was second to none in the AFL.

Billy Joe, fullback, Denver Broncos

Tobin Rote reminded me of Earl Morrall later in his career. They knew the game, and his arm was gone, but he had a lot of savvy and knowledge of what needed to get done. Rote made the Chargers the team to beat in '63 and '64.

Fred Arbanas, tight end, Kansas City Chiefs

I was a Tobin Rote fan when he was back in Detroit since that is where I grew up. With San Diego he was really good at changing plays at the line. He could read things real fast. It was like having a coach on the field.

John Hadl

Tobin had been around for a long time and was a great guy. We were roommates at camp and on the road and I can remember talking game plans in bed night after night. He was a really good teacher and would nit-pick about things that made quarterbacks great. He was immediately accepted by the team because of his age and reputation. He had the respect of all the players and was a smart quarterback at the line. Maybe my best memory of him was that when we had some time on the road, he taught me how to play gin. Those were the only two years I played with him, and I haven't played gin since.

Getting to know his receivers was just one of the new challenges facing Rote when he arrived with the Chargers. Learning the complicated play book and timing pass patterns was another. That is where Rote's leadership also shone. He was always studying and staying late to work with the receivers. He just wanted to do well and win.

Lance Alworth

When he got here I thought he was an old man. I was twenty-three and he was thirty-five, but we gave him a lot of respect because of his reputation. He was not in the best shape and showed his age, but he was really smart. He was calling his own plays in the huddle and in the beginning we all thought, "Oh boy, here we go." Sid had a pretty complicated system, too, so we didn't know what to expect or how he would adapt but everything he called was working. He saw stuff when he walked to the line like nobody else and could audible based on what he saw. He kept getting the attention of the other players because they were seeing him pick defenses apart and that his play calling was working. He really taught us a lot about how to play the game.

All the extra work did pay off in the end as he led the AFL in pass completion percentage, yards per attempted pass, and passer rating. Those personal numbers, along with the Chargers top offensive rating and league championship, also earned him a spot on the All-AFL Team as well as the AFL Player of the Year Award. It would be safe to say that without his presence, the Chargers would not have won the championship. His passing statistics can measure his on-field value, but what could not be seen was what he meant to the team off the field. His resume got the player's attention right away; they knew of him and his success in both the NFL and CFL, and his calm and friendly demeanor gave him even more credibility. They also knew him as a team player, mentor, and encouraging teammate. In those regards, he was a perfect fit for a team with a young roster that had loads of talent. It was almost as if they were waiting for someone to come in and show them the way. The way to work, prepare, and win. Tobin Rote was the right man on the right team and at the right time in 1963.

Game 2: Foreshadowing

Boston Patriots
Saturday, September 14, 1963 (Night), at San Diego
Balboa Stadium
Attendance: 26,097

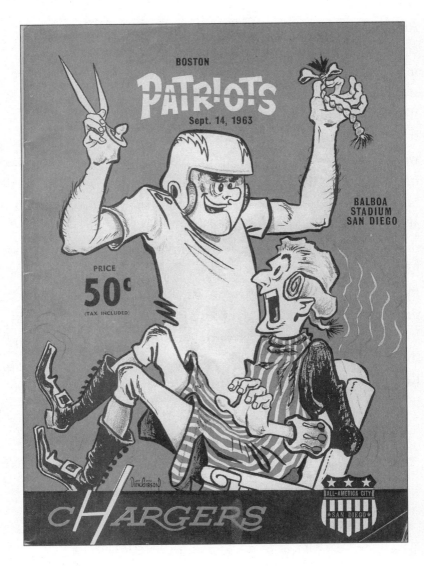

There was no more determined team in the AFL in 1963 than the Boston Patriots—and for good reason. In 1961, the Pats won their last four games of the season only to finish a game behind the eventual AFL champion Oilers who defeated them in a pivotal game in Week 10. Still, an Oiler loss on the last day of the season would have deadlocked the two teams at the top of the division.

Included in that 1961 season was an opening day 21–20 loss to the Titans last year and a last-second Blanda field goal that earned Houston a 31–31 tie later in the season proved to be the pivotal games that could have turned the season's outcome around for Boston. Another point or two was the only difference.

In 1962, Boston trailed Houston by a half game heading into that final weekend. A loss by Houston to the Jets would give the Patriots the title if they could beat the winless Oakland Raiders. But the Oilers did not lose, and Boston again had to settle for a second place finish. For Boston, the 1963 season was going to be the time to end the *IF ONLY* scenario, just as the 1955 Brooklyn Dodgers swore that there would be no more "Wait 'til next year" cries.

In many ways, preparing for the Patriots would be similar to preparing for the Bills. Both teams had stubborn defensive lines that always finished in the top three in the league. Boston was being especially tough against the run, and had finished 1st and 2nd in that area the past two seasons. Their front line included the best set of defensive ends in the AFL with Bob Dee and Larry Eisenhauer, both of whom were quick, aggressive, and All-AFL 1st or 2nd Team selections for previous three years. Eisenhauer posed and especially complicated blocking assignment as the "wildman" could hardly be contained consistently by one lineman. Tackle Dick Klein was pushed out in favor of Houston Antwine, who was tried at offensive guard as a rookie. Antwine would make the All-AFL Team in 1963 and the All-Time AFL Team at the end of the 1969 season. Veteran Jess Richardson, who may be remembered more as the last player to wear a helmet without a facemask than for his play, was an important cog in the Patriots defensive wheel. So too was top backup Jim Hunt who could have been a starter on many teams in the league.

Like Buffalo, Boston had a very active and above average trio of linebackers. Tom Addison was another perennial All-AFL selection and maybe over those three years the best outside linebacker in the AFL, and Jack Rudolph was not only steady, but one of the hardest hitters on the team. Starting at middle linebacker was Nick Buoniconti, who was selected to play in the 1963 All-Star Game and made the All-AFL Team in five of the next six seasons, as well as an All-Time AFL Team selection. Nick moved into a starting role at the end of his rookie season last year, prompting the team to trade the previous starter, Archie Matsos. He may have been inexperienced, but he was an active and mobile middle backer. Another area where the Pats resembled the Bills was in their defensive secondary, where they too were vulnerable to deep passes. Including 1963, the secondary of Dick Felt, Don Webb, Ron Hall, Ross O'Hanley, and Chuck Shonta were the worst team in the league at defending the pass, finishing dead last in 1961 and 1962, and gave up over 200 passing yards a game over the three seasons.

In part, their poor showing was the result of the All-Star play of their front seven. Teams came to realize that it would be much easier to pass on the Patriots than enter into hand-to-hand combat with their front four. So from 1961–1963, the Boston secondary defended more passing attempts than any other team in the AFL.

Offensively, their line was strongest at guard with Charley Long, an all-league tackle in '62 who moved to guard for '63 to take advantage of his swiftness in leading sweeps, and Billy Neighbors, a master at blocking fundamentals and conditioning. Neighbors made the All-AFL Team in '62 and '63.

Jim Colclough was the fastest of their receiving corps, which included Gino Cappelletti, the best kicker in the league, and tight end Tony Romeo. Larry Garron became the best of the runners since Ron Burton had injured his back against Oakland in their August 4 exhibition game. Where the Patriots outshone most other teams was at quarterback with Babe Parilli. At thirty-three, Parilli was another senior citizen like Tobin Rote, but finished 2nd in the AFL ratings among quarterbacks in '61 and '62. Since he moved from Oakland to Boston in '61, the Patriots had been a factor in the East. In their visit to San Diego in August, the Pats lost 50–17 with Tom Yewcic and Parilli splitting the time and Hadl and Breaux filling in for the injured Rote.

To beat Boston, the Chargers would need to keep Parilli's throws underneath their secondary and key on Larry Garron coming out of the backfield. Offensively they would have to challenge the secondary and confuse the front line using traps and screens in order to keep the pressure off Rote and allow him some time to connect with his receivers. Using his backs on swing passes had become a favorite short yardage call for Rote. He would also need use Kocourek more as a pass blocker to hold off Boston's blitz-happy linebackers.

THE UNCROWNED CHAMPS

It was a change of pace for San Diego on September 14, when they hosted the first regular season game under the lights of Balboa Stadium. It was also the first time the league would host more games on Saturday night than on Sunday afternoon. The Broncos were also playing a night game in Houston with only Oakland hosting the Bills on Sunday, while the Chiefs and the Jets were idle.

* * *

After Boston took the opening kickoff, it took both teams nearly the entire first quarter to get a 1st down. When the Patriots finally did, they put together a 12-play drive from their own 43 to the Charger 29 that ended with a 35-yard field goal. The Chargers offense was still in reverse with 6 yards of offense as the first quarter came to an end. Each time the Chargers had the ball

Keith Lincoln (22) returns a punt 47 yards that set up the Chargers' first touchdown.

they faced a fourth down needing more than 10 yards to make a first down, and were forced to punt.

Then when Boston punted from their own 43 in the second quarter, Keith Lincoln woke up the offense by returning Yewcic's punt right back to the original line of scrimmage with a 47-yard return.

They were on the scoreboard one needing to make up play later, as Tobin Rote connected with Lance Alworth for a 43-yard touchdown. That quickly, with two explosions, the Chargers led, 7–3.

It wouldn't take long for the Chargers second score, either. After the Chargers blocked a 42-yard field goal attempt, Rote sent Paul Lowe on a sweep to the left side. He then stopped short and threw a long pass to Jerry Robinson who took the completion 71 yards for another touchdown. That long strike lengthened the team's lead to 14–3. After looking so out of sync offensively to begin the second quarter, their trademark lightning strikes from all over the field stunned the Boston sideline.

Parilli was then forced off the field with a pinched nerve after being thrown to the ground by Earl Faison, reinjuring the collarbone he'd broken in Houston the previous year. Tom Yewcic relieved him and, on the next possession, drove them fifteen plays before he dove over the goal line from the 1-yard line, putting Boston back in the game, 14–10. Later in the quarter, Parilli checked back in and took his team to the Chargers 3-yard line before giving way to Cappelletti on 4th and goal to attempt a 10-yard field goal. Cappy, the second leading scorer in the league in '62, missed the kick as time ran out in the half. One problem the Chargers needed to fix before they returned to the field was their penchant for being penalized. Just as they did against the Bills, the Chargers were putting themselves in a hole by being flagged five times for 45 yards. By contrast, Boston had kept themselves out of trouble with only 5 yards in penalties.

As expected, the Chargers were having trouble running the football against Boston. On nine carries, they were held to only 25 yards gained. For the most part the Patriots were equally unsuccessful getting through Faison, Ladd, Gross, and Petrich. They ran the ball 23 times and were averaging only 2.8 yards a carry for the half. And with all the difficulty the Chargers were having in the first quarter, coupled with the quickness of their scoring in the second, they threw only eight passes in the half. It looked to be more of a defensive struggle for both teams as they readied for the second half.

The Chargers offense continued to sputter in the third quarter, but was bailed out twice with interceptions by Charlie McNeil and Paul Maguire on the Patriot's first two possessions of the half. After the McNeil interception, Rote started a mini-drive with short power runs by Gerry McDougall and quick passes to Alworth. And when Gillman decided to go for it on 4th and 1 from the Boston 32, he sent McDougall into the middle of the Patriot line. This time, Don Rogers and company gave him just enough room to keep the drive alive. On the next play, however, Rote fumbled and Boston was back in business. Tom Yewcic stayed in to quarterback the Patriots, but this time the defense shut him down and forced a punt. And, just as they started the second quarter with Lincoln's 47-yard punt return, this time it was Alworth's turn to start the surge. He fielded the ball at the San Diego 6-yard line and took off through the Boston coverage, racing 61 yards to the Pats 33. Another lightning strike for a big play.

John Hadl now relieved Rote and was also met with frustration by the Boston defense and got nowhere, bringing Maguire back out to punt. Coach Mike Holovak kept Parilli on the bench as Boston took again. On 2nd and 10, Yewcic was pinned in the pocket, but then escaped for a 19-yard jaunt to the Boston 39. Larry Garron broke loose for 28 yards to the Chargers 32 and it looked like Yewcic was going take the Pates in for six until Earl Faison and Bob Petrich met him in the middle of the field before he could release a pass and dropped him for an 8-yard loss. The drive ended when Cappelletti split the uprights and reduced the Charger lead to one, 14–13, with 10:37 left in the game.

The Chargers needed to take some time off the clock and also needed a drive that produced some insurance points. Using Keith Lincoln, who had been used sparingly in the first two games, to produce their longest run of the day on a sweep that netted 16 yards. Hadl followed with a 12-yard slant to Robinson that led

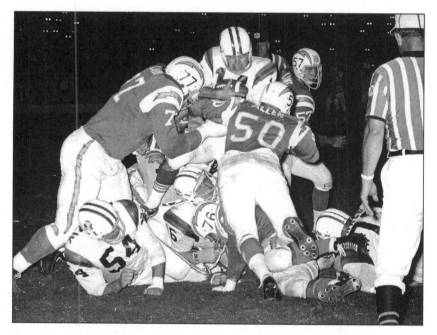

Ernie Ladd (77) and Chuck Allen (50) stop Boston's Tom Yewcic.

to George Blair increasing the San Diego lead to 4 points with a 31-yard field goal.

Both teams refused to let the other gain any momentum through the game and made every first down a struggle. Babe Parilli returned to the field with seven minutes left in the game, and faced another 4th and 1 from the Charger 40 to keep Boston's drive alive. Coach Mike Holovak decided that this was the time to take a chance, gain the elusive momentum, and give the Pates a chance to take the lead. He gave the sign to go for it, knowing he needed more than a Cappelletti field goal to win. As Parilli handed to his fullback Jim Crawford, the ball squirted loose, and although Parilli fell on it, they had to give the ball up on downs. Unable to move themselves, the Chargers had to kick it right back as Maguire punted into the end zone from 45 yards away.

Starting what would most likely be their last chance to score, Holovak again sent Yewcic out to start the drive from their own 20. Three straight completions to rookie Art Graham advanced the ball to the 42, but they would advance only six more yards before a fourth down incompletion gave the Chargers possession of the ball with 17 seconds to go.

On the game's final snap, John Hadl fell on the ball giving the Chargers their second victory of the season by defeating another contender from the East. Defeating both Boston and Buffalo on successive weeks was no small accomplishment. Both teams were preseason favorites and came at the Chargers with everything they had. Rote and Hadl handed off only 19 times for the day and threw only 20 passes, completing 7. It was the big play that Gillman stressed so often that won this game for San Diego. Lincoln's 47-yard punt return, Alworth's 43-yard touchdown catch, Paul Lowe's 71-yard touchdown pass to Jerry Robinson, and finally Alworth's 61-yard punt return that led to Blair's field goal accounted for all the Charger scoring. The offense struggled but was picked up by a defense that gave up yardage without yielding many points, and special teams that stung Boston with big plays. Chuck Allen was especially active with 22 tackles, as was Henry Schmidt, who had 10 in a supporting role. After their first two weeks of play, Sid Gillman's Chargers were exactly where they wanted to be. After the upcoming bye week, the Chargers would host the defending champion Chiefs at home.

Boston Patriots	3	7	0	3	-	13
San Diego Chargers	0	14	0	3	-	17

Bos-FG, Cappelletti 35
SD-Alworth, 43 pass from Rote (Blair kick)
SD-Robinson, 71 pass from Lowe (Blair kick)
Bos-Yewcic, 1 run (Cappelletti kick)
Bos-FG, Cappelletti 36
SD-FG, Blair 31

Charger Statistics:

Player	Rush Att	Yds	Avg	TD		
Keith Lincoln	8	39	4.9	0		
Paul Lowe	4	6	1.5	0		
Gerry McDougall	7	31	4.4	0		
	Pass Att	Cmp	Yds	TD	Int	Long
Tobin Rote	12	5	105	1	1	43
John Hadl	8	2	17	0	0	
Paul Lowe	1	1	71	1	0	71
	Rec	Yds	TD	Long		
Dave Kocourek	1	5	0	5		
Lance Alworth	4	76	1	43		
Gerry McDougall	1	21	0	21		
Jerry Robinson	2	83	1	71		

Interceptions: McNeil, Maguire
Tackles: Allen 22, Schmidt 10, Gross 8, Mitinger 7, Faison 7

Around the AFL: Oakland (2–0) beat Buffalo (0–2), Houston (1–1) defeated Denver (0–2), while Kansas City and New York were idle.

Earl Faison and Ernie Ladd

By 1959, pro football was gaining on baseball to displace it as America's favorite sport. The Colts vs. Giants overtime championship game the previous year captured the attention of fans across the country who were now demanding more coverage, stories, and games to watch. With stars like Johnny Unitas, Jimmy Brown, and Tommy McDonald, the publicity agents emphasized those on offense much more than on defense. That's what fans wanted, and what brought them into the stadiums as the fifties came to a close. As the New York Giants defense became more and more dominant and even cheered for more than their ineffective

Earl Faison (86) and Ernie Ladd (77) in their favorite position: hovering over a quarterback they had just sacked.

offense, there was a shift in what was drawing fans interest in the early sixties. New York defensive end Andy Robustelli even suggested that the offense should pay to get in the game and *Sport Magazine* glamorized Giants middle linebacker Sam Huff's with an article about his Violent World on defense. Another thing fans were enamored with was player size and the controlled violence of the sport, especially from the defense. Besides Huff, another defensive player who was drawing a lot of attention in the early sixties was the biggest man in the NFL, Colts defensive tackle Gene "Big Daddy" Lipscomb, who stood 6'6" tall and weighed 286 pounds. Pictures of Lipscomb always showed him dwarfing offensive linemen or raising his arms up to knock down a pass. To many opponents those arms were so large they looked like the uprights of a goal post. It was common knowledge for those inside the game that it may be the offense that puts fans in the seats, but it is the defense that wins championships.

* * *

When the AFL started play, one of the criticisms of the league was that it played very little defense and passed too much. But with teams like the Buffalo Bills, Boston Patriots, Houston Oilers, and San Diego Chargers, that was not the case. In 1961 when San Diego marched out their oversized defensive front line with rookies Ernie Ladd and Earl Faison, the interest in defense and size became a point of interest in the new league as well. Faison came to the Chargers as their first pick (seventh overall) out of Indiana as a two-way star at end. He also played on the Hoosier's basketball team. He was selected by the Detroit Lions in the NFL draft as well, but not until the fifth round and the 66th overall choice. He chose to sign with the AFL on New

Year's Eve in 1960 after playing in the East-West Shrine Game in San Francisco. Standing 6'5" and weighing in at 260 pounds, Faison was as big as "Big Daddy," but was not the biggest line-man on the Chargers. That status belonged to Ernie Ladd, who stood 6'9"and packed in 315 pounds. His chest size measured 52 inches, had a 39-inch waist, 20-inch biceps, 19-inch neck, and wore size 18D shoes. He was the biggest player in pro football and he played as big as his frame. It was no secret why he was referred to as "The Big Cat." One only needed to catch a glimpse of him in action to appreciate how nimble and quick he was for his enormous size. A defensive tackle from Grambling, Ladd was the Chicago Bears 4th pick and the Chargers 15th. Like Faison, he was also a basketball player in college, and together with the Chargers they became the most talked about front four in foot-ball and the two most glamorous defensive players in the AFL.

During their rookie season, they were to be the subject of a national magazine feature article while the Chargers were on an

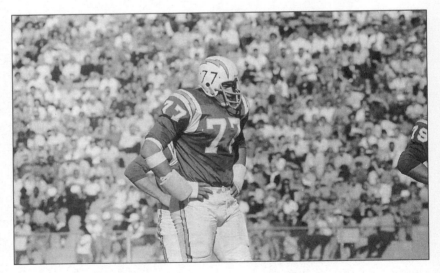

Ernie Ladd

100

Earl Faiscn (86)

11-game winning streak, and were described as "The Fearsome Foursome" by the *Sports Illustrated* writer. But before the story was pub_ished the win streak ended and the magazine never ran the story. Shortly afterwards, the Los Angeles Rams front line of Deacon Jones, Merlin Olsen, John LoVetere, and Lamar Lundy were being referred to by the press with the name previously reserved for the Chargers front line.

Besides the two first-year monsters on the original "Fearsome Foursome" were defensive end Ron Nery and tackle Bill Hudson until 1963, when Hudson was part of a trade with Boston and Nery was traded to Houston. Taking their place were two rookies who were larger than the men they replaced. Bob Petrich from West Texas played with unbridled energy, and George Gross from Auburn was nicknamed "Mr. Muscles" for his enormous size and strength. Not only were both players bigger, they were also younger and much faster, making the fearsome factor even more ferocious.

From 1961 to 1965, Faison and Ladd played in the league championship every year except 1962, when Faison injured his knee and Ladd dislocated his shoulder. Coincidence? Seeing as everyone knew that the Charger defense started and ended with Ladd and Faison, it seems pretty likely that their absence played a significant role in the Chargers '62 downfall. So no one was surprised that after Gillman grew tired of their annual salary disputes and cut ties with them after 1965 that the Chargers never returned to the AFL Championship game. After being released, Ladd signed with Houston and Faison moved on to Miami.

Together, Ladd and Faison made up the fiercest two pass rushers in football and, in their early days together, were able to just pass rush using their brute strength and were unable to be stopped by one blocker and many times even by two.

Len Dawson, quarterback, Kansas City Chiefs

With Ladd and Faison, the Chargers front four was really hard to avoid and even see over. I remember on third and long situations Ladd would be talking at me on the line, telling me he knew I had to pass and that he was coming to get me. It was because of those two that Hank Stram created the moving pocket, because they were so big and rushed so fast and hard that he had to get me away from them. We tried to play-action pass to hold them on the line and then roll the pocket away from them so I could see the receivers. You never heard much from Faison unless it was his footsteps bearing down on you, but those two guys were just so big and athletic that they just ran over people.

Dick Harris

Ernie was like a brick wall. He was 6'9", over 300 pounds, and had no gut like most of the big guys who had big bellies hanging over their belts. Ernie was trim and fast. He played basketball in college and was always looking to win at everything; cards, pool, you name it. He and Lincoln use to play some really competitive ping pong games back at Rough Acres.

Ed Budde, guard, Kansas City Chiefs

When I had to play across from Ladd, he was the biggest guy I ever saw. He was strong as an ox and the best defensive tackle I ever played against.

Len Dawson

Ladd always felt that Sid Gillman never paid him what he was worth. He really knew the value of money and use to be a pro wrestler in the off season. When he came to Kansas City in 1967, he told me that one time he was in Japan wrestling when training camp started so he wasn't there with the team. When Gillman contacted him about why he wasn't there, Ladd told him that he was making more money wrestling and that if he paid him what he was worth then he wouldn't have to have a second job and he'd be in camp on time. He knew he had the upper hand on Gillman.

Ernie Ladd, a.k.a. "The Big Cat."

With most teams being right-handed (running to their right side), Gillman would put Ladd and Faison together on that side at times to deter teams from running in that direction. It really created some tough match-ups, and when the two were side-by-side you usually needed three or more men to contain them.

Ed Budde

Ernie was the biggest guy I ever saw and did not have an ounce of fat on him. Just the sight of him could make you cringe, knowing you had to play across from him. And he used to like to talk to you on the line. He used to tell me, "Budde, I can put you out of the game anytime I want to. But I like you so I think I'll let you stay in today." There was probably more truth to that than I'd like to admit. When he got down in his stance, I would see these big veins and muscles popping and all I could think of was that it was going to be a very long day. We had some tough battles back then, but we all had respect for each other even though we didn't always like each other.

I remember being in the locker room shaving one day and all of a sudden I hear the guys behind me chattering about us just trading for Ladd. I'm saying to myself "Oh man, he and I are going to go at it right when he gets here," and just then he turns the corner to where I was with this big old smile on his face and says, "Hey man, how's it going? Man we really had some battles, didn't' we?" He could be just as easy-going off the field as he was nasty on it.

Boston center Jon Morris even commented that when Ladd played in front of him that he was so big he blocked out the sun, the linebackers, and the goalposts. And that it made him feel like he was being locked in a closet.

Art Powell, split end, Oakland Raiders

Ernie was like a mountain: big but very trim. Just a big old farm boy. The Chargers would put him over center to clog it up because you needed two guys to block him. I'd watched him get up with the guys he'd tackle or linemen he'd knock down and when they were side-by-side everyone else looked like little kids next to him.

As a rookie, Ladd had the advantage of playing against men who were physically smaller than him, and he relied mostly on his size and strength to move them out of the way. But as they became more familiar with his physical style, he knew he'd have to continue to develop his skills and moves to keep up his level of dominance. One adjustment he had to make was to curb his temper. And once he was able to make that adjustment, he saw an improvement in his defense. As a rookie he worked with Chuck Noll, who was in charge of the linebackers and front defensive line. Noll worked with Ladd to change his pattern of just knocking over his blockers. He would then rush in as tall as he could. Noll, showed him that by changing his angle to be lower, he would be even harder to block. As a result, his rush got stronger and he could get into the backfield faster, as well as chase runners down on angles more efficiently.

When interviewed later in his career for *Sport* magazine, Ladd told Bill Libby that aside from his size, his greatest asset was his ability to move left or right quickly. He continued that he wasn't a guy who got a hunk of weight and headed in a straight path and couldn't turn, and admitted that it had taken him years to develop the basic fundamentals without using brute strength. He also felt that he would not have made it as a rookie if he wasn't big and strong and knowing that he had a lot of things to learn. That kind of approach is what enabled him to play in the All-Star Game from 1961–1965, and make the All-AFL Team in 1961, 1964, and 1965.

Billy Joe, fullback, Denver Broncos
Avoiding Ladd and Faison was always my goal as a runner. I'd try to go wide or have a trap play called for me, then come back inside a little bit just to keep them guessing. It was usually an exercise in futility to try and run inside on them consistently. We also tried to throw quick passes on

them because they rushed so hard and fast. Our offensive line would prepare for them and have a plan to block them, but when you are dealing with players that big and talented you just couldn't contain them. I was a big back out of college, 250 pounds and was a shot putt throwing champion and always lifted weights, so I felt I was pretty strong. I was usually kept in to help block them on passing plays. They were tough, man, real tough.

Libby also described Ladd as having a corner on being ornery. "Ladd's intemperate independence has been a headache to the Chargers ever since he joined them." Libby wrote. Of which Ladd said, "I've always been bold. In my rookie year when I asked for a half day off and they didn't give it to me, I took it anyway." He could be equally as mellow and nice, but when he was ornery, you did not want to be in the same area code. For four years he was unstoppable playing defensive tackle.

Bobby Bell, Kansas City Chiefs' Hall of Fame linebacker

I was the long snapper for the Chiefs on punts and field goals. When I was a rookie, the first time we played the Chargers I went in and got the ball to snap it. Then I looked up and there was Ernie Ladd and Earl Faison head up in front of me on the line. Ladd gave me a look, kind of like he might be kidding but he might not be kidding look, and said, "hold on, rookie, we're going to knock you back into Dawson's [the field goal holder] lap." With each one on both my shoulders I did what I could to hold my own. They were really great players.

Billy Joe

Faison was faster than some halfbacks. He was really mobile and a punishing pass rusher. The thing that was so great about him was that if you got by him he was fast enough to run you down.

Fred Arbanas, tight end, Kansas City Chiefs

Earl had a great temperament. He really never got too upset about anything. He didn't seem to like to do much talking on the field either, but I'll tell you what; if he didn't injure his knee that second year he'd be in the Hall of Fame. No one player could block him. I remember one play, maybe in

Earl Faison signs an autograph for a young fan.

'62, when I was a rookie and we were playing the Chargers in Dallas. Jerry Cornelison was the tackle aside of me and I forgot the snap count. "Chicken Hawk" as we called him, had Faison on his shoulder. I whispered to Jerry as we got down in our stance, "What's the count?" He said "Two" and right then Faison nailed "Chicken Hawk" at one and a half. He just destroyed the play and knocked the helmet off Cornelison. Back in huddle, JC was putting his helmet back on and looked over at me with this deadly look and said, "I'll never give you the count again." Earl also had great hearing.

Dave Hill, offensive tackle, Kansas City Chiefs

Earl Faison was unbelievable. I used to try to talk to him at the line and one time I remember him saying, "You better watch out, Hill. I'm going to trick you this time." I just stayed down in my stance and said, "Earl, I've played you so much I know all the tricks in your book." Then I'd give him a fake like throwing my arm out as if I was going one way and sometimes he'd go for it.

He was so gifted that sometimes he would slack off. He was best defensive end I ever played against. Back then his knee injury would never go away. He was a great pass rusher and was the quickest guy I ever played [against]. If I could get close I could hold him, but he would give me a great head or shoulder slap and get by me, so I tried to get him to the outside next time. We had a real love-hate relationship.

They had a pretty good team all around but their front four was absolutely great, maybe the best of their time. We would pull a guard and try to trick them into going the opposite way and then run a counter play. I think at times Earl's quickness became a weakness, too. If we were going to run a play that went off-tackle, sometimes I would drop back like it was going to be a pass and he'd run right by the runner. Or I'd have to pull outside with a head fake to move him that way; otherwise I couldn't block him straight up. I'd have to come up with ways to trick him like he was trying to trick me. If I didn't do those things I wouldn't have been able to play against him.

When Ladd hurt his knee, too, he became disenchanted with Gillman as a GM and his contract, and requested to be traded. He and Gillman were always at odds, and Ladd made his feelings known that he thought Gillman let his GM position influence some of his coaching decisions. Ladd wanted Gillman to just be the coach but knew that was never going to happen. Even though Ernie loved him as a coach, by 1965 their relationship was headed down a river of no return. Ladd, as did some other players, felt that Gillman the GM caused Gillman the coach to lose key players, which ultimately broke up the championship team. Tensions grew to be so bad that Ladd started the '65 season on indefinite suspension for holding out with Faison, and threatened to play out their contract option and become free agents.

It was an interesting contrast with Ladd and Faison. Ernie was the talker at the line and made no bones about his ornery demeanor, and Earl, who was his equal and maybe even more so on the field, rarely said a word to those he played across from. He was liked as much for his mild demeanor as Ladd was feared for being the opposite. But both All-Stars bonded more with each than any of the others. They often roomed together on the road and even endured Rough Acres by sharing a cabin. It was

Ladd who also relied on his buddy to calm his temper during games.

Their relationship and All-Pro status also gave them what they felt was leverage during contract time, much the same way that Dodgers future Hall-of-Fame pitchers Sandy Koufax and Don Drysdale would do in 1966 in their highly publicized contract holdout. After sitting out six games in the 1962 season with a knee injury, Faison reported late to camp after his own contract dispute. The dispute seemed to drive a deep wedge into his relationship with his coach and created a problem that never went away. And just like it did with his defensive line mate Ernie Ladd, at times it effected Gillman's decisions about him. Although Faison was a consistent All-Star, he never felt as though he was being compensated fairly, and year after year Gillman, Ladd, and Faison would butt heads when negotiations would begin. Gillman was stubborn, Ladd ornery, and Faison determined, and no one came close to backing down.

On January 15, in 1966, Ladd and Faison were traded to the Houston Oilers, but the trade was voided by Commissioner Foss when he discovered that Bud Adams had illegally tampered with the two Chargers by approaching them while they were still under contract. The tension never subsided after the trade was nullified, and with Faison's performance suffering because of back problems and the bitterness surrounding his contract, Gillman released the All-Star, who signed with the expansion Miami Dolphins the next day. As a free agent, Ladd returned to Adams and signed with the Oilers. As quickly as the Chargers liked to strike for a touchdown, their two best and most notable defensive stars were gone after leading them to four championship games in five years, including the last three in a row. Quietly the rest of the team had to wonder if they would still be on the team if Gillman the coach had negotiated the deals, as opposed to Gillman the GM.

They had come a long way from the days when Sid described Faison's hits as sadistic and stated that no one would ever run over Earl Faison, who he saluted as the best defensive lineman in the league. Then, when the man whom they called "The Tree" injured his knee in 1962, things slowly began to unravel. Once praised for his quickness, strength, and intelligence, and predicted to reach greatness, Faison, although still one of the most dominating defensive players in the AFL, started to hedge on some game situations to favor his injured knee. Some felt that it was a mental thing and noted that his pride, interest, and ability never waned. Some said that there were times when Faison would take plays off rather than stress his knee unnecessarily. But when it came to rushing the quarterback and tackling runners, Faison still excelled. Gillman even said that if he ever got over the tendency to favor the knee, that there would be no stopping him. Faison of course felt that Gillman should have been backing up his confidence with a bigger contract. As long as Faison and Ladd were wearing lightning bolts on their helmets, the Chargers never had to worry about how to stop the run, or who was going to be able to get to the quarterback. The answer always pointed to "The Tree," and "The Big Cat."

Len Dawson
San Diego had the best front four I ever played against with Ladd and Faison, and that includes the Minnesota Vikings Super Bowl team with Carl Eller, Alan Page, and Jim Marshall.

Game 3: Making a Statement

Kansas City Chiefs
Sunday, September 29, 1963, at San Diego
Balboa Stadium
Attention: 22,654

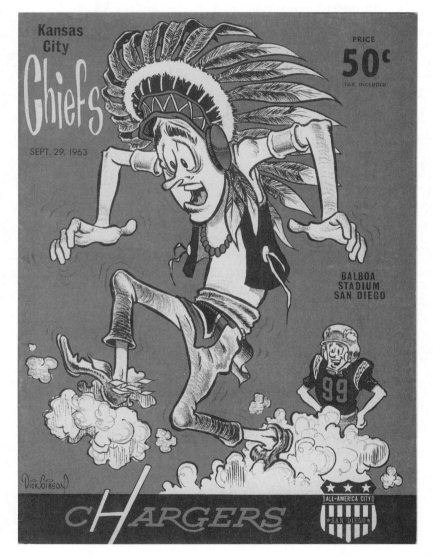

If you want to be the champions, you have to beat the champions. The Dallas Texans won the right to call themselves the champions by beating Houston 20–17 in the second overtime period of the 1962 Championship Game, which was the longest game ever played in professional football history.

Shortly after becoming the AFL Champions, league creator and Dallas Texans owner Lamar Hunt realized that his hometown was not big enough to support the two professional football teams that shared the Cotton Bowl. Courted by community leaders in Kansas City, Missouri, Hunt officially moved his team to the Midwest in February and renamed them the Kansas City Chiefs to honor both the region's heritage and the city's top recruiter, mayor H. Roe "The Chief" Bartle.

The move was good for the franchise, but did not sit well with a large contingent of the team's players. Seventeen roster players had played their college games in the Southwest Conference or had ties with Texas, and some others used their championship checks to purchase homes in Dallas. Before the new Chiefs could even think about mounting a title defense, they needed to repair the hard feelings among many of their Texan players who opposed the move. They also needed to heal the despair in the aftermath of the death of popular rookie teammate, Stone Johnson, which was the result of a kickoff block in an exhibition game on August 31 played in Wichita against the Houston Oilers. The two matters seemed to haunt the Chiefs all year.

Despite the irritation with their transfer to the Midwest and while still grieving for their teammate, the defending champions were on target when they kicked off the 1963 season with a visit to Denver to play the resurgent Broncos. The Broncos stampeded out of the chute the previous year with a 7–2 record, so the Chiefs knew there was a need to focus. When the opening whistle blew, the team responded as never before, killing all hope for Denver that they may have turned the corner and would make a run at the Western title. The Chiefs rained down on the Broncos almost more than they were rained upon on the gloomy, wet opening night with a 59–7 pummeling, reinforcing the talented Kansas City franchise that they could pull together under extenuating circumstance and play perhaps even stronger because of them. Their second game in Buffalo two weeks later caught them a bit stale, though, and required a second half surge to score the game's final 17 points to earn a 27–27 tie. Facing their third straight game on the road, and with some players still wrapping up loose ends in Texas, there were also issues that Stram needed to be concerned about. Another concern (besides playing the undefeated Chargers) was his team's inability to run against the Bills, grinding out only 49 yards on 22 carries with Len Dawson picking up 28 of those while scrambling outside of the pocket.

The self-made Kansas City squad, put together by Hank Stram, included only one former NFL player (Dawson) and started the season with a mix of old and new on the defensive front. They now featured defensive end Mel Branch and defensive tackle Jerry Mays, both All-AFL players, and two rookies who would end their careers with Hall-of-Fame inductions, tackle Buck Buchanan, and end Bobby Bell. This group presented coach Madro's retooled offensive line with new guards Sam Gruneisen and Pat Shea, their third straight challenge against an outstanding defensive line. Both guards were among six who were used in last year's injury-riddled season and, although young and inexperienced, they had already shown signs of coming into their own. Unretired backup Sam DeLuca and rookie Walt Sweeney offered depth for the two starters. The Chiefs liked to move Mays over center when they used three linemen and four linebackers, so how well center Don Rogers could hold him off would be key to any Chargers success in giving Rote time and keeping him safe. Defensive tackle Paul Rochester, a starter the previous year, was also difficult to handle and matched up with Pat Shea in a wrestling match of the team's strongest man. Bobby Bell sat the Chargers game out with an injury, so Buck Buchanan moved over to take the defensive end spot. Going head-to-head with Ron Mix would be an education for the Grambling rookie, since Mix was usually matched up against Earl Faison in practice and was no stranger to handling big men.

* * *

After starting Bob Jackson and Keith Lincoln in the backfield for the first two games, Gillman was starting both Lincoln and Lowe together against the Chiefs with the hope that the tandem would help their offense catch fire. They had scored only 31 points in their first two games, and although Tobin Rote had completed 23 of his 41 passes, the team's longest completion to date had been thrown by Paul Lowe. One player who had been playing especially well was wide receiver Jerry Robinson, while filling in for Don Norton. Norton was not due back until late October, so it was crucial for Robinson to continue to be a deep threat and keep teams from concentrating on just stopping Alworth. When Alworth was injured after the fourth game of the '62 campaign, Robinson stepped in and caught 21 passes the rest of the way.

Taking over in Norton's absence, the speedy wide receiver had caught 4 passes for 128 yards and a game-breaking 71-yard TD pass from Lowe.

Defensively, the Chargers would have to contain the most balanced offense they had seen so far. Kansas City had a quarterback who could throw short and long, and who could effectively run out of trouble. This was a big concern for Noll's group. Their backs presented additional problems with rookie-of-the-year fullback Curtis McClinton, the inside force, and the elusive Abner Haynes, the team's outside threat. Haynes could also run from the slot and wide receiver set and catch passes anywhere on the field. Tight end Fred Arbanas was a great blocker who averaged 16 yards a catch in '62. Bud Whitehead who was filling in while Dick Harris recovered from injury would be the man with the most pressure, having to deal with 6'3" possession receiver Chris Burford. Through two games, Burford had already caught 15 passes (11 against Buffalo) for 4 touchdowns. His flanker partner was Frank Jackson, who converted from halfback to take advantage of his speed. He'd caught 5 passes in each game, but did not play in the August 3 exhibition game against the Chargers, so rookie Dick Westmoreland was seeing him for the first time. The Chargers were unable to concentrate on any single area since the Chiefs were so balanced. If they took away Burford, Arbanas would step up. If they stopped Haynes, McClinton would power through. And if they double-teamed Burford or Jackson, the other one would draw weaker coverage. In short, the Chargers defense would have their hands full and the offense would have to play a much more penetrating game than they had thus far. How well they ran ball against the Chiefs was the key to the entire climate of the game.

All week long, San Diego had been waiting for some relief from the 100-degree heat that suffocated the area. So when a 10-mph breeze dropped the game time temperature down to a tolerable 80 degrees, the respite was a welcome sign for good things to come. The Chiefs 1–0–1 record was negligible, knowing that their tie was no fluke against a very good Buffalo team that took the Chargers the distance without Cookie Gilchrist on opening day. Everyone knew that this would be an important division match-up for the two Western foes.

As 22,000 onlookers sat in Balboa Stadium on what was described as a sultry Sunday afternoon the Chargers were looking to make a statement against the defending AFL Champions. And on the Chiefs first possession of the game, the Chargers defense emphatically made their statement. After stopping Kansas City fullback Curtis McClinton for a 1-yard gain on their second play from scrimmage, linebacker Paul Maguire created the first break of the game by intercepting his third pass of the year and gave the Chargers possession at their own 49-yard line.

Although the Chargers punted on their first possession to open the game after first testing Lowe and then Lincoln on sweeps, there was no cause for concern as Gillman was notorious for "testing the waters" early in the game to see what the defense was doing to counter his play calls. On their second try, they threw an incomplete pass to Alworth and lost yardage on a swing pass to Lincoln. Although they went three and out both times, Gillman was getting a feel for what kind of adjustments his offense would need to make.

Bobby Hunt, safety, Kansas City Chiefs

The Chargers used their first series or two to test the defense. They tried to isolate a back on a linebacker or corner and see if they could beat them on a pass and would feel Alworth out on a safety with a deep route.

Many times Gillman would test out teams to see what kind of coverage they were in or how they would react on certain plays. He wasn't interested so much in what happened around the ball, but in what was happening away from it, to give him an idea of what else might work.

Faison brings down Abner Haynes.

San Diego made another statement on Kansas City's second possession after Faison pulled Abner Haynes down from behind for a loss to bring up a 3rd and long situation. Forced out of the pocket by a big pass rush, Dawson was stripped of the ball. Faison, in hot pursuit, recovered the fumble and gave the Chargers a 1st and 10 at the KC 25. Another sweep by Lowe netted 5 yards and, on the next play, the Chargers beat the Chiefs coverage down the right side with a 19-yard touchdown pass to Dave Kocourek.

Right before the end of the first quarter, the Chargers created another turnover when Charlie McNeil intercepted Dawson again at the Chiefs 47. Then on the third play of the second

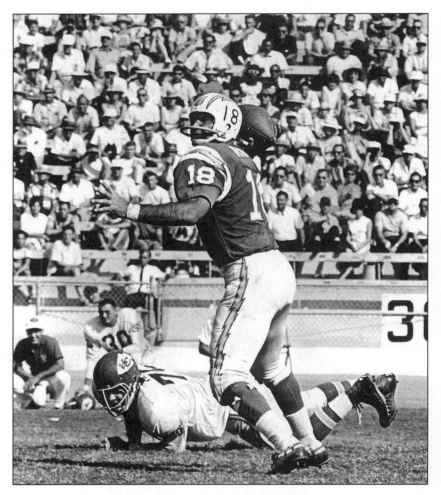

Tobin Rote throwing a touchdown pass to Dave Kocourek.

quarter, Rote caught the Chiefs in a zone coverage mistake and hit Kocourek alone down the left sideline for a 35-yard score and a 14–0 lead.

After KC put together a few first downs, the Chargers forced another punt and Rote put together the team's best drive of the half. Five consecutive runs by Lincoln and Lowe for 23 yards gave them two more first downs. After overthrowing Jerry Robinson deep, the Chargers put on a deluge of plays that took them into the end zone for the third time. Lowe picked up 25 yards aided down field by crack back blocks from Lincoln and Alworth; another completion to Kocourek took them 16 yards closer and two more sweeps by Lowe gained 17 additional yards. On 1st and 10 from the 15, Rote threw his third touchdown pass of the game by using deception to confuse the Chiefs. He lined Kocourek up on the right side, sent Lowe on a circle pattern to the left, and then hit Lincoln with a swing pass to the vacated left flat. Twelve yards later Lincoln cut inside to avoid attempted tackles by Dave Grayson and Johnny Robinson and took the ball in for six more points.

It took 14 minutes and 50 seconds for Kansas City to put points of their own on the scoreboard, and as the half ended the Chargers were firmly in charge, 21–3. Defensively it was the best half of football San Diego had played in some time, allowing only 20 yards rushing, 57 passing, intercepting three passes, and recovering a fumble. Offensively the results were just as good and the Lincoln and Lowe tandem was showing great results with 96 yards gained. Rote completed 6 of his 10 passes for three touchdowns.

The lightning was still striking for the Chargers on their first drive of the second half with Lincoln and Lowe sharing runs on six of the next ten plays and picking up five first downs. But the drive was halted when Rote was sacked and George Blair missed

Keith Lincoln runs against the Chiefs.

a 35-yard field goal attempt. The period would end without any more scoring. When the clock hit zero to end the fourth quarter, the Chargers had won their third game in a row, 24–10, and took over leadership of the West.

After the game, Sid Gillman could hardly contain himself and called the win a "Great, great, victory. It's our greatest victory yet, we had fine offense and a tremendous defense. . . . We controlled the ball for 8:45 in the third quarter. . . . It was our best all-around effort, we are mighty happy."

Hank Stram gave credit to the Chargers by calling them a "great team," and felt that his team was not able to handle the outstanding defensive effort by the daunting front four, saying, "You win games up front and that's where they won it, they controlled things up front."

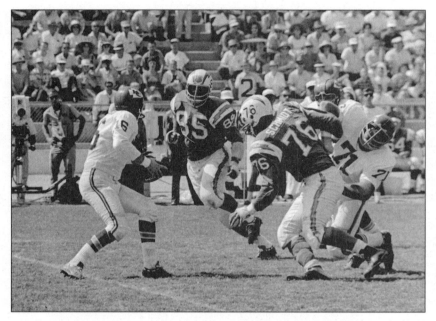

Hank Schmidt (76) and Bob Petrich (85) ready to sack Len Dawson.

Chris Burford, split end, Kansas City Chiefs

The Chargers always gave us trouble. That 1962 year was an anomaly; they still had all that good talent that was injured the year before. Hank Stram was a great coach, but sometimes he was stubborn with our game strategy. He didn't want to admit any weakness, and just wanted to jam things down a team's throats and beat them at their strong points. He believed if you beat them there, you take away their confidence and you can then dominate them . . . but it didn't work every time. In that game, it was the wrong strategy.

The Chargers defense was just outstanding against the defending champions and completely shut down their running game.

123

THE UNCROWNED CHAMPS

Fourteen times the Chiefs tried to penetrate the foursome and picked up only 27 yards. That forced Dawson into a lot of passing downs, which was instrumental in the Chargers forcing four turnovers. The Chiefs offense never got on track and scored only a lone field goal in the last 10 seconds of the first half and a 2-yard touchdown pass with 90 seconds left in the game.

| Kansas City Chiefs | 0 | 3 | 0 | 7 | - | 10 |
| San Diego Chargers | 7 | 14 | 0 | 3 | - | 24 |

SD-Kocourek, 19 pass from Rote (Blair kick)
SD-Kocourek, 35 pass from Rote (Blair kick)
SD-Lincoln, 16 pass from Rote (Blair kick)
KC-FG, Brooker 28
SD-FG, Blair 38
KC-Arbanas, 2 pass from Dawson (Brooker kick)

Charger Statistics:

Player	Rush Att	Yds	Avg	TD		
Keith Lincoln	14	59	4.2	0		
Paul Lowe	17	91	5.4	0		
	Pass Att	Cmp	Yds	TD	Int	Long
Tobin Rote	16	10	127	3	1	35
John Hadl	3	2	41	0	0	
	Rec	Yds	TD	Long		
Dave Kocourek	3	71	2	35		
Lance Alworth	2	16	0	8		
Jacque MacKinnon	1	13	0	13		
Jerry Robinson	2	40	0	28		
Keith Lincoln	4	28	1	16		

Interceptions: McNeil, Maguire, Allen
Tackles: Petrich 9, Allen 7, Westmoreland 7, Ladd 6, Blair 6

Around the AFL: For only the second time in the season, every team was in action. Houston (2–2) evened their record by keeping Buffalo (0–3–1) winless with a 31–20 win. New York (2–1) took over the top spot in the East by handing Oakland (2–2) their second loss in a row, 10–7, and Denver (1–2) got their first win of the season by shocking Boston (2–2), 14–10.

Dave Kocourek

Dave Kocourek was big enough to play tight end, with a frame of 6'5" and 240 pounds, and quick enough to play wide receiver.

As an original member of the Los Angeles Chargers, he never had a marquee name like Paul Lowe, Jack Kemp, Keith Lincoln, or Lance Alworth, and never gained the Hollywood notoriety some of his teammates did. But he was a big-time performer when given the call, always there to throw a key block or make a clutch catch. He played a steady game mostly in anonymity, starting out in 1960 as a flanker so teammate Howard Clark could be slotted at the tight end position, where Kocourek was better suited to play. He led the team in receptions over their first two years and then, after making the All-Star team in 1961 while splitting his time between flanker and tight end and catching 55 passes for 1,055 yards, he was moved to tight end in 1962 to take advantage of his blocking prowess. He continued to be an All-Star every year through 1965, and was either a 1st or 2nd team all-league selection at tight end over the same period.

Bobby Hunt, safety, Kansas City Chiefs
When we were in zone defense, I had to cover Kocourek. He was a good possession receiver and a strong blocker. Once he became a tight end they didn't send him deep as much, but when he caught those short passes he could take them a long way.

Their backs were such good receivers that Kocourek sometimes was asked to block more than usual, maybe more than he should have. If they had thrown to him more he might have been the best tight end in football. But even so he was right up there with the best.

In his six years with the Chargers, Dave caught 218 for 3,720 yards and 21 touchdowns. He also holds the distinction of playing in more AFL Championship Games (7) than any other AFL player. When the league became part of the NFL after the 1969 season, Kocourek was voted to the All-Time AFL 2nd Team.

Cornerback teammate Dick Harris remembers him best as one of the players he had to scrimmage against in practice.

Dick Harris

I loved playing for Chuck Noll. He let me be a free spirit and practice the bump and run before it became popular. I started doing it on our receivers in practice; just coming up to the line and popping them. Back then you could do pretty much anything to a receiver until the ball was in the air. Well, I started doing it to Kocourek when he still played flanker and he really got on me. He said I was getting too concerned with banging guys instead of covering them and that if I would just start covering people that I wouldn't get beaten so much. He was the only one who told me what I needed to hear and I thanked him for it later.

"Big Dave" caught 23 passes in 1963 while being nagged all year with lingering injuries. Paul Lowe referred to him as "Iron" because, in Lowe's words, he was an "iron man" for playing hurt no matter how much pain he was in. He was always on the field for the team.

As a tight end who loved to block, Kocourek also reaped the benefits of playing for Sid Gillman, who liked involving his tight ends in five-man passing routes. The Chargers were so dangerous on the outside that teams could not cover them man-to-man, so they had to play zone more often. That helped Kocourek because

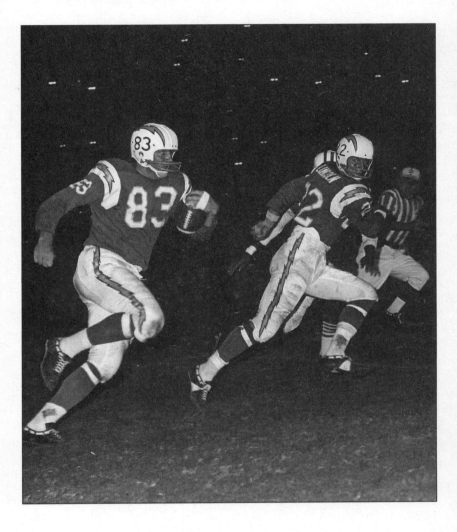

he was great at finding seams in the secondary and getting open deeper than most tight ends were able to. His 17-yard-per-catch career average as a Charger is a testament to that. What Gillman liked most about him was how quick he was at firing out to block so that he could contain the defensive ends. And when running pass routes, he was able to run stop-and-go patterns as expertly as anybody.

When newspaper and magazines would describe him, they always used words like hard-working, rugged, sure-handed, and steady. Kocourek could always be counted on, year after year, for that steady blocking and sticky pass catching. He never looked for attention or praise, saying instead that his teammates' respect was what made him most satisfied.

There is a scene in the movie *Field of Dreams* that can best sum up Kocourek's football life. When "Shoeless Joe" Jackson retires to the cornfield for the last time, he turns to Ray Kinsella and pays him the sincerest compliment an athlete can receive from his peers. He looked him straight in the eyes and said "Hey, Ray . . . you were good." In a nutshell, that, too, can be said straight up about Dave Kocourek . . . "He was good."

Game 4: Giving One Away
@ Denver Broncos
Sunday, October 6, 1963
Bears Stadium
Attendance: 18,428

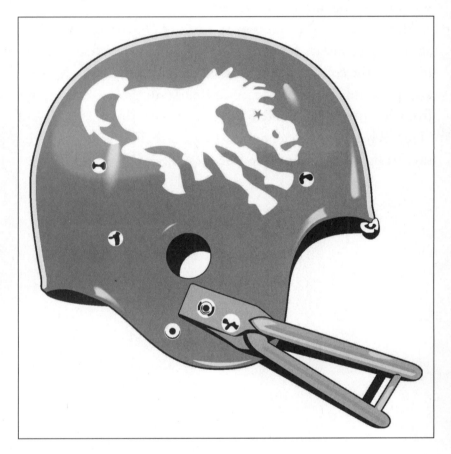

In their first two years in the American Football League, the Denver Broncos found themselves looking up from the cellar at the rest of the Western Division teams. With records of 4–9 and 3–11, it was only the makeshift Raiders that posted a worse history. A change in coaching in 1962 under the leadership of former Charger assistant Jack Faulkner started moving things in the right direction, as he had a strong desire to change the culture of the losing franchise. Beginning with the burning of the most despicable-looking uniforms in pro sports, the brown and gold went up in flames along with their haphazard approach to the game.

Faulkner brought in new orange and blue uniforms and a game plan that changed weekly to utilize the team's strengths, hide its weaknesses, and adapt to their upcoming opponent. The turnaround caught the league by surprise, and it wasn't until the Broncos led the West with a 7–2 record that the rest of the division adjusted, sending Denver into a tailspin that saw them lose their last five games of the season. Still, their 7–7 finish was a marked difference to their disappointed past.

The game plan over the first three years in Denver was pretty simple: Pass to Lionel Taylor. If that worked, then keep passing to him. If it didn't work, then pass to him until it did work. There was relatively no running and definitely no inside force to be reckoned with. That changed, too, in 1963, with the arrival of power runner Billy Joe. A 250-pound fullback out of Villanova, Joe was the runner that Denver needed to force defenses from rushing their passer with abandon. Faulkner planned on making him the feature back in the offense to take the pressure off Taylor and force the defenses to be more conservative with their blitzing and pass rushing.

Billy Joe, fullback, Denver Broncos

Faulkner was an excellent coach. He interacted well with players and gave me the opportunity to be the

131

featured back in the running game as a traditional power fullback. Donnie Stone was the halfback and I had to beat Bo Dickinson out for the position. Dickinson was the fullback the previous season, and Coach Faulkner wanted a bigger, stronger fullback to bulk up the position. Hewritt Dixon was also a rookie and I had to beat him out, too. I had a really good exhibition season and that was the deciding factor to how we would start the season.

In their opening day loss to Kansas City, the rookie carried nine times and picked up 61 yards while the Broncos got annihilated. The problem with the offense now was not just throwing to Taylor, it was *who* would be throwing to Taylor. In that first game, Frank Tripucka, their sore-armed senior citizen quarterback, threw four passes and had two of them intercepted before he was pulled in favor of rookie Mickey Slaughter.

In their second game, another loss, Tripucka threw eleven passes and had three intercepted before he not only retired to the bench, but retired for good. His 1,277 AFL passes and a career that began fifteen years had finally taken its toll and Tripucka knew it was time to hang up his cleats. Down to just rookies under center, Faulkner hired second-year man John McCormick, a punter/quarterback who had just been cut by Minnesota, and tossed him to the lions (actually, it was the Patriots) only days after arriving. Now with less than ten days on board, McCormick was drawing the start against the visiting Chargers.

It must have been quite shocking to the Boston Patriots a week earlier when the 0–2 Broncos hosted them after Denver spent their off-week licking their wounds from having 59 points scored on them by Kansas City and then falling six points short in Houston. The extra time to prepare apparently worked in their favor, as they came back from a 10–0 deficit in the third quarter to win, 14–10. Newly acquired John McCormick and Lionel Taylor teamed up for a 72-yard touchdown in the final period to stun the 2–1 Patriots and bring home their first win of the season.

Gillman had no scouting on the new Bronco thrower since he'd only thrown 18 passes for the Vikings in 1962 as a backup, and attempted only 7 passes against Boston. But he was confident his defense would be able to frustrate McCormick with pass rush pressure while also keeping an eye on the hard-running rookie Billy Joe. Joe had accumulated 164 yards rushing in three games for Denver and was giving them the inside bulk they had so desperately sought.

Billy Joe

While we were preparing for the Chargers, Coach Faulkner would be very serious about the game. He gave us a lot of insight as to what the Chargers would do based on how they would line up. I guess out of respect for his former boss he wanted to show coach Gillman that he was a good coach and how much he learned from him. It was a special week before that Chargers game. Having been their former defensive coach, he showed us what they would do from different defensive set-ups and how to react to certain coverages. He knew their tendencies and what they would do from certain places on the field. He really wanted to win against them.

Billy Joe showed he was the real deal on his first carry by taking off through the middle of the Chargers defense on a draw play for 16 yards. But his early impact was short lived, and he fumbled on the next play. Chuck Allen recovered the ball and gave the Chargers possession at midfield. Then the pattern of the game started to develop. In what would be the Chargers worst effort of the season, the first of their seven turnovers shifted the game's tide. After fielding Jim Fraser's punt at the San Diego 25, Keith Lincoln fumbled after a 7-yard return and the Broncos Tom Nomina recovered it at the 32. Four plays later, Gene Mingo started off the day's scoring with a 37-yard field goal. Thirty-two seconds after that, the Chargers took the lead and Lincoln quickly reprieved himself by catching a 39-yard touchdown pass to go ahead 7–3.

A minute later, that lead increased to 13–3, after Charlie McNeil intercepted his third pass of the season to set up a touchdown on the Chargers next play, a 31-yard pass to Paul Lowe, though George Blair's extra point attempt was blocked. Denver returned to score with a nine-play drive that covered 79 yards driven by Billy Joe and Donnie Stone most of the way. After stopping the league's best running team a week earlier, the Chargers were having trouble stopping Denver's inside game. Seven times in a row the Broncos sent Joe left and then Stone right inside their tackles with success. The drive started with a 14-yard screen pass to Joe, and he then picked up 2 yards going left, followed by Stone running into George Gross for a pickup of 1. Then it was Joe left for 9, Stone right for 18, and Joe left for 13 more. After two more short bursts by the duo, McCormick threw into the end zone for tight end Gene Prebola to close the San Diego lead to 13–10.

One area that the Chargers were still struggling with was their punting game. During the preseason, Gillman had given Lincoln

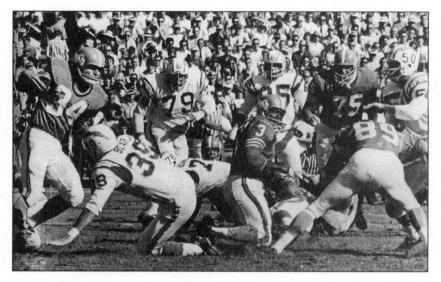

George Blair (39) moves in to stop Denver's Donnie Stone (34).

and Hadl a look at the punter's position, but they were unable to unseat the incumbent Paul Maguire. Although he had two punts of over 50 yards in his first three games, Maguire was averaging less than 40 yards on his fourth down kicks. After another Charger drive stalled, a punt from his own 24 slid off the side of his foot, giving Denver a first down inside the San Diego 43. Four more short plunges into the heart of the front four, followed by a couple of incompletions, had Mingo attempting another 37-yard field goal that fell wide left, but there was concern that the Broncos were gaining momentum and even their missed scoring attempts were keeping the Chargers deep in their own end.

Denver showed that they were not intimidated by the Charger defense and knew they could move the ball against them. As the Chargers took over at their own 20 after the missed field goal, Rote looked to strike quick and long. He sent Alworth flying down the right side and hit him at the 50, and Alworth never

135

stopped running until the Chargers had an 85-yard touchdown and a 10-point lead.

Although Denver was having success running the ball and keeping it away from the Chargers offense, Rote was using the long ball to keep his team ahead. Three touchdown passes of over 30 yards underlined their proficiency for scoring from anywhere on the field. Their penchant was also for doing it before the Broncos could adjust defensively. Of their five touchdowns on the day, four were on first down and the other was a second down play.

Lance Alworth

That's the way we played. We had so many guys who could break off long plays that we didn't need long drives that took a lot of time off the clock. We knew when we got the ball that sooner or later someone would break something for a long gainer that would either score or set up a score.

Charger trips to Denver always seemed to bring out the best in the Broncos and made the Chargers look very average. Back in August, the Broncos handed San Diego their first exhibition loss in four years, and their three previous regular season games there were always tight. The Broncos were enjoying their continued resurgence this day, and being behind by 10 points didn't appear to cause them any feelings of inferiority. On the ensuing kickoff, Gene Mingo returned the ball to the 38-yard line and, using the experience and savvy of Lionel Taylor against the inexperienced Dick Westmoreland, McCormick hit his split end four times for 64 yards and another Denver touchdown on a seven-play drive just before the half ended to separate the teams by only 3 points.

Each team gave the ball away twice in the first half with San Diego attempting only seven runs that picked up 28 yards. Denver's running game was giving Gillman fits, though. Eighteen attempts had gained 90 yards already after holding the Chiefs to less than 30 for an entire game the week before.

For the Chargers, the second half would be their worst of the year. The usually reliable Lincoln fumbled twice more on kick returns, giving him three special team fumbles for the afternoon and each time handing Denver a chance to convert. As he fielded the opening kickoff of the second half, Lincoln had a great return to the 35-yard line until he fumbled, with Denver's John McGeever recovering the ball. The defense held again, but Mingo kicked his second field goal of the day to tie the score at 20–20.

Kicking off this time, Mingo caught the Chargers by surprise with an onside kick that McGeever also recovered at the San Diego 39. The Broncos had the momentum while the Chargers looked dazed and confused. The Broncos drove down to the 18 where Mingo kicked another field goal. Denver now had a three-point lead.

There was still 9:18 left in the third quarter and, with the way the Chargers could break away runs and long passes, there was no panic to speak of. Then two more turnovers gave Mingo his fourth field goal and Denver a six-point lead. Rote had not only thrown an interception, which Denver did not convert on, but he also fumbled at his own 13. Lucky for him and the Chargers, the defense bailed him out by holding the Broncos to Mingo's fifth field goal. The defense was keeping Denver at bay by holding them to 3 points after the turnovers and, under the circumstance, being behind by only six points after five turnovers averted what could have been a bigger disaster. Now they just had to stop giving Denver good field position, since they were putting points on the board nearly every time they crossed midfield.

As the fourth quarter began, Gillman had seen enough. The Chargers failed to score in the third quarter and Rote was obviously off his game, so he sent in John Hadl to try and change the tempo. It paid off immediately with a 19-yard touchdown pass to Lincoln. Somehow the Chargers, who had been playing so poorly and had handed Denver one scoring opportunity after another, regained the lead, 27–26, with nine minutes left in the game.

Unshaken, the Broncos stampeded back, and John McCormick went after Westmoreland again with his savvy end, Taylor. Taylor had been relatively quiet except for the one drive he scored on, but it was almost as if he were playing a game of cat and mouse with the rookie. When he shook him off at midfield this time, McCormick led him long down the left side line and he scored on a 49-yard TD pass. Denver had again regained the lead.

Taylor was the consummate possession receiver. He rarely outran defenders and so relied on deception and crisp, exact moves to break free. Over the first three years of his career he had frustrated many defensive backs with his ability to get open.[6]

---

6   In fact, of the 816 passes caught by Bronco players from 1960–1962, 33 percent found safety in the hands of Lionel Taylor. Against the Chargers this day he caught 7 of John McCormick's 18 completions (39 percent) for 142 yards. At the end of the '63 season, his four-year total accounted for 34 percent of the Broncos receptions.

Taylor was a guy who brought it every game and never took a play off. He was the Denver offense in their early days, and could very easily have been nicknamed "Mr. Consistency."

The Chargers fumbling ways returned when Lincoln fielded the ensuing kickoff and coughed it up again. Denver recovered and Donnie Stone snuck through the usually tight defense to score on a 39-yard run for a touchdown.

Hadl's second possession ended in still another turnover, as Denver's Goose Gonsoulin intercepted his pass and scored from 43 yards out. By scoring 21 points in the last five minutes, the Broncos had broken the game wide open and now led 47–27 with four minutes remaining.

For the entire second half, Denver had been able to start drives off of turnovers and four of their six scoring plays were

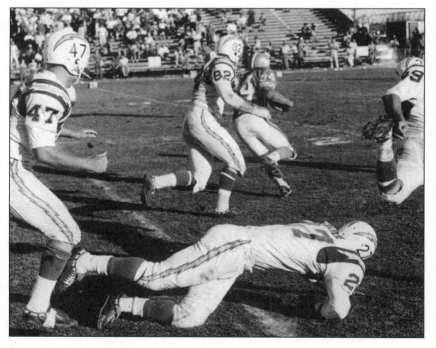

Donnie Stone enroute to a 39-yard touchdown.

results of Charger miscues, including their let down on the onsides kick recovery.

It wasn't that Denver was a particularly good team when you sized them up player for player and position by position. Their only real advantage besides Lionel Taylor was on defense with both safeties—Gonsoulin and former Charger Bob Zeman—but that was where it ended. Most teams came into Denver expecting to win, and most times they did. In 1963, they were the third-worst rushing and the worst passing team in the AFL and gave up more passing yards than any other team in the league. Some suggested in this game that the difference was coach Faulkner, who was on Gillman's staff in college, as well as in the NFL and AFL. He was so familiar with the Chargers that he was able to prepare his team for everything they would encounter. No matter what people hypothesized, the biggest factor in this game was the seven Charger turnovers. Three interceptions and four fumbles were just too much to overcome and gave Denver great field position, which enabled them to convert them into 23 points. Time and again Gene Mingo was able to turn a fumble or interception into 3 points and accounted for 20 points by himself on five field goals and five extra points. It was Denver's brightest moment and San Diego's lowest of the season.

In spite of the Chargers possession lapses, their offense did showcase their ability to strike quickly and from long range, which in turn gave them the confidence to be able to not only score but come back swiftly from any deficit. Of their twelve touchdowns this year, only one came from inside of 16 yards with eight from more than 30. Their offensive outbursts were not necessarily designed to gain large portions of real estate, but they had so many game-breaking players that any one of the five could score on a given play. Against Buffalo, Paul Lowe ran for 48 yards; against Boston, Alworth's score came from 43 yards away and Robinson's from 71. When they defeated Kansas City, Dave Kocourek scored on receptions of 19 and 35 yards and, at Denver, four of their five touchdowns started from over 30 yards away, with two covering more than 50 yards.

Defensively, the Chargers were challenged to keep the game close after the each error. They were able to hold the Broncos to just three field goals after the first five turnovers, breaking down for a lone touchdown after the sixth giveaway. The last turnover, Gonsoulin's interception return for a 43-yard touchdown, finally put the game away. Before Denver, the Chargers had given up only one touchdown in each of their first three games and none from over 4 yards. Denver exposed some holes in the fortress that would need plugging in the coming weeks. Taylor's long score from 49 yards and Stone's 39-yard run were issues that were particularly troublesome. They also needed to repair their mishandling of kick returns and cut down on interceptions. Through their myriad of errors, Denver was able to score more points in the fourth quarter than the Chargers allowed in any of their first three games. The midnight oil would be burning in the film room this week until Gillman found the remedies to get his Chargers back on track. Saying that "When you give 23 points away through turnovers you are not going to win," and, "You better protect the football above everything else." The message for the week was obvious: *The test of champions is how well they adjust and are able to come back after an off game.* The test would come next week when they hosted the New York Jets.

THE UNCROWNED CHAMPS

San Diego Chargers	13	7	0	14	-	34
Denver Broncos	3	14	9	24	-	50

Den-FG, Mingo 37
SD-Lincoln, 39 pass from Rote (Blair kick)
SD-Lowe, 31 pass from Rote (kick failed)
Den-Prebola, 12 pass from McCormick (Mingo kick)
SD-Alworth, 85 pass from Rote (Blair kick)
Den-Taylor, 24 pass from McCormick (Mingo kick)
Den-FG, Mingo 41
Den-FG, Mingo 26
Den-FG, Mingo 13
SD-Lincoln, 19 pass from Hadl (Blair kick)
Den-Taylor, 49 pass from McCormick (Mingo kick)
Den-Stone, 39 run return (Mingo kick)
Den-Gonsoulin, 43 int (Mingo kick)
SD-MacKinnon, 54 pass from Hadl (Blair kick)
Den-FG, Mingo 21

Charger Statistics:

Player	Rush Att	Yds	Avg	TD	
Keith Lincoln	8	62	7.8	0	
Paul Lowe	6	42	7	0	
Lance Alworth	1	-7	-7	0	
	Pass Att	**Cmp**	**Yds**	**TD**	**Int**
Tobin Rote	17	11	230	3	2
John Hadl	6	3	87	2	1
Keith Lincoln	1	0	0	0	0
	Rec	**Yds**	**TD**		
Dave Kocourek	1	8	0		
Lance Alworth	4	114	1		
Keith Lincoln	4	73	2		
Paul Lowe	2	28	1		
Jacque MacKinnon	2	68	1		
Jerry Robinson	1	26	0		

Interceptions: McNeil

Around the AFL: The Chargers stayed in first place with a 3–1 record. And in beating Houston (2–3), Kansas City (2–1–1) moved into second place behind the Chargers. Buffalo (1–3–1) shutout Oakland (2–3) to win their first game, and dropped the Raiders to the bottom of the West. New York (3–1) held off Boston (2–3) to stay on top of the East. The two division leaders were scheduled to meet each other next week in San Diego. Denver's win over San Diego lifted their record to 2–2.

Dick Westmoreland

Dick Westmoreland was a walk-on defensive back who came to training camp with the Chargers looking to make the team and

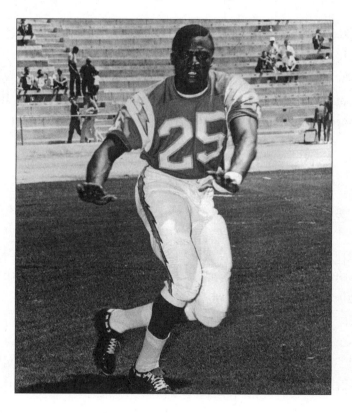

left with a starting spot at the cornerback position. If there was a defensive rookie-of-the-year award at the time, it would have been his. He finished second in the voting for the annual ROY voting, right behind Broncos fullback Billy Joe. He also made the AFL's 2nd Team All-League squad. Drawing rave reviews from his teammates and coaches, Westmoreland was the most energetic player in camp and, according to cornerback mate Dick Harris, was the most interested and attentive rookie he had ever seen. Sid Gillman was quoted as saying that Westmoreland only had one bad game all year, which was the one against Denver. But he learned a lot from that game, and wasn't the first to be "schooled" by Lionel Taylor.

Dick Westmoreland

Lionel was a smart player and always ran precise patterns. We did bump and run even before it had a name or was popular, and Taylor liked to play ticky-tac, using his hands a lot. If I tried to bump him he'd tug my shirt or something to throw me off-balance.

Sid came after me and Petrich at practice after Denver and told us we'd stunk that week. When we watched films together as a team, he tore into us. That was his way of getting you to improve and keep you working hard. He'd mock you if you got beat to motivate you to play better. You had to play well so you wouldn't be mocked during film sessions.

Westmoreland was 6'1" and 190 pounds, out of North Carolina A&T, whose life goal had always been to play professional football. It was with that, and only that thought in mind, that he came to San Diego and in his own words, "I wasn't going to go home with that goal not being accomplished." His size and speed allowed him to be quick off his receiver's first moves and guard them as tightly as he did.

Dick Westmoreland

Charlie McNeil took me under his wing in camp; he looked out for me and everyone was just pulling for me. They liked the way I came into camp and just busted my tail. I was tackling and stopping the pass and that got everyone's attention, especially coach Noll's. I didn't even know what I was doing, I just wanted to play and be good.

As a rookie I tried to hit people harder than most other backs. You have to want to hit people and I gotta be able to stop them by myself out on the corner. I had to be in the right mind set so I was always looking to learn. This was my dream so I did what they taught me to do.

Dick played behind linebacker Paul Maguire and defensive end Bob Petrich on the right side, drawing coverage mostly on players like Taylor, Art Powell, Gino Cappelletti, and Charlie Hennigan.

Dick Westmoreland

There was a lot to learn that first year and I covered some really good receivers. I remember covering [Houston receiver] Charley Hennigan one time when they were near the end zone. When the ball was snapped he just relaxed like it was a running play, so I did too. Then he took off and slanted at the goal line. Man, he tricked me, but when the ball was thrown to him it hit the goal post and I was saved. I learned not to relax no matter what on that play.

Another thing I had to do was learn how to get around the pulling guards. The Bills had Billy Shaw, who went into the Hall of Fame. He was a great pulling guard. My job was to force my way inside and I would try to juke him so he couldn't get set and I could get the drop on him. I'd fake in and go out or something like that. I thought I had the advantage because I could see where the runner was going, so I could do things like that. And if the runner was Cookie Gilchrist, I really had to be ready. Tackling him was like taking on a freight train.

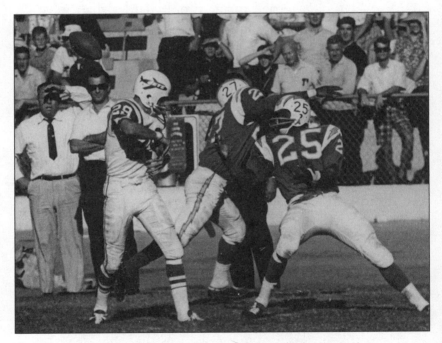

Dick Westmoreland (25) and Charlie McNeil (27) knock down a pass intended for Bake Turner.

I needed to be strong to the inside and force the receiver to where I wanted him to go. In the end zone most patterns were to the inside so we had to force them out. You had to keep adjusting and learning. I liked to take chances, too, and get off the receiver. I'd try to blast forward and pick the pass off. When I'd do that, sometimes I'd tell McNeil to cover for me; that I was going after it. We tried to communicate what we were doing all the time.

After making the All-AFL 2nd Team his first two years, Dick played only four games in 1965 and ended up on the expansion draft list the following spring. Selected by the new Miami Dolphins, he led the AFL in interceptions in 1967 with 10.

Game 5: Showing Their Mettle
New York Jets
Sunday, October 13, 1963, at San Diego
Balboa Stadium
Attendance: 27,189

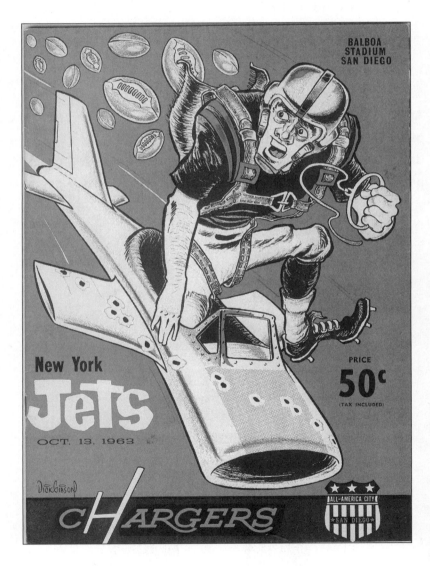

As the "new" New York Jets flew into San Diego, their 3–1 record was quite a surprise after having beaten division rivals Houston and Boston, as well as the improved Oakland Raiders. All the teams that sat below them in the standings were preseason favorites, so for the Jets to be the only team in that division with a winning record was definitely unexpected.

The new business plan under the leadership of majority owner Sonny Werblin was to purge everything Titan (the rival's previous name) about the franchise he purchased from the league and build a winning operation. He hired former NFL champion Baltimore Colts coach Weeb Ewbank as his on- and off-the-field leader, opened his check book, and told his new coach to build a championship team, cost being no object. It would not be easy, but Werblin's plan called for changing everything about the organization from top to bottom. The new direction had everyone enthusiastic and optimistic about the future. New, too, would be a stadium (scheduled to open in 1964) near LaGuardia Airport, prompting Werblin to rename his new team the *Jets* and purchase new green and white uniforms for their attire. Also new were seven starters on offense and five on defense.

From the team that had not yet recorded a winning record and had finished 5–9 in '62, the New Yorkers had several new faces in key positions to blend with the old at the start of the season. They replaced their leading receiver, Art Powell, who signed with Oakland with Bake Turner, and also inserted Charger castoff Dick Wood at quarterback. Sherman Plunkett, a Charger starter in '62 at tackle, and Charger draft pick Gene Heeter, a tight end also found their way into the new Jets lineup. Offensively through their first four games the Jets were relying on Turner, Don Maynard, and fullback Mark Smolinski to generate yards through the air. On the ground, though, except for Smolinski's 100-yard opening day against Boston, the Jets as a team had not run for more than 65 yards in any of their last three games. Their top two ground gainers from the last two seasons, Dick Christy and Bill Mathis, ran with Smolinski at halfback but neither had found their groove thus far. In building a defensive plan to stop the Jets, Noll and Gillman agreed that Ewbank would have to take to the air to try and beat them. Even though they gave up over 200 yards rushing to the Broncos, the Chargers knew they could control the line of scrimmage and stop the anemic Jet running game just as they had with Kansas City. The focus at practice during the week leading up to the game was on keeping Wood from feeling comfortable in the pocket and tightening up the secondary.

Like the Chargers, the Jets were starting three rookies on defense—including two in the secondary—which could explain why they were giving up over 260 yards of total offense per game, including over 170 through the air. With the Chargers propensity for scoring by using long passes and running sweeps, Gillman planned to keep the Jets defense busy by going full throttle with his arsenal of speed and talent.

The biggest issues for the Chargers was to avoid duplicating the disastrous run of turnovers that directly led to their loss and tightening up the right side pass defense where inexperience hurt them as well in Denver. Yet on the game's first three possessions, San Diego was back to digging themselves into a hole. Paul Lowe fumbled the team's first possession, and the Jets took possession at their own 49-yard line. On their first play from scrimmage, the Jets tested the vulnerable right side of the Chargers pass defense, sending Bake Turner long and started the

Jets quarterback Dick Wood scrambles under pressure.

scoring off with a 51-yard touchdown pass. Lowe erred again on their next possession by throwing an interception on a halfback pass. Dick Wood immediately went long again on first down and this time hit Don Maynard for 39 yards. Two San Diego turnovers and two New York plays for 90 yards and a touchdown looked frighteningly familiar to the previous week. Thankfully, the defense tightened up and the second Jets opportunity ended with a missed field goal.

Lowe was visibly upset and his confidence was in need of a boost, and Rote was aware enough to give his back a chance to pick himself back up. On the next Charger play, as he took a handoff on a sweep to the right side, Lowe burst through an opening that took him 40 yards downfield. Two plays later, he caught a 17-yard pass that led to George Blair's 28-yard field goal. The quarter ended with the Chargers trailing 7–3.

On their first possession of the second quarter, Rote was knocked down as he threw and his pass floated into the hands of Jets defensive tackle Chuck Janerette for another interception, which they converted into 3 more points. Three Chargers turnovers in the game's first sixteen minutes led to all of New York's points. As predicted, the San Diego defense was holding the Jets ground game in check, but the ball protection and pass defense were still haunting them after two quarters. Another thing that was still driving Gillman batty was Maguire's punting. Twice they called on him to kick the Jets deep into their end, and both times he failed to move them back more than 30 yards. Gillman was at his boiling point as the teams left the field at the half.

The Jets had tried to balance their attack in the first half to keep the Charger defense guessing, running the ball 12 times for 46 yards and completing 6 of 9 passes for 115 yards. Without the three turnovers, the New York offense was only able to muster up a missed field goal the entire half. Protecting the ball better was imperative for the Chargers, who were able to penetrate the Jets defense for some big plays. Although they picked up over 200 yards of offense, Rote was not able to get them into scoring position more than once throughout the half. The message from Gillman as his team returned to the field was to stick to the game plan and have confidence that their talent would pick them up.

Judging by the Jets' first possession, the message appeared as though it had gotten through. On the first play, Bob Mitinger, filling in for Faison at defensive end, knocked down Wood's pass attempt. Then Ernie Ladd dropped Wood for a 7-yard loss and John Hadl was sent in to change the Chargers fortunes. As a college quarterback, Hadl ran an option offense and many times would opt to keep the ball himself instead of handing off or pitching out to another back. On the first two plays of the second half, Hadl, who was named the AFL's Player of the Week for his performance in this game, ran first for 9 yards and then faked an inside hand off to Lincoln, faked another pitch to Lowe, and split two Jets defenders for a 33-yard gain. He was also the beneficiary of an additional 15 yards when a Jet piled on too late. On that play, the Chargers moved from their own 25 to the Jets 27. Lowe then followed Shea and Gruneisen on a sweep to the left side for 17 yards. From the 8-yard line, Hadl then hit Dave

Dave Kocourek catches a touchdown pass over Jet Bill Baird.

Kocourek for a leaping catch between Bill Baird and Dainard Paulson for the Chargers first touchdown of the afternoon to tie the game at 10–10.

Hadl ignited the offense again after the defense held the Jets to a three-and-out by passing to Lincoln for 40 yards, and then put the Chargers ahead by calling for a halfback pass from Gerry McDougall who threw to Alworth for an 11-yard touchdown.

The Chargers pass defense had been tightening up as Gillman demanded. But the officials thought that it was little *too* tight. Aided by two pass interference calls (one which negated an interception in the end zone), the Jets took the lead, 20–17, as the third quarter ended.

For the second game in a row, the Chargers trailed after three quarters and needed to make their own breaks. Paul Maguire gave them one after a stalled drive in which he stuck a punt on the Jets 1-yard line. From there the defense smothered Smolinski and Mathis on three runs, and the Jets had to return the ball to the Chargers. Starting another drive to the end zone, Paul Lowe added to the 161 yards he gained on the day by breaking another sweep around right end for 30 yards. Hadl then connected with Jacque MacKinnon for 17 yards. As the drive continued, Hadl picked up seven more on a scramble and then handed to Lowe on a blast up the middle for a 7-yard touchdown. The Chargers retook the lead, 24–20, with nine minutes left in the game.

The Jets knew that they needed to solve the Chargers defense in order to beat them. Stringing together a series of short yardage pickups on a 12-play drive, the Jets put themselves on the San Diego 13 where they faced a 4th and 8. The fact that kicker Dick Guesman had missed on field goal attempts of 47 and 13 yards earlier in the game may have influenced Ewbank's decision to go for it with more than enough time to get the ball back. Turning down the chance to pull within one point of the Chargers, the Jets threw to Bake Turner in the end zone to take the lead, but a huge pass rush batted Wood's pass into the air for an incompletion. San Diego took the ball over on downs at their own 20. The defense had come up big again with the game on the line, and again the front four's pressure had played the biggest part.

Bob Petrich, Chargers defensive end

It all starts with the defensive line. Walt Hackett was our line coach and Noll was the coordinator. They were really good teachers and got us prepared with film and practice. Earl Faison taught me to read and react as a rookie and said, "You'll learn over time what else to do." Reading the blocks of offensive linemen came from watching film and drilling over-and-over. I'll tell you, having Ernie Ladd aside of me really helped too. I had outside responsibility on the blind side. Most teams were right handed in those days, meaning they lined up with the tight end on their right side of the line. Team's didn't go weak side running as much and with Ladd there it was even less. Sometimes they would move Ernie to the left tackle spot just to keep teams from running to the strong side. The hash marks were wider then so we had to run farther to the other side, but our coaches were big on pursuit. Our strongest suit, though, was the pass rush. Big Ernie and Earl were like huge wrecking balls coming in, and Schmidt was known as the wedge buster because he was so strong that he just rammed through blockers. Even George Gross, the other rookie on the front four, was called Mr. Muscles because he was so strong. So rushing the passer was our strength and that helped the secondary be better at coverage because we made the quarterback release the pass sooner than they wanted.

With less than two minutes to play, the Jets got another chance to win after another good Maguire punt put them at their own 20-yard line, needing a touchdown to win. A completion to Bake Turner moved the Jets 20 yards closer and then the defense dug in to shut them down. Charlie McNeil knocked away another pass to Turner, followed by Wood being knocked to the ground by Ladd. Then his third down pass was knocked down by Petrich. On 4th and 10 from the 40, Wood tried one last pass for a

Gerry McDougall picking up a few of his 56 yards against the Jets.

first down but linebacker Frank Buncom knocked the ball away to give the Chargers their fourth victory of the year.

It was a satisfying win for Gillman and a good showing for both the offense and defense. They allowed only two scores off of the three turnovers in the first half and showed their mettle by scoring 21 points in the second half behind a superb effort by John Hadl, who completed 8 of 12 passes for 134 yards. Paul Lowe came back from a slow start to have his best day of the year, averaging 10 yards a carry and picking up 161 yards. Gerry McDougall also had his best game by picking up 56 yards on six carries and completed his only pass for a touchdown.

The offense had their best output of the season, totaling 510 yards, with 287 rushing and 223 passing. The defense returned to their dominating play on the line of scrimmage by giving up less than three yards a carry and only 24 rushing yards in the entire second half. The 4–1 Chargers and the now 3–2 Jets stayed on top of their respective divisions, and were still the only two teams in the AFL with winning records.

New York Jets	7	3	10	0	-	20
San Diego Chargers	3	0	14	7	-	24

NYJ-Turner, 51 pass from Wood (Guesman kick)
SD-FG, Blair 28
NYJ-FG, Guesman 44
SD-Kocourek, 8 pass from Hadl (Blair kick)
SD-Alworth, 11 pass from McDougall (Blair kick)
NYJ-FG, Guesman 32
NYJ-Smolinski, 2 run (Guesman kick)
SD-Lowe, 7 run (Blair kick)

Charger Statistics:

Player	Rush Att	Yds	Avg	TD	Long	
Keith Lincoln	13	33	2.5	0	5	

Paul Lowe	16	161	10	1	40	
Gerry McDougall	6	56	9.3	0	19	
John Hadl	4	38	9.5	0	33	
	Pass Att	**Cmp**	**Yds**	**TD**	**Int**	**Long**
Tobin Rote	13	10	78	0	1	19
John Hadl	12	8	134	1	1	37
Paul Lowe	0	1	0	0	0	1
Gerry McDougall	1	1	11	1	0	11
	Rec	**Yds**	**TD**	**Long**		
Dave Kocourek	3	42	1	22		
Lance Alworth	4	54	1	19		
Paul Lowe	4	18	0	17		
Jerry Robinson	4	26	0	12		
Keith Lincoln	2	40	0	37		
Gerry McDougall	1	26	0	26		
Jacque MacKinnon	1	17	0	17		
Interceptions: none						
Tackles: Allen 12, Mitinger 7, Ladd 5, McNeil 5, Westmoreland 5						

Around the AFL: The Boston Patriots (3–3) evened their record by scoring a touchdown in the fourth quarter to hand the Oakland Raiders (2–4) their fourth loss in a row, 20–14. The Houston Oilers (3–3) also evened their record by scoring 26 points in the first half to drop the Denver Broncos (2–3) under .500 with a 33–24 victory. The Buffalo Bills (2–3–1) earned their second win in a row by knocking off the Kansas City Chiefs (2–2–1), 35–26.

John Hadl

John Hadl

Sid Gillman really had an eye for talent. He knew what he wanted in coaches, scouts, players, everything. He had

one scout named Don Klosterman who he sent down to see me at Kansas back in '61 when I was a senior. You have to remember that at Kansas back then we threw about five passes a game. Well, the day Klosterman comes down to see me at practice we are going through passing drills and I'm having a great day, hitting receivers on the run, long, short, you name it. I guess he liked what he saw because he went back to Gillman and told him to draft me. I really don't know what would have happened if we didn't have passing drills that day or if I had only had a mediocre showing. But it was Klosterman who saw something in me that day. And I guess Gillman knew that Kosterman knew what he was doing because he picked me. Sid was like that. He saw talent in the people he hired and he let them do their job, otherwise he would not have hired them in the first place. I'm glad he took Klosterman's advice.

John Hadl became a San Diego Charger in 1962 and looked forward to learning how to be a professional quarterback from Jack Kemp, the Chargers starter in 1960 and 1961. Hadl was originally a running back at Kansas, and it was at his suggestion that he was tried at quarterback to run their option offense. With options to handoff, run, or pitch out, he was rarely called upon to throw. In fact, most times when he was asked to put the ball in the air it was while rolling out as opposed to from the pocket. In his junior and senior years, Hadl became the first Kansas player to be named an All-American two consecutive years. As their quarterback, in 1960 and 1961, he threw only 190 passes in 20 games, averaging less than 10 per game. He admittedly had a lot to learn in his first pro training camp, and roomed with Kemp to absorb as much of his cerebral training as possible. When Kemp dislocated a finger on his throwing hand in the second game of the season, Hadl was called into action much sooner than he imagined. Upon entering the game, he was asked to do something he had never done before in a game: throw passes from the pocket . . . and a lot of them. It was a learning experience for the rookie who shared the job with journeyman Dick Wood after Kemp's dislocation sidelined him for the rest of the year. But it was Hadl who played the bulk of minutes and, under the circumstances, played as well as could be expected. He was even voted "most valuable offensive back" by the San Diego fans.

When he learned of Rote's signing with the Chargers, instead of being a disgruntled starter, Hadl was excited about the possibility of learning from him the same way he was about being mentored by Kemp. He had often said that he really learned how to be a pro quarterback under Rotes' tutelage and used the opportunity to learn valuable lessons in game management and strategies from the knowledgeable veteran.

In 1963, he was used as the team's "middle reliever and sometime closer," as he was called upon to come in and change the pace and momentum of a game for either short stints or to carry the team the rest of the game and lead them to victory. His first call came against Denver when the Chargers trailed the Broncos in the fourth quarter. Hadl was able to put his team ahead briefly with a touchdown pass, and then threw another later in the quarter. While his impact was felt against Denver, his biggest contribution came on October 13, as the Chargers hosted the first place New York Jets. Stalled offensively, trailing, and without a touchdown at halftime, Hadl started the second half in relief and made an immediate impact on his first two plays by running for over 40 yards. He then sparked the offense by completing 8 of his 12 passes and led the Chargers to three second half touchdowns and a comeback win. For his inspiring performance, Hadl was named the AFL's Player of the Week.

By 1964, he had improved significantly and in the second week of the season, after Rote had posted a 110.3 passer rating the week before, Hadl (in relief) checked in as the league's top rated passer with a 97.5 rating. He led the league again in week five with a 118.2 rating when the Chargers topped Boston, and followed that up with a 111.6 rating the following week in a win over Denver. As Rote's persistent bursitis kept him on the sidelines more and more, Hadl's consistently strong performances had lifted the Chargers into the division lead—which they would never relinquish. He started 8 games in all and finished the season with over 2,000 yards passing and was the second-highest rated quarterback in the league.

In 1965, Hadl led the league in passing yards and was the AFL's top rated quarterback, spearheading the league's most efficient offense and taking the Chargers to another championship game. After finishing second in 1966 to Len Dawson, he kept his Chargers in the Western Division race in 1967 and 1968, when he again was the league's top passer, and lead the team to 8–1–1 and 9–3 starts before finishing third both years.

With receivers like Lance Alworth and Gary Garrison, San Diego was among the top passing teams in both '67 and '68, and also had their running game ranked among the league's top five over the same time.

But John Hadl was hardly a natural, and the heights to which he rose and the accomplishments he was able to attain were the bounty of his hard work and the endless hours put into crafting his skill, mastering his position, creating game plans, and studying film. For most of his career he would not take a day off, spending Monday going over film and the rest of the week practicing and staying late to break down videos and performances while planning for the next game with his coaches. His relationship with Sid Gillman is remembered as being a give-and-take partnership that would often involve lively discussions, loud debates, arguments, and even threats that were most often won by the coach. But Hadl never backed off. He may not have won many battles when going head-to-head with the man he most respected, but he would not give in until he had his say and fought with every fiber of his being for what he believed in. And that was the same way in which he played the game.

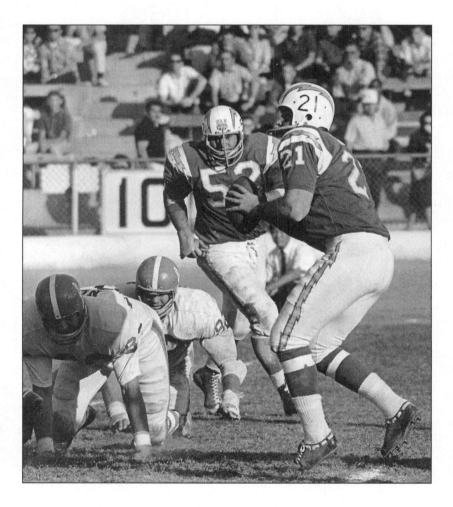

Game 6: Second Half Lightning

@ Kansas City
Sunday, October 20, 1963
Municipal Stadium
Attendance: 30,107

One and a half games separated the Chiefs and Chargers when the two teams met on a cloudy, rainy Sunday in late October. Since they saw the Chiefs three weeks earlier, KC had beaten the Oilers handily and lost a high scoring game to Buffalo, both times running for more than 120 yards and passing for nearly 200. The key to beating the Chiefs would again depend on the Charger defense's ability to stop the running game, with which Hank Stram always like to establish first. But Stram was fearful that having the same strategy this time would be playing into the San Diego front four's strength that yielded only 27 yards when they last met. Inter-Division games were always significant, even this early in the season. A San Diego win would give them a 2.5-game lead on the second place team but a loss would tighten the race to only a half game. Battle strategists would suggest that the second time two opponents meet, the loser of the first game has the advantage because they can review what went wrong previously, make adjustments, and devise a plan based on fixing what is needed to change the result. The winner, on the other hand, knows what worked but is also aware that their opponent will plan to stop whatever it was that produced the victory. The chess match between Stram and Gillman would be nothing new for the rival's eighth meeting, with the advantage so far on the Chargers side with a 5–2 record.

San Diego felt that they were in a much better position than the Chiefs after putting up over 400 and 500 yards of total offense in Denver and against the Jets, while knowing that they previously had been able to hold off the KC running game. A big pass rush, active linebackers, and heads-up pass coverage was the order of the day for San Diego, and as before, they would depend on Petrich, Gross, Schmidt, Ladd, and Faison to first stop Curtis McClinton and Abner Haynes and then pressure Len Dawson. Dawson always felt the Charger front was the best he faced and made sure to utilize his moving pocket as often as possible.

Chris Burford, split end, Kansas City

The Chargers always gave us good games. They had that strong front line. Hank would run a moving pocket because of the big front four to get Dawson away from them. He hated to lose—particularly against Gillman—who he had a real rivalry with. Heck, he seemed to have a rivalry with everybody. He'd go to extremes to win.

Another factor that aided the Chargers previous win against Kansas City was forcing turnovers early in the game that led to scores. Offensively, the Chargers used a balanced running (154 yards) and passing game (140 yards) to keep the KC defense at bay with Paul Lowe pacing the ground game with 91 yards. The plan would be the same for their second meeting.

Len Dawson

Their passing and running game was really balanced. It was hard to figure out what they were going to do so you couldn't overplay one player or area.

Bobby Hunt, safety, Kansas City

Gillman had been getting great personnel through the draft and had what he wanted in a team after three years. But of all the players, Alworth was the key that put them over the top. You had to stop Alworth first and then their running game. Lowe and Lincoln, they were the cream that year. You had to stop both of them because if you concentrated on one, the other would bust loose.

Gillman was a little ahead of the other coaches on offense and they played really tough team defense.

Outside of Ladd and Faison they really didn't have any superstars but they all covered their areas and covered for each other really well and had great pursuit.

The rain was a factor in the Week 7 match-up, and both teams played conservatively in the first quarter, running twice as much as they passed. As they did in Week 4, Kansas City kept trying to penetrate the Chargers front line. Ten of their first twelve plays were on the ground, gaining less than three yards on seven of the attempts. With an abundance of running plays, the period ended with both teams having just two possessions and no score. The sloppy conditions were also forcing more tentative play calling and changes in game plans. When the teams changed sides to start the second quarter, both defenses had given up only two first downs as the offenses were looking to get a better grip on the ball and surer footing underneath them.

After three more punts by Paul Maguire, the Chargers caught their first break when Chuck Allen intercepted Dawson's pass at the KC 38 and ran it back to the 15-yard line where Dawson knocked him out of bounds. Unable to put together any offense, Gillman sent Hadl in to take the Chargers in from 15 yards away, but he, too, was unable to find his footing. George Blair was then sent in to get his team on the board, and made a 29-yard field goal. After falling behind 3–0, the Chiefs found a sudden burst of incentive to get on the scoreboard themselves and came right back and scored two plays later. Abner Haynes pulled in a pass over the outstretched arms of Charlie McNeil, broke Blair's tackle attempt, and scored on a 73-yard pass play to take the lead into halftime.

The San Diego thoroughbreds were slipping and sliding on offense and had negative running yards for the half. The good news was that the Chiefs were having similar issues, gaining less than three yards a clip on their 19 rushing attempts. So far the two top Western teams were using a punting strategy to jockey for position, sending their kickers in eight times to try and get a field position advantage. The task in the locker room would be to figure out how each team would make adjustments on the muddy turf to put some points up in the second half.

Gillman used the intermission to revise his plan of attack for the final two quarters. When Tobin Rote returned to work, he moved his team 70 yards in six plays, using five passes—three to Alworth—with the final catch covering 44 yards for a score that gave San Diego the lead, 10–7. But again, the lead didn't hold for long, as Tommy Brooker tied the score with a field goal on the Chiefs' next possession.

Bobby Hunt

Our usual coverage had one man on the tight end or, if we were in zone, I had the deep area in the middle and right side. I played left safety so I liked playing zone on the Chargers so I wouldn't have to cover Alworth. Johnny Robinson was at left corner and had him on short coverages and I didn't have to pick him up until late or not at all if he crossed. We had very little double-teaming in our defense and the wide receivers didn't flip from side to side much, either, so when we played the Chargers and I had to cover Alworth it made for a long, difficult day. They also had a lot of guys who could catch passes so there was always a pretty good load to cover all over the field. Their backs were really good at getting open on short routes and flat passes that started in the backfield.

It was evident that Gillman wanted to use the right side running strength of Shea and Mix against the rookie left side of Kansas City to get his ground game rolling. On their next series, Lincoln and Lowe started picking up yardage in big chunks. This set up two long passes to Robinson and Alworth, moving the Chargers 79 yards to the KC 7. The final play of this 86-yard touchdown drive had Paul Lowe following Mix and Shea again all the way into the end zone.

Paul Lowe

Their second touchdown of the third quarter had the Chargers leading 17–10. Mixing up their calls was opening up the San Diego offense after trying to play conservatively on the ground in the first half. The adjustment called for their backs to swing wide and in opposite directions, forcing the linebackers into pass coverage and leaving more room for Robinson and Alworth to maneuver. For Alworth, it was like a break out party. In his first eight professional games he had never caught more than four passes and only once did he gain more than 100 yards. This was a a career day for the speedy flanker, hauling in 9 passes for 232 yards and two touchdowns.

Lance Alworth
For some reason I was able to hang onto the ball in bad weather. I was able to get open in the slosh and was too afraid to *not* catch the ball. If you dropped passes, you didn't always get thrown to again.

At a time when they had to step up their game, the Chargers played their best second half of the season by putting up 35 points and holding the Chiefs to only 10. The key to victory was Gillman deciding at halftime to open up the offense. While the offense put the points on the board, it was the brute force of the defense that set up the team's first score of the fourth quarter and opened the flood gates. KC had advanced to the Charger 13 when Hank Stram's determination clouded his judgment and may have given the Charger defense the impetus to put the game away. Forcing the issue with eight minutes still on the clock and the Chiefs trailing by only one touchdown, Stram decided to go for the first down on 4th and 5. The defense dug in and held, giving the offense a spark that appeared to get them untracked for some of their quick striking gains. Lincoln picked up 15 yards around right end to start the drive and Alworth brought it to an end by leaping over Duane Wood to catch Rote's pass at midfield and run it in for a 73-yard touchdown. The Chargers now had a two touchdown lead.

The Chiefs followed with a 10-play drive that again got them to within a touchdown, but the Chargers continued to strike from long distance. Lincoln took a pitch out around the left side for 76 yards on San Diego's next play, and the quick striking offense was again up by 14 points.

Bobby Hunt

No other team had two backs that could break the game open or take over a game like the Chargers. So you had to stop both, not just one of them. You couldn't outscore them without stopping those guys. They had so many weapons that you had to stop them all because the one that you didn't stop would beat you.

The last score of the day was triggered by defensive pressure on Dawson that led to George Blair intercepting and returning the ball 40 yards to inside the KC 30. Paul Lowe finished it off with a 21-yard run around the left side to seal the victory, 38–17. The win pushed the Chiefs 2.5 games behind in the standings.

Overcoming the elements and the Chiefs supportive, partisan crowd was a big accomplishment. As well as the fact that they had done this all against the defending champions. The Charger defense led the way, giving the Chiefs only 17 points and again holding their runners in check. In their two match-ups, the Charger defense had held the mighty Chiefs running game to only 105 yards on the ground. And outside of the seven-turnover game in Denver, no one had scored more than 20 points on the Chargers in their other five games. For all of the attention the offense was receiving, the defense was the unheralded backbone. They were continually containing the opposition and forcing them to settle for field goals after getting favorable field position. In six games, the defense had given up 10 touchdowns and 11 field goals.

The offensive catalysts of the day were Lance Alworth and Keith Lincoln. Of the 17 Charger pass completions, nine were to Alworth, who accounted for 232 of the team's 281 receiving yards. His two touchdowns picked up the bulk of the yardage as well, going for 44 and 73 yards. Lincoln shouldered the lion's share of the rushing game by gaining 127 of the team's 147 ground yards. For Lincoln, it was the second time in his career that he'd cracked the 100-yard mark and his first of the season. Together, Alworth and Lincoln accounted for 90 percent of the Chargers total offensive output.

Hank Stram later said, "The big plays were the difference. . . . Those two passes to Alworth and Lincoln's run were what stopped us. . . . They have a very explosive team, and their backs all run the 100 in under 10 seconds. They have a well-seasoned team now that has come into its own."

Gillman, as expected, was ecstatic with the win, saying it was their best game of the year. As for how his team came out in the second half, he commented, "We just went to work on them. If Tobin had gone to work on them in the first half as he did the second, we would have scored just as much then." He also noted, in reference to Hadl's replacing Rote in the first half, "If one can't move us, then we'll go to the other. We have two wonderful quarterbacks." And when asked about his defense, he just smiled and said, "We have a damn fine defense." But he was cautious enough to know that at even at 5–1 the Chargers had to keep things in perspective. When asked if he thought his team had just sewn up the West, he emphatically stated, "No! If we feel we've got it won we'll go down the drain so fast it won't even be funny." He and everyone on the team were aware that relaxing now would negate all the planning, bonding, and enduring they had accomplished at Rough Acres Ranch back in July and August. And *nobody* was going to risk that.

San Diego Chargers	0	3	14	21	-	38
Kansas City Chiefs	0	7	3	7	-	17

SD-FG, Blair 29
KC-Haynes, 73 pass from Dawson (Brooker kick)
SD-Alworth, 44 pass from Rote (Blair kick)
KC-FG, Brooker 36
SD-Lowe, 7 run (Blair kick)
SD-Alworth, 73 pass from Rote (Blair kick)
KC-Arbanas, 7 pass from Dawson (Brooker kick)
SD-Lincoln, 76 run (Blair kick)
SD-Lowe, 21 run (Blair kick)

Charger Statistics:

Player	Rush Att	Yds	Avg	TD	Long	
Keith Lincoln	10	127	12.7	1	76	
Paul Lowe	11	42	2.2	2	21	
Gerry McDougall	1	-9	-9	0	-9	
	Pass Att	Cmp	Yds	TD	Int	Long
Tobin Rote	22	16	266	2	0	73
John Hadl	4	1	15	0	0	15
	Rec	Yds	TD	Long		
Lance Alworth	9	232	2	73		
Paul Lowe	3	11	0	8		
Jerry Robinson	3	36	0	17		
Keith Lincoln	2	2	0	3		

Interceptions: Allen, Blair
Tackles: Allen 9, Karas 8, Gross 8, Westmoreland 8, Schmidt 7, Buncom 6

Around the AFL: Houston (4–3) used 21 second-quarter points to move into first place and keep Buffalo (2–4–1) in last with a 28–14 victory. Boston (4–3) moved into a first place tie with Houston by drubbing Denver (2–4), 40–21, and Oakland (3–4) bounced back from four-straight losses by knocking New York (3–3) out of first place in the East with a 49–26 win. Oakland moved ahead of Kansas City (2–3–1) into second place in the West, and would travel to San Diego (5–1) to meet the first place Chargers the following week.

Chuck Allen

Chuck Allen was the defensive quarterback of the Chargers, but if you were to ask him about the role he played, you'd find out that he just wanted to be one of the guys. Humble almost to a fault and always quick to deflect any attention from himself to his teammates, Chuck stated that the Chargers played together as a unit, and credits the Rough Acres experience for a lot of it. Everyone knew their responsibilities and did their job, Allen will tell you. There was absolutely no "I" on their defense, and everyone communicated on the field and covered for each other.

Allen led the Chargers in tackles from his middle linebacker spot in 1963, and seemed to be everywhere the action was—whether it was going north or south, east or west—he could cover enough ground to always be around the ball. He was second on the team with 5 interceptions and even scored a touchdown when he ran 42 yards to pay dirt with a recovered fumble.

Chuck Allen

We had to work hard for what we got. We had a lot of talent but couldn't just walk out on the field and think we'd win. We had to go out and play up to our potential. Nobody was going to give us anything. We were prepared for everything and were hardly ever fooled by what a team did. Our coaches, Chuck Noll and Walt Hackett, worked out the plan and got us prepared for what teams would want to do against us. We watched more film than anybody out there at the time. We all had jobs to do and nobody was any more a leader than another. We all did what we did together and, like everyone else, I just had a job to do and did it.

Noll would call the defense from the sideline but he had enough confidence in me to let me do what I thought would work from the field. They also prepared us for what personnel we'd be going against and what they could do or how they'd want to try to beat us. He had pretty good fortune, too, with what they taught us.

We based our defense on down and distance and with zone or man coverage. The personnel the other teams had also determined what we'd do with our defensive set ups. Sometimes a team would have one really good receiver and just an average other guy so we'd over shift to one side or change coverage based on where each receiver was setting up or what the offense wanted to do with the players they had. The coaches pretty much scouted all of that stuff from watching film and then they'd go over our assignments in the meetings.

We played mostly a 4-3 defense, but sometimes used different looks. We'd move people around and put them on different linemen to confuse them. Or we'd run stunts or give them different formations to change their blocking assignments and open something up for another defensive guy. For example, I'd tell Ladd to slice the gap to the inside instead of being head-up on the guard. My responsibility then would be to plug up the vacated area. If the guard would follow the tackle inside, then I'd be able to shoot up the gap untouched. If the guard stayed put, then I'd make him come after me and Ladd could bust things up inside. We'd do a lot of things based on what the offensive formation was and we'd send our line in different directions at different times. We didn't have to blitz that much because our pass rushers were so good. We'd do it occasionally just to have the other team think about it, but most times we just let those front guys do what they did best.

Scrimmaging against our offensive line really helped us, too. They were smart and talented, well coached. Hey, if we could stop the best offense in the league at practice it was a real accomplishment, so we had to be ready to play every day at practice. That gave us enough confidence to stop anyone.

Allen made the All-AFL Team as a rookie in 1961 and again as a 2nd teamer in 1962 and 1964. How he was not selected in

THE UNCROWNED CHAMPS

1963 is a mystery because to some it was his best year. He was also named to the West All-Star Team every year through 1964. He was a player's player, a teammate's teammate, an All-Star, and league champion. He played with his heart on his sleeve and with the valor of a Knight. Chuck Allen was a leader on the field and relished the relationships he had with his teammates off it. And when his day's work was done, all he hoped for was to have the respect and regard of his fellow defenders.

Game 7: The Formidable Foe

Oakland Raiders
Sunday, October 27, 1963, at San Diego
Balboa Stadium
Attendance: 30,182

THE UNCROWNED CHAMPS

After three years, the Oakland Raiders had finished with records of 6–8, 2–12, and 1–13. The team that was put together hastily after the original Minnesota franchise backed out of their league commitment at the last minute, the Raiders franchise was desperately seeking stability and, more importantly, respectability.

The disorganization and ownership infighting had finally been resolved. Now that Wayne Valley and Ed McGah were firmly in control, the Raiders' prepared to embark on their fourth season with their fourth head coach. Wunderkind Al Davis took over the dual roles of head coach and general manager, giving him unilateral control of the team and its front office. Under the futile leadership of Eddie Erdelatz (6–10), Marty Feldman (2–15) and Bill Conkright (1–8), the Raiders stumbled through a 19-game losing streak that was only ended by a victory over a disinterested Patriots squad on the last weekend of the 1962 season. With the assurance that he would have of enough time and money at his disposal from the ownership, Davis was ready to mount an Oakland renaissance. Davis, the boy genius fresh out of Sid Gillman's coaching paddock, left no stone unturned on his quest to lift the Oakland franchise out of the AFL's crypt and transform its image from rag-tags to that of a formidable foe.

New, too, was the team's look. Gone were the nondescript black and gold uniforms in favor of silver and black, resembling those worn with honor by Army's West Point Cadets. Perhaps most importantly was the new team motto of "A commitment to excellence," created by its aggressively confident leader. Davis also brought in a new offensive philosophy, preached, taught, modeled, and demanded *Pride and Poise* under all conditions, and even cut his two starting tackles, Charlie Brown and Jack

Stone, a week before the season began because he was dissatisfied with their performance in preseason games.

With the Davis renaissance came a new attitude, an aggressive and precise game plan, and several new faces that were looking for a new beginning. To start the season, Davis employed nineteen new players on the roster. Archie Matsos, a two-time All-League and All-Star linebacker came over from Buffalo to shore up the defense. From New York came two-time All-League and All-Star receiver Art Powell, considered the most dangerous deep threat in the AFL.

To guide his team on the field, Davis was using both Tom Flores, who in 1960 was the AFL's leading passer and in 1961 was second in completion percentage, and Cotton Davidson, who was the starter in Flores' absence the year before. Through their first six games the alternating quarterback system seemed to push both throwers to elevate their game. Anchoring the line was All-League center Jim Otto and bolstering their running game was Clem Daniels, who was the league's fourth league rusher in '62 and averaged 5.0 and 4.8 yards per carry the previous two seasons. With Powell and Olympian Bo Roberson as the wide receivers, the Raiders had quite a bit more balance on offense than in seasons past.

Davis' challenge was to shore up a team that finished last in total offense and gave up 157 more points than it scored. Davis claimed he didn't want the job as much as he wanted the challenge, and in that regard he got exactly what he wished for.

His attention to detail and game preparation was unlike anything the Raiders had seen before. And his philosophy for winning was unequalled. After defeating the Oilers in their season opener, Davis' "Pride and Poise" boys knocked off the

Bills, 35–17. But when Boston arrived the following week, the Patriots were more prepared to face the resurgent Raiders than their first two victims. In their previous meeting, the final game of 1962, the Patriots became the first and only team in the AFL to be shut out all season by the team that hadn't won a single game. Now, coinciding with star halfback Clem Daniels sitting out with a deep thigh injury, the Raiders were caught short, 20–14. Then on their three week sojourn east, with Daniels being used sparingly, the results were the same, losing in New York, 10–7, Buffalo, 12–0, and Boston, 20–14, in succession. Returning to the West Coast with a 2–4 record, the new Raiders appeared to look like the team of old. With Daniels back at full strength and running for a team record 200 yards, the silver and black set a franchise record by scoring 49 points in beating the Jets for their third victory of the season. Next up was a trip down the coast to take on the 5–1 Chargers, a team they had never beaten.

For the second week in a row, the Chargers were facing the team on their heels. With the comforts of Balboa's blue skies, dry turf, and 79 degrees making the day more suited for their type of game than the soggy conditions in Kansas City, the team captains, Mix and Karas, met with Cotton Davidson at midfield to conduct the pregame coin flip. San Diego won the toss and chose to receive. Davidson selected to defend the North side of the field and kicked off to the South so that the Chargers would be heading into the 7-mile-per-hour wind on their opening drive.

The Chargers were not taking the Raiders for granted in this first meeting of the Davis era. They knew that their defense would be hard pressed to stop the explosive and balanced Raider offense that featured big game players Clem Daniels and Art Powell.

Both Daniels and fullback Alan Miller were being used in dual roles and were catching passes out of the backfield much the way Lincoln and Lowe were for the Chargers. Davis had learned the Gillman system well and was using it to his full advantage in transforming his Raiders. Powell would pose the biggest threat they had encountered thus-far, as he was not only fast and elusive, but had the size and force of a tight end. Dick Westmoreland would have to be on top of his game against Powell and the confident rookie was excited about the chance to cover the big Oakland end.

Gillman's offense was also a cause for trepidation for Al Davis. He had recruited, signed, coached, and helped develop many of the stars that were now the core of the Chargers attack. He knew better than anyone that they had a knack for gaining steady yardage and had the fire-power to demoralize their opponents with game-breaking plays. Lincoln and Lowe, now settled in as running mates, had traded off gaining 100 yards on the ground the previous two weeks. Lowe had the reputation from his past and present performances, while Lincoln, coming of off his scintillating performance against the Chiefs, was making the Chargers that much more difficult to defend. As Kansas City experienced, stopping just Lowe was no longer the only method for shutting down the San Diego running game.

Don Norton was still a week away from returning to the lineup after sitting out the entire year, which gave Jerry Robinson another start at split end. Robinson posed enough of a threat to keep secondary's balanced. Now if Tobin Rote could get off to a good start in the first quarter, the Chargers could distance themselves from the West the way they did in 1961 when they locked up the division by early November.

Keith Lincoln bursting through the Raiders defense.

It didn't take long for the Chargers to break off a quick burst, testing the deep pass coverage and then giving the Raiders their first break of the game. Keith Lincoln picked up where he left off in Kansas City by busting 21 yards up the middle on a draw play the first time he touched the ball. Rote then tested Fred Williamson's coverage on Alworth deep, but the throw fell incomplete. On his next toss, Rote was intercepted by linebacker Archie Matsos, then lateraled to safety Claude Gibson, who was tackled at the San Diego 25-yard line. Three plays later, Art Powell was in the end zone and the Raiders had a 7-point lead three minutes into the game.

The veteran Rote was unrelenting in his effort to get the Chargers into the end zone. His long career had taught him not to panic and to stay the course. It was all about execution and the Chargers offense was designed to sail a steady course and use the occasional gusts to blow by opposing defenses. On the ensuing kickoff, Lincoln's return gave team Rote the ball at their 43. Using Lowe and Lincoln's 17 and 13 yard bursts off tackle put George Blair in field goal range and he nailed a 23-yarder to get the Chargers on the board.

When the Chargers got the ball back with good field position, Rote connected with Alworth for 15 yards. That was followed by a 10-yard run from Lowe and a 32-yard touchdown catch by Alworth. Steady sailing with a few gusts put San Diego ahead, 10–7. Later in the quarter, Rote steered into trouble again with two more interceptions by Freddie Williamson. Williamson returned the latter one to the 30-yard line which led to another Raider touchdown. The lead had changed back to the Raiders, 14–10.

Gillman was known to grow impatient and, when he thought the team needed a change of pace, would bring in Hadl to test the waters to see if he could kick start the offense. He also wanted to give Rote a chance to see the defense in action from the sidelines for a series or two before re-entering the game. Hadl offered a more mobile option as well, being able to run out of trouble even if his throwing accuracy was not on Rote's level. Young and unafraid, Hadl took over on the Chargers next possession and in three plays put the Chargers back ahead, 17–14, by connecting with Jacque MacKinnon on a 69-yard touchdown pass. The half ended after Charlie McNeil intercepted Flores and Hadl returned the favor by throwing one right back to the Raiders.

While the Chargers four interceptions spoiled several drives and tarnished their 274 first-half yards (139 on the ground and 135 in the air), Paul Lowe was enjoying another good day after being held to 24 yards on 11 carries the week before, by gaining 84 yards in the first half. Lincoln was also having a fine day rushing, but was being used sparingly and getting a lot of attention from the Oakland defense. His four carries netted 38 yards and opened up more opportunities for his running mate by making deceptive fakes as Lowe ran counters off-tackle.

The Raiders started the second half with Cotton Davidson at quarterback, a common occurrence from Davis. After an obligatory hand-off to Daniels on the first play of the half, he dropped back and floated a swing pass intended for Alan Miller and read perfectly by cornerback Dick Harris. Harris snatched the ball out of the air and raced 23 yards untouched for a touchdown to start the quarter. George Blair, however, missed the extra point for the second time in the season. It was a miss that would come back to haunt them later in the game.

Another Chargers miscue gave the Raiders more points late in the third quarter. Keith Lincoln, so deft in his play the week before, fumbled again with Oakland recovering. The turnover led directly to another touchdown, their third of the day off San Diego mistakes.

After Art Powell scored again following a San Diego field goal, the Chargers found themselves on the short end—but only briefly. Making up for his earlier fumble, Lincoln bolted off tackle for a 51-yard touchdown that put him over 100 yards rushing for the second consecutive game. The fourth quarter run regained the lead for the Chargers at 33–28. In the past, the touchdown would have put the game away, but Davis' boys were not finished. Leading the

Ernie Ladd stops Clem Daniels.

Raider offense for the entire second half, Davidson got the ball back for one final drive with less than three minutes to go. From the Oakland 37, Daniels' final run of the day netted 41 of his 125 yards and gave the Raiders a first down at the San Diego 22.

Scrambling to the 9-yard line, Davidson gave himself another first down with barely under two minutes to play. He then put the Chargers on the ropes with a knockout punch, finding little-used halfback Glenn Shaw for a touchdown. The catch delivered the Raiders their first win of any kind against a Charger team with a one-point victory, 34–33. The missed extra point by Blair ended up being the difference between a loss and a tie.

For the second time, multiple Charger turnovers and mistakes were their worst enemy and directly affected the outcome of the game. Five interceptions, a missed extra point, and a fumble were too much to overcome and foiled the Chargers' brilliant display of 480 yards on offense (with Lincoln and Lowe combining for 212 yards on the ground). The Chargers played good enough to win, but careless enough to lose.

Their record of 5–2 still led the division, but two inter-division losses in four games was a clear reminder that they had to bring their "A" game and be ready to play each week.

As was the practice in the AFL, when the West Coast teams traveled East, they would be scheduled against Buffalo, Boston, and New York on consecutive weeks to avoid the constant drain of coast-to-coast travel. With the season at its midpoint, it was time for the Chargers start November with a trip to New York City. All the Eastern teams were tied up in knots vying for the lead of the division and all needed to win down the stretch, as did the Chargers. From the looks of things, the trip east would be the tell-tale part of the season.

| Oakland Raiders | 7 | 7 | 7 | 13 | - | 34 |
| San Diego Chargers | 10 | 7 | 9 | 7 | - | 33 |

Oak-Powell, 20 pass from Flores (Mercer kick)
SD-FG, Blair 23
SD-Alworth, 32 pass from Rote (Blair kick)
Oak-Miller, 5 pass from Flores (Mercer kick)
SD-MacKinnon, 69 pass from Hadl (Blair kick)
SD-Harris, 23 interception return (kick failed)
Oak-Craig, 39 pass from Davidson (Mercer kick)
SD-FG, Blair 36
Oak-Powell, 46 pass from Davidson (Mercer kick)
SD-Lincoln, 51 run (Blair kick)
Oak-Shaw, 9 pass from Davidson (run failed)

Charger Statistics:						
Player	**Rush Att**	**Yds**	**Avg**	**TD**	**Long**	
Keith Lincoln	15	130	8.7	1	51	
Paul Lowe	12	82	6.8	0	25	
Gerry McDougall	3	16	5.3	0	9	
	Pass Att	**Cmp**	**Yds**	**TD**	**Int**	**Long**
Tobin Rote	14	6	67	1	4	32
John Hadl	6	2	82	1	1	69
Paul Lowe	1	1	29	0	0	29
	Rec	**Yds**	**TD**			
Lance Alworth	3	50	1			
Jerry Robinson	1	6	0			
Jacque MacKinnon	3	111	1			
Keith Lincoln	2	11	0			
Interceptions: McNeil, Harris (2)						
Tackles: Allen 10, Petrich 10, Blair 8, Ladd 7, Faison 5						

Around the AFL: New York (3–3–1) tied Denver (2–4–1), 35–35, on Saturday night. Houston (5–3) held onto first place in the East by scoring all of their points in the second half and downing Kansas City (2–4–1), 28–7. Buffalo (3–4–1) inched themselves closer to contention and knocked Boston (4–4) out of first, beating them 28–21 with a touchdown in the fourth quarter. Oakland (4–4) ended a four game losing streak to even their record with their 34–33 victory over San Diego (5–2).

Bob Petrich & George Gross

The two "little guys" on the defensive line of the Chargers in 1963 were Bob Petrich (6'4", 250 pounds) and George Gross (6'3", 270 pounds), both rookies with big ambitions. Petrich

Bob Petrich

was drafted in the 6th round by the NFL's New York Giants (as an offensive tackle) and in the 11th round by the Chargers (for defense). Gross was an 8th round selection of the St. Louis Cardinals (NFL) and a 16th round pick by San Diego. At the time they were drafted, the Chargers front four consisted of Ron Nery, Bill Hudson, Ernie Ladd, and Earl Faison, all younger than twenty-eight and widely touted as the best in the league and the original fearsome foursome. The Giants also had the best front four in the NFL, featuring Jim Katcavage, Dick Modzelewski, Rosey

George Gross

Grier, and Andy Robustelli, and were led to a 12–2 season by offensive tackles Rosey Brown and Jack Stroud. The youngest of the lot was Katcavage at twenty-eight. St. Louis started Joe Robb, Don Owens, Frank Fuller, and Luke Owens, with all but Robb past their prime. So it was not an easy decision to decide which team offered the best chance for the two to break into the starting lineup. The NFL was infamous for holding rookies back for a few years, while the AFL, still in its infant stages, was promoting new talent and fresh faces regularly.

It was to their credit that Gross and Petrich selected the Chargers under the circumstances of knowing that both NFL teams that drafted them had most of their starters over thirty years of age, while the Chargers were five years younger at each position. With Ladd and Faison as the luminaries of the group, they were not about to be moved out either. When the two first-year players arrived at Rough Acres Ranch to start their professional careers, they were not as concerned about becoming starters as they were about just making the team.

Bob Petrich

I had an old film of Gino Marchetti, the All-Pro defensive end of the Baltimore Colts and would study it over and over so I could mirror his moves. I was glued to the film and studied it all the time. Ernie Ladd used to call me "Gino" because I was so intrigued by Marchetti. I also played against Ernie Wright our left tackle in scrimmages and he was so good—one of the best in the league—so I

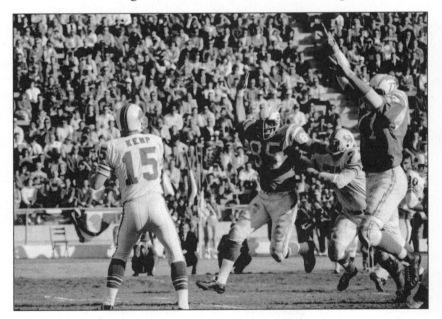

had to continue to work on moves and get better. When you practice against the best, you have to be on your game at all times. Otherwise, you look like you are being outplayed. That made me a better player.

Petrich was always going hard in practice, like a Pete Rose–type player, always hustling and bringing his all on every play. Ron Mix noted one day that it felt like Petrich never turned his motor off. But that's was why he made such a quick, positive impression on the coaches and probably why they felt they could trade Ron Nery, the man who was in front of him on the depth chart, to Houston.

Bob Petrich

It was drilled into me that defense starts with the front line by [Charger defensive line coach] Walt Hackett. He taught me a lot. Earl Faison helped me a lot, too. He told me how to read and react as a rookie. He said pass rushing was learned with experience and that I would understand over time what needed to be done. He showed me how to fight off blocking linemen and how to get around them. We watched a lot of film and were being drilled on techniques over and over. Ernie Ladd and George Gross would play aside of me depending on what set we were in. When it was Ernie, with his reputation, skill, and size, he was always double-teamed which helped me. I would have outside responsibility on what has become known as the "blind side." Most teams set the tight end on the right and then would run that way more often. Teams didn't go weak side as much, so when they would run to the right it was away from me, which meant more running for me because the hash marks were wider then and we had to run farther across the field on all those sweeps.

We would run two types of defense for running and passing games. It was my job to make sure the runners couldn't get to the outside. I tried to protect the linebackers and take out the blocking on sweeps so they could come up and make the tackle. On passing plays we would not blitz that much because we had really good pass rushers. We trained hard on the rush and on things like not beating your guy too soon because they would put a back on you the first time you beat your guy, then you were double-teamed the rest of the game. On 3rd and long downs, I'd jab and cross over to the inside to rush harder and faster. Earl Faison used to look at me in the huddle and say "meet you at the quarterback." There were times when we'd get there at the same time and I'd get the brunt of Earl's hit.

Petrich was an active defender from the get-go and wasted no time becoming an impact player. After the Chargers first seven games, only middle linebacker Chuck Allen had more tackles.

Bob Petrich

We always felt that when things weren't going well on offense that we had get them the ball back as quickly as possible. Our whole purpose was to make the other team go three and out. I remember an interview that the Boston Patriots coach did and he said we were the hardest team to scout because we rushed the quarterback so hard and so fast that they couldn't do anything to stop us. They would double Ladd all the time and that made the other offensive linemen's jobs harder because they had nobody to back them up. Everyone on our front line was really strong; we just didn't have any weak links. And if they tried to run away from Ernie they had to deal with "Mr. Muscles," George Gross on the other side.

Gross was born in Romania and lived for a time in a refugee camp in Austria during Russia's occupation of his country. He later moved to New Jersey where he learned to play American football and wrestle. His nickname, "Mr. Muscles," came from his propensity for weight lifting. Teammates would gawk at George when he would walk into the weight room and start

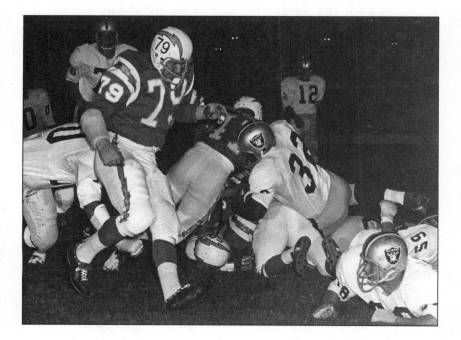

pumping iron of nearly 300 pounds over his head in reps of 10. Then he'd ask when the workout would start because he had just finished his warm-up.

Bob Petrich
I've known two guys in my life who were strong beyond comprehension. One was George Gross.

Dave Hill, tackle, Kansas City Chiefs
George Gross was a big, strong guy. I never saw anyone stronger. He could run like a deer too, at 270 pounds, he'd run like a 4.9, 40-yard dash. I played in college at Auburn with him and he used to say "My heart is not in football." He played because he knew he was good at it and could have been so much better, but he just didn't love it. He had great ability. He wrestled in college and was an SEC champion, so he knew how to get people off balance and get by them or shrug off blocks. He was quick as a cat and strong as an ox.

To his other front line mates, Gross was considered the man with the soft heart, but he could also hit like a sledge hammer. For the first part of 1963, to keep all the linemen fresh, he would alternate at tackle with Ladd and Hank Schmidt, and by midseason he was among the top five tacklers on the team.

Having such a large and controlling front line was a big reason why the defense had 14 interceptions by midseason and were the unsung heroes of the Chargers mid-year 5–2 record. Rookies Bob Petrich and George Gross were as responsible for that as much as any other player was.

Game 8: Polo Grounds Blowout

@ New York Jets
Saturday, November 2, 1963 (Night), at New York
Polo Grounds
Attendance: 20,798

Halfway through the season, the Chargers held the best record in the AFL and a game-and-a-half lead on the second place Oakland Raiders. The team's report card at midseason was Dean's List–caliber and they were only in need of a little tweaking here and there to satisfy their coach as they entered the second half of their schedule. The running game was nearly flawless with Lincoln and Lowe firing off double digit runs regularly while the passing game was consistently mixing in long gainers with their steady stream of aerials. The defense was relentlessly choking off drives and scoring threats, displaying their muscle, agility, and tenacity. Reducing their turnovers and getting more consistent punting were the two biggest areas that Gillman prioritized for improvement as the Chargers headed to New York's Polo Grounds for the last time before the Jets moved into their new home next season.

A friendly early season schedule had the Chargers playing five home games in the first half of the season, which meant that they only had two of their final seven games left at Balboa. It also meant that it was time to embark on their annual three-game sojourn to the Northeast. They would be playing three teams that were jockeying for the Eastern Division lead: New York on Saturday night, Boston the following Sunday, and wrapping up the trip a week later in Buffalo. The Jets and Patriots had both spent time in the catbird seat and Buffalo had recently found the edge they were missing in the opening month to make themselves a factor. The trip would not be easy and, after a one-point loss to Oakland, the Chargers were chomping at the bit to get back on the field to start the home stretch.

The Polo Grounds, home of the Titans/Jets since their arrival in the AFL, had fallen into disrepair after being abandoned by the New York Baseball Giants in 1958 (after the 1957 baseball season) and because of the lack of attention (and funds) given to it on former owner Harry Wismer's watch. The Jets were playing their last season there now that a new home (Shea Stadium) was under construction and scheduled to open in 1964. Everyone hated coming to Coogan's Bluff and its ancient relic that was dimly lit, attracted small crowds, and had an uneven, often dangerous playing field. And the locker rooms were downright archaic, offering cramped quarters and outdated accommodations. But knowing that this would be their last visit to this dungeon-like facility made the trek almost nostalgic. Ewbank's team had flown to San Diego three weeks earlier as a first place team with a 3–1 record, and now hosted the Chargers as the third place team behind Houston and Boston with a record of 3–3–1. The Jets liked to play their home games on Saturday evenings so they wouldn't have to compete with other New York sporting events that were on Sunday's billet. And during the entire span the AFL (from 1960–1969), the Chargers would play only two Sunday games in New York.

Rolling up over 500 yards of total offense—more than 200 yards both on the ground and in the air and holding the Jets to 63 yards rushing in their previous meeting—the Chargers had controlled nearly every aspect of the game except the scoreboard. Even though they moved the ball offensively and the defense resisted any movement by the Jets in Southern California, the Chargers were determined to use their output with more efficiency this time around. They would also be welcoming back split end Don Norton to the lineup for the first time all season. Norton had injured his shoulder at Rough Acres participating in the summer weight lifting program and had yet to make an appearance. His return relegated Jerry Robinson back to the bench as a spot sub for both Norton and Alworth.

The chilly 41 degrees and wet turf of the Polo Grounds reminded the Chargers that for the next three weeks there would be no 70 degree days or warm air flowing through the stadium as it did in Balboa. And on evenings like this one, in the Jets damp and dingy arena, the air seemed more frigid than cool. Fending off the elements as well the Jets, Patriots, and Bills was always an extraneous side effect of playing in the Northeast, and only focused performances would get them through the month unscathed.

The Jets took possession first and picked up two quick first downs on Mark Smolinski runs through the middle of the Charger line and a 15-yard pass over the middle to Ken Gregory. Dick Wood was then dropped for a 13-yard loss by Hank Schmidt and called upon Curly Johnson to punt them out of trouble.

On the Chargers opening drive, Lance Alworth started the evening off by out-leaping his double coverage on an underthrown pass for a 62-yard gain on San Diego's second play of the game. Setting up what appeared to be a sure-fire 7-point lead. But three plays later they succumbed to another costly fumble on the Jets 11. As they had done many times this season after a turnover, the Chargers defense shut the Jets down and gave the offense the ball back near midfield. Leaning to the pass on this series, Tobin Rote moved the Chargers on a quick touchdown drive, set up with a 21-yard pass play to Lincoln before connecting with Paul Lowe for an 11-yard touchdown pass four minutes into the game. When Emil Karas then recovered Dick Wood's fumble at the Jets 43-yard line with 1:57 left in the first period, Tobin Rote deployed his offense on another drive to the end zone.

Two plays after the teams changed ends, Dave Kocourek scored from 14 yards out. The defense followed the score by shutting the Jets down for their third consecutive three-and-out. Looking to take advantage of rookie Tony Stricker's inexperience, Rote, on the first play of the Chargers next series went deep and connected with Alworth again, this time for 49 yards to the Jets 28. Four plays later, Paul Lowe sprinted around right end to put his team firmly ahead, 21–0, with a TD run of 11 yards. Another fumble recovery by Karas when the Jets faced a 2nd and 13 situation led to three more Charger points to give them a 24–0 lead with five minutes left until intermission. The deepest penetration the Jets could muster in the first half was then engineered by Galen Hall, who had replaced the ineffective Dick Wood. Hall used short passes to move down field to the Chargers 35-yard line until Dick Harris stepped in front of Bake Turner at the goal line for an interception with less than two minutes left in the half. Content with a 24–0 lead, the Chargers ran out the clock in the remaining seconds. With renewed focus, the Chargers had everything working offensively and defensively in the first half.

Lincoln and Lowe had already run for 70 yards and Tobin Rote was hotter than he had been thus far this season. He completed 11 of his 18 passes for 221 yards through the air in only two quarters. Alworth was also burning the Jets defenders and accounted for half of the Chargers' passing yardage on three receptions—all of them by leaping over rookie defender Tony Stricker. The defense, flexing their intimidating size and muscle, held the Jets to less than 100 yards of total offense at the midway point. It was the most dominating display on both sides of the ball in one game all season.

Before many of the 20,000 fans had returned to their seats following the intermission, Alworth had already picked up 54 more yards on two more receptions and the Chargers had seven more points at the end of his 28-yard touchdown catch, opening up a 31–0 advantage three minutes into the third quarter.

Sid Gillman and Tobin Rote discuss strategy during a time-out.

By the end of the quarter, they increased that lead to 38–0 after Harris recovered the third Jet fumble near midfield where Rote continue to dissect the Jets with a 13-play drive which he ended with a one yard sneak across the goal line. In running up their best offensive output of the season, the Chargers ran for over 150 yards and passed for nearly 400 more, stinging the Jets for a whopping 528 yards in total offense and lighting up the scoreboard with 53 points. It was by far Rote's finest day, completing 21 of 29 passes for 369 yards and no interceptions.

Being nearly perfect the second half, he connected with his receivers on 10 of 11 passes. Not to be outdone, the defense held the Jets to 39 yards rushing for the night on 14 carries. Unable to negotiate their way through the Chargers run defense, the Jets were forcing the ball to the air, necessitating quarterbacks Dick Wood and Galen Hall to throw 41 times. Dick Harris intercepted two of them, giving him four in his last two games. He also set up another Chargers scoring drive by returning Dick Guesman's short field-goal attempt to the Charger 19-yard line. After another long drive that covered 81 yards in nine plays, Gerry McDougall pushed the ball across the goal to give San Diego a 45–0 lead.

As a result of their loss to Oakland, the Chargers appeared to be re-energized—or it at least caused them enough anxiety to refocus their eyes on the prize. Not only did they cut their turnovers down from six to one from the previous week, but they forced four turnovers against the Jets and were now a plus one through eight games. To this point in the season, they have given up the ball 21 times and recorded 22 takeaways for themselves. As the rest of the year unfolded and the last six games intensified, the Chargers improved their takeaway differential by another eight, forcing 23 more turnovers in their remaining games. They had started the road trip in the best possible way: by dominating their opponent in all aspects of the game and scoring the most points in one game in the franchise's history. It was a good opening result to the road trip that was either going to make or break their run to the top of the league. And it had everyone in a renewed state of mind as they headed to Boston, where they would have to escape the Patriots lockdown defense.

THE UNCROWNED CHAMPS

San Diego Chargers	7	17	14	15	-	53
New York Jets	0	0	0	7	-	7

SD-Lowe, 11 pass from Rote (Blair kick)
SD-Kocourek, 14 pass from Rote (Blair kick)
SD-Lowe, 11 run (Blair kick)
SD-FG, Blair 18
SD-Alworth, 28 pass from Rote (Blair kick)
SD-Rote, 1 run (Blair kick)
SD-McDougall, 3 run (Blair kick)
NYJ-Wood, 4 run (Guesman kick)
SD-Robinson, 8 pass from Hadl (Kocourek pass from Hadl)

Charger Statistics:

Player	Rush Att	Yds	Avg	TD	Long	
Keith Lincoln	11	62	5.6	0	16	
Paul Lowe	16	79	4.9	1	16	
Gerry McDougall	2	6	3	1	3	
Tobin Rote	2	10	5	1	9	
	Pass Att	**Cmp**	**Yds**	**TD**	**Int**	**Long**
Tobin Rote	29	21	369	3	0	62
John Hadl	2	1	8	1	0	8
	Rec	**Yds**	**TD**	**Long**		
Lance Alworth	5	180	1	62		
Jerry Robinson	1	8	1	8		
Don Norton	4	41	0	14		
Keith Lincoln	2	44	0	23		
Paul Lowe	5	40	1	16		
Dave Kocourek	3	34	1	14		
Gerry McDougall	2	30	0	20		

Interceptions: Harris (2)
Fumble recovery: Karas (2)

Around the AFL: Buffalo (4–4–1) moved out of the East's basement and squared their record by winning a close one in Denver (2–5–1), 30–28. Boston (5–4) spanked first-place Houston (5–4), 45–3, to move into a first-place tie with the Oilers and set up a battle of division leaders next week when the Chargers invaded Fenway Park to play the Patriots. With their loss to San Diego (6–2), New York (3–4–1) fell into last place in the East. Oakland (5–4) stayed in second place behind San Diego by downing Kansas City (2–5–1), 10–7, handing the Chiefs their fourth loss in a row.

George Blair

George Blair, San Diego safety/kicker

I was a backup kicker in college at Ole Miss and only remember getting one chance to kick a field goal in a game . . . I missed it and never got another chance. I then went to play for the Chargers the first year they were in San Diego as a defensive back in 1961. Our kicker was Ben Agajanian, who had been kicking in the NFL since the forties (he was now forty-two years old). He kicked for the Chargers in 1960 and made probably half his field goal tries (he made 13 of 24 attempts). One day at a training camp practice early in the week, I was with the defense doing drills and the offensive line coach, Joe Madro, came over to where we were. He called out to me, "Hey Mississippi, don't you kick?" When I said yes he said, "Come with me." He took me down to where Agajanian was practicing and told me I was now the backup kicker and to stay there and practice with Ben. A few days later I came out to practice and went right to the kicker's area and saw that I was alone. When I asked around about where Ben was, I was told he'd just gotten cut and that I was now the number-one kicker. I hadn't really kicked in games since I was in high school and now I'm the kicker on a pro team.

George was a backup defensive back in both 1961 and '62, along with being the kicker. In 1963, he stepped into a starting role at what became known as the strong safety spot. He was the only DB on the team in '63 that played his position all season without being injured. All the other starters—Charlie McNeil, Dick Westmoreland, and Dick Harris—spent time sitting out with injuries.

George Blair

In college we played mostly zone pass defense, so when I got to the San Diego I basically had to learn how to play defense. Chuck Noll was our defensive backs coach when I got there and he was really good at teaching the system. I think he liked playing zone more than man, though.

I wasn't that big at 5'11" and 195 pounds, so I covered mostly guys who were bigger than me. Most times it was the tight end on the right side and I was the left safety. I really had to be a good tackler or they'd run over me. Sometimes, too, I'd have to cover wide receivers if they lined up in the slot, like Charlie Hennigan of the Oilers. I hated covering him. He wasn't that fast but he could really run a great pattern and never dropped the ball. He was one of the tougher guys I had to go up against.

After making less than 50 percent of his attempts that first year (13–27 FGA), Blair came back in 1962 to set a record by making 85 percent (17–20 FGA) of his tries. In 1963, he converted on 61 percent (17–28), which included 15 of 22 attempts from inside the 40-yard line.

George Blair

I was a straight-on kicker and used one of those square-toed shoes when I kicked. That meant I was changing shoes every time I had to go in to kick, then would come out and change the shoe to go back in to play defense. Sometimes I'd have to miss a play or two while I changed.

Back then the goal post was on the goal line and the hash marks were wider so it was a little more difficult to make field goals, especially those extra points. They were so close you had to get the ball up really quick. It took me a while to make that adjustment, too, because in high school and college you could use a tee to kick from. In the pros, if it wasn't a kickoff, you couldn't use a tee. You had to kick a little differently from close range then you did from farther away.

Blair's 1963 season was the only one of his career in which he was a defensive starter for the complete season. Five games into the 1964 season he injured his knee and sat out the rest of the year.

George Blair

I was still playing both ways in 1964, kicking and at safety. We were playing in Boston and I came up to the line for run support and their flanker, Gino Cappelletti, came down and clipped me from behind and my knee went out. I tried to come back the next week against Denver but it just didn't work. It hurt too much and that was it. That's what ended my career. I went back to Ole Miss and finished school and helped coach the football team.

But I have really good memories of that '63 team. I thought we had an excellent offense. I don't think anyone could have stopped us. We really had excellent personnel. Sometimes we'd turn the ball over more than we liked, but that's football. You just adjusted to the situation. Sometimes you had games like that. We were all out there trying and that's all you wanted.

Our defense was really good, too. Maybe they didn't get enough credit. We just all got along so well. Nobody was a problem and as a player you wanted to play your best for everyone on the team. That was always in the back of our minds.

Game 9: Lucky 13!

@ Boston Patriots
Sunday, November 10, 1963, at Boston
Fenway Park
Attendance: 28,402

After their last visit to the Polo Grounds, the Chargers made their first visit to Fenway Park, legendary home of Ted Williams and the Boston Red Sox.

Prior to moving into Fenway, the Patriots roamed the city of Boston for a home like a stray cat. Harvard Stadium, Boston

College, and Boston University all hosted home games during the team's first three seasons. Now in their fourth year, it seemed reasonable to make their fourth home a permanent one. The set up at Fenway spread the gridiron across the baseball diamond from the right field bullpen to the third base line, and set up the visitor's benches in front of auxiliary seats that extended out from left field's "Green Monster" wall to within ten yards of the player benches.

The game-time conditions on the second Sunday in November were worse than the Kansas City rain weeks earlier, and gloomier than their last night in the Polo Grounds. This meant that the Chargers would have to fight the weather as tenaciously as the Boston Patriots, who were deadlocked with Houston at 5–4 at the top of their division. Always fierce against the run, the Boston defense again put the Chargers running game on lockdown, as the rain-soaked field was clearly no venue for San Diego's thoroughbred backs to utilize their wide-open running. Lincoln and Lowe were held to a season low 36 yards in the muck that gave no player stable footing. This was a defensive tussle on both sides of the ball, with the Chargers offense producing the game's lone touchdown. Boston produced their points on two field goals and had a chance at three more without connecting.

The first time San Diego had possession, they drove from their own 28 to the Boston 5, with most of the yardage picked up on three consecutive passes to Alworth that netted 60 yards. When the Boston defense tightened, kicker George Blair missed a chip shot field goal attempt from the 12-yard line; he was clearly affected by the rainy conditions.

Boston had some early success moving the ball as they took over at the 20 after the missed attempt and drove to the San Diego 42.

211

The drive ended when Larry Garron was stripped of the ball by George Gross after picking up 6 yards, and Dick Westmoreland threw himself on top of it for a drive-stopping recovery.

It was on this possession that the Chargers put up their only points of the dreary afternoon. Driving from their own 36, Lincoln ran for 14 yards followed by Norton gaining 9 on a pass reception. A Boston penalty and Paul Lowe busting up the middle for 7 yards moved the Chargers to the Boston 18. Rote then connected with Alworth on a stop-and-go pattern for their first touchdown . . . but somebody on the San Diego line moved and the touchdown was called back, moving the Chargers back to the Boston 23. On the next play, Alworth's number was called again—this time on a play that Rote had not called all year. First, he rolled out to his left and faked a pass to Don Norton, and then he turned to the right and hit his flanker on a screen pass behind the line. Alworth weaved and sprinted through the Boston secondary after being sprung by Sam DeLuca's down field block, escaped a tackler at the five, and scored the day's only touchdown as the first quarter came to an end.

The Pats ensuing drive ended with Gino Cappelletti missing his first goal attempt from 38 yards away. Boston's next possession was halted by another fumble after Cappelletti picked up 18 yards. On their next drive, Chuck Allen intercepted the ball at the San Diego 25. All three San Diego possessions in the second quarter ended with Paul Maguire punting the ball back to Boston. When the half ended, the story lines for the first two periods were Lance Alworth's eight pass receptions and San Diego's three takeaways that stopped Boston drives and kept them off the scoreboard.

Lance Alworth

That day in Fenway it was really raining. I remember I had a pretty good day and it appeared I was the only one who could catch the ball. I can't explain why, I just could.

It was fun playing in Fenway Park. That was the first time we played a game there and it was the first time I ever played a game where I was aware of the fans in the stadium. Our benches were right next to the fans and, as we'd come off the field, they'd be screaming at us and we'd be hollering back at them. That was an unusual day. I don't ever remember people being in the stands except for that day in Fenway.

The rainfall throughout the game made the conditions increasingly difficult and the understandably slippery ball-handling resulted in seven turnovers between the two division leaders. With both offenses at a disadvantage running the football, it appeared that passing was the better option. Babe Parilli was 8 for 12 passing in the first half, but was unable to get his team on the scoreboard. Tobin Rote was equally successful, hitting on 11 of his 16 passes with one scoring connection through two quarters.

For the rest of the day the storylines continued to be about Alworth and the dominating defensive play by both San Diego and Boston.

Boston came out blazing in the second half with two long gainers after the kickoff, first with Art Graham catching a 25-yard pass, followed by Larry Garron rumbling for 20 more yards. An incomplete pass and an offensive pass interference penalty then pushed them back 15 yards. Their opening drive finally ended with Cappelletti putting the Patriots on the board with a 35-yard field goal, which put pressure on the Chargers to answer. Tobin Rote again went back to Alworth, who caught his ninth pass for 13 yards, followed by Keith Lincoln picking up 10 more on a draw play through the blitzing Boston defense. On the eleventh play of the drive, on 4th and 1, George Blair's field goal attempt from 41 yards hit the upright and bounced back onto the field, giving Boston possession at their own 20.

Photo courtesy of the Boston/New England Patriots.

Babe Parilli throws against the Chargers.

Parilli got his team three points closer on the next possession, engineering the Pats' best drive of the afternoon by moving them all the way down to the Charger 18 before needing Gino's right foot to get them on the boards. Cappelletti kicked another field goal, shrinking the Chargers lead to a single digit as the end of the third quarter neared. The score now stood at 7–6.

Rote continued to use his only weapon, Alworth, to move the Chargers. After his 10th reception moved the ball to the San Diego 47, Rote's next pass was intercepted by Mike Suci to end the third quarter.

Both teams had played as carefully as they could under difficult conditions that had players skidding and sliding with every step. Seven turnovers (five by Boston) did somewhat tarnish the herculean efforts the players put forth, but under the circumstances it could have been much worse. Every play on each possession challenged ball carriers and receivers to protect the pigskin with the highest degree of security. And with the score 7–6 at the beginning of the fourth quarter, the pressure on the place kick holder and his importance in the game's outcome was also magnified.

After Suci's 15-yard interception return gave Boston the ball on the Chargers 34, the San Diego defense rose to the occasion—just as it had been doing all season. Two incompletions and a 9-yard loss halted the Patriots drive and gave Cappelletti another opportunity to give his team the lead with a 37-yard field goal. But this attempt was stymied by a wobbly center snap that caused the hold to be a bit off-center, driving the kick low and giving the Chargers a reprieve and the ball at their 20-yard line.

The footing continued to be an issue for the Chargers as they tried to take time off the clock, hold onto the ball with first downs, and avoid the desperation pass rush of the Patriots. The results were not good, losing 12 yards on three plays. Twenty-two yards short of a first down, they again looked to Paul Maguire to stretch the field with a fourth down punt. Even the center snap and the punter's catch became dangerous at this venture.

A fair catch at midfield gave Parilli another shot at taking the lead from 50 yards away. On first down, it appeared that the Pats were ready to take control when Babe completed a quick turn-in pass to Art Graham at the Chargers 42. But as quickly as the rookie pulled the pass in, it was ripped away by Chuck Allen for his second interception of the game, giving the Chargers the opportunity to take more time off the clock and maybe even more distance on the scoreboard.

The Chargers offense now moved into their slowdown mode and Alworth's 11th catch moved the ball six more yards, but that was all they could muster as the Pats' defense held yet again. Maguire returned to punt Boston closer to their own end. Both teams failed to move the ball throughout the final quarter, making the punters the best weapon to regulate field position. Six of the game's nine punts occurred in the fourth quarter and gave the game the mood of a chess match; making moves to set up other moves and then hoping those moves would result in more advantageous situations later in the game.

Another Boston fumble, recovered by Chuck Allen at midfield, further dimmed the Patriot's hopes and took more time off the clock. But San Diego failed to move the ball, and again Maguire was called upon for his fourth punt of the quarter.

Moments later, when Boston was still unable to move the ball, the first of two nearly game-breaking disasters occurred as Tom Yewcic prepared to punt from his own 21. The center snap from

Jon Morris sailed over his head and into the end zone. Racing to recover the ball, he was able to avoid the Chargers rush and kick it away without incident, escaping a possible game-ending mistake. The second near-disaster happened on the following play, with Paul Lowe losing control of the handoff and Boston's Bob Dee recovering it at the San Diego 42-yard line. The Patriots still had another chance to take the lead. Parilli then walked onto the field for what would most likely be his team's last and most crucial drive of the game. On first down, he sent Garron on a sweep, where he was swarmed under by the Chargers front line for a 6-yard loss. On 2nd down and 16, Harry Crump gained only 2 yards on a draw play, bringing up 3rd down and 14 from the Chargers 46. Sending his receivers deep, Parilli was looking to catch San Diego in a prevent defense and threw a screen pass to Crump. But the Chargers were waiting for him and brought him down before he could even get started and a 2-yard loss, bringing up a 4th down and 16 situation with the ball resting at the San Diego 48-yard line.

Gino Cappelletti, arguably the AFL's best field-goal kicker, had never attempted a field goal from that far away. And with the sloppy field rippled with mud, Cappy was now being asked to win the game from 55 yards away. Throughout the 1962 season he had attempted field goals from between the 40- and 50-yard line twenty-three times, and was able to convert on only three of them. Now, from a spot he had never tried from before, in terrible weather conditions, this kick was for the win and to maintain first place in the division. This time the snap and the hold were perfect, but as it rose above the Chargers outstretched arms, Cappy's kick fell well short of the crossbar and rolled harmlessly into the end zone. As the Chargers took possession at their own 20-yard line with just under two minutes to play there was still a slim chance for Boston to get the ball back if they could hold the Chargers and force another punt. To hold on and run the clock out, the Chargers needed to move the ball and pick up a first down or two—something they had been unable to do since their first possession of the second half. A play-action pass completion to Lance Alworth, his 12th of the game, picked up 5 yards and Paul Lowe's only catch of the day netted 11 more to the San Diego 36, giving the Chargers only their third first down of the half. As time continued to tick off the clock, Rote handed to Lincoln on a draw that picked up 5 yards, then off-tackle where he lost 3. Facing a 3rd and 8, Rote then made his gutsiest—or maybe craziest—call of the day. With under a minute to go, he launched a long "sideline and go" pass to Alworth that silenced the Fenway faithful, connecting with his flanker for 50 yards. The catch moved the ball to the Boston 14-yard line and gave Alworth his 13th reception—tying the AFL record for most receptions in a game (which was originally set in 1961 by Houston's Charlie Hennigan). It also forced Boston to take their last time-out with less than 30 seconds left in the contest. The Pats' only hope now was to create a fumble and throw a bomb for a game-winning touchdown. When Paul Lowe cradled Rote's deliberate handoff on the next play, losing 3 yards, the clock ran out to end the most exciting and gut wrenching game of the year.

Dominating play by both defenses only accentuated Alworth's spectacular performance (he was thrown to 18 times and caught 13, the highest numbers in his Hall of Fame career) in a game that had the player's emotions running high and fans on the edge of their seats. On every play and each possession of the final thirty minutes, the tension only mounted. According to Boston coach Mike Holovak, the Patriots defense played its finest game against San Diego that day. In their two games against San Diego, Boston's defense had given up only 24 points, while the Chargers held the Patriots to one touchdown and four field goals in eight quarters. The Chargers had also surrendered only 13 points in their last two games. San Diego may have been outgained by a more balanced Boston offense, but they showed that their identity wasn't driven only by their offense. Today was their defense's finest hour and gave them a win that kept the needed distance between themselves and their division pursuers.

One of the marks of a good football team is being able to win when they underperform and when the conditions are less than ideal. What the Chargers showed against Boston was that they were able to block out and overcome the elements and grind out the tough yardage, and even though they were occasionally let down on one side of the ball, they were able to pick up the slack from the other side. On the road to winning a championship, these things become necessities that require more than just talent. They necessitated a feeling of esprit de corps, and the experience of having endured even tougher conditions before. They were the result of careful planning and exceptional leadership, developed in places like Rough Acres Ranch. As the Chargers headed to War Memorial Stadium to play the surging Buffalo Bills, they were rife with the knowledge that they could rise to the occasional, no matter how difficult the situation. By winning in Boston against an excellent and talented team, the feeling was that the Chargers had won more than just a football game that day.

| San Diego Chargers | 7 | 0 | 0 | 0 | - | 7 |
| Boston Patriots | 0 | 0 | 6 | 0 | - | 6 |

SD-Alworth, 27 pass from Rote (Blair kick)
Bos-FG, Cappelletti 35
Bos-FG, Cappelletti 25

Charger Statistics:

Player	Rush Att	Yds	Avg	TD	Long	
Keith Lincoln	11	36	3.3	0	14	
Paul Lowe	8	0	0	0	7	
	Pass Att	Cmp	Yds	TD	Int	Long
Tobin Rote	29	17	252	1	1	50
John Hadl	3	1	6	0	0	6
	Rec	Yds	TD	Long		
Lance Alworth	13	210	1	50		
Don Norton	4	37	0	11		
Paul Lowe	1	11	0	11		

Interceptions: Allen (2)
Fumble recovery: Allen, Glick, Westmoreland

Around the AFL: With San Diego's (7–2) win in Boston, the Patriots (5–5) dropped from first to third place in the East as Buffalo (5–4–1) won their third straight game, beating Denver (2–6–1), 27–17. Houston, who had shared the lead with Boston, held off the Jets (3–5–1), 31–27, to take over sole possession of first place. Oakland (6–4) continued their winning ways with their fourth in a row by beating Kansas City (2–6–1) for the second consecutive week, 22–7.

The Legend of Jimmy Jones

Following their win in Boston, the Chargers flew into Niagara Falls to set up camp at the Hotel Niagara in preparation for their next opponent: the Buffalo Bills. The short trip allowed the team to use the extra time to relax and even let their hair down for a few days and nights. The team-bonding effect that coach Gillman was so determined to create during camp was in full flight by mid-November. Of course, winning brings a team together more than anything, so it was no surprise that after arriving at the Falls the team leaders decided to host a gathering of sorts. Having no gas station to hang out as they did back in Boulevard, California, the boys had to improvise and create their own temporary watering hole. Thanks to Jimmy Jones, the team had one of their best parties of the season. One of the players was put in charge of finding a place where the team could gather and "debrief" about the Patriots game. Explaining to the desk clerk their need for a large meeting room, the hotel was able to accommodate the squad immediately and *voilà*, the Chargers had their "debriefing" room. When asked whom the room should be billed to, the answer from the requesting player was to charge it to the Chargers' Jimmy Jones.

Now you won't find the name Jimmy Jones on any San Diego Chargers roster, nor will you find it on any team directory in 1963. And yet Jones is one of the most cherished members of the Chargers championship team. Conning their way into a rented room and charging it to the organization would not in itself have been a problem had it all gone as planned. And if the boys had just had their fun and then retired to their rooms for the evening, all would have been okay. But when you put a group of professional football players in a room to let off steam and consume the libation of choice, there are times—like this night in Niagara Falls—when everything does not go according to plan. At some point during the evening, one of the Chargers players had an altercation with a guest at the hotel and chased him into a bathroom. The guest locked the door behind him to avoid what he assumed would be a heavy whooping. The fuming player was not going to let a locked door stop him from getting his satisfaction and proceeded to rip the old-fashioned oak door off its hinges. Luckily, his teammates intervened before any further damage—to the room or the guest—could take place.

The next morning, as Gillman was preparing for the day's practice, he was interrupted by hotel management to find out where they could find Jimmy Jones so that he could pay for the room, food, drinks, and damages to the tune of $2,000. Gillman hit the roof and told the manager the Chargers don't, and never have, had anyone named Jimmy Jones on their team or under their employment.

Addressing his team at practice that afternoon, a seething Gillman lined them up and began his interrogation to find out who was responsible for the charge and to identify who the "real" Jimmy Jones was. He moved about the practice field asking each group, "Who is Jimmy Jones?" No one came forward, and he knew no one would. He should have known that on this Chargers team, no one was about to break ranks. Still, Gillman insisted later that he knew who Jimmy was the entire time. Fifty years later the secret remains safe, and no one outside of the tightly knit championship Chargers knows the true identify of Jimmy Jones.

Lance Alworth

Never underestimate the wisdom of fatherly advice. Take it from Lance Alworth, who credited it with paving the way for his journey to the Pro Football Hall of Fame. Recruited out of

Brookhaven High School in Mississippi by the New York Yankees as a center fielder, Lance's father encouraged him to turn down the chance to play professional baseball for the opportunity to get a college education. According to Lance, it was the best advice he ever got.

As a three-sport athlete at the University of Arkansas, Alworth led the nation in punt returns in 1960 and 1961. He was an All-American halfback, broke the World Record for the 100-yard dash (9.4) during track practice, and was a three-time Academic All-American who earned his degree in English and Business Marketing before leaving the Arkansas campus for the Chargers.

Lance Alworth

If I didn't make it in football, I was going to go to law school. I also had an interest in archeology, so that was a possibility as well.

To be sure, Alworth never thought he had much of a chance to make it in pro football beyond his specialty of returning punts. But Al Davis and Sid Gillman saw something more than a special teams' player for the man who would become known as "Bambi" during his rookie year. What the Chargers coaching staff saw in Alworth was incredible speed, soft and sticky hands, and the ability to leap above defenders to pull down passes. It was their plan to use him as a flanker rather than at his college position of running back. College football in the early sixties was a running game, and Alworth was plenty good at it, averaging 4.2 yards per carry over three seasons as a Razorback. Although he caught only 37 passes in college for a 17-yard average, it was there that his professional career would earn him fame.

It was fullback Charlie Flowers who dubbed Alworth "Bambi" for his graceful leaping ability and his quickness and speed during training camp in 1962. Then, after catching 10 passes in his first four games, he pulled a quadriceps muscle while place kicking in practice and spent the rest of his rookie year in rehab. So Alworth was more than anxious to resume his career when he reported to Rough Acres Ranch in July with a clean bill of health.

Essentially a rookie again in 1963, Lance came into his own by making an immediate splash, catching 61 passes and averaging 20 yards per reception. Beyond earning a championship ring, he was named the UPI (*United Press International*) Player of the Year and was selected to the All-AFL 1st Team. He would also be selected for that group every year through 1968. He led the AFL in receptions three times and was voted onto the All-Time AFL 1st Team as a flanker.

Charlie Hennigan, flanker, Houston Oilers

Alworth was the best receiver I ever saw. He had such a tremendous and graceful way of running a pattern. He'd take a defender past his spot and then come back behind him to catch the pass. I loved watching him. When our defense was on the field, I would stand on the sidelines and just watch him play. He was amazing.

Billy Joe

Alworth could have played anywhere and been a star. He had speed, hands, was a great leaper, and could cut on a dime.

Alworth excelled at catching the football with a unique, cradling style. He would protect the ball by cushioning it with his body.

John Hadl

Lance caught the ball with his body when no one else was doing it that way. I can't ever remember him dropping a pass either.

Lance Alworth

We were playing against Oakland in 1963, and Freddie Williamson, who was a really good defensive back, was always chirping at me and trying to get into my head. One time he must have gotten in there because my concentration was broken and I dropped three balls. I never said a word to the defense; when I dropped a pass I figured out that I was taking my eye off the ball because I was trying to run before I had control. I needed to make sure I had control first. So from there I came up with a simple drill that I ran through in every practice, and it helped me immensely over the course of my career. In the final seven seasons of my career, I didn't fumble the ball once in 356 touches (341 receptions, 15 rushes).

I would have our quarterbacks throw me passes in practices from 10 yards away. Just drill me with passes from my groin to my head. Instead of simply catching the passes and tossing them back, I concentrated on watching the ball, catching the ball, and tucking the ball. It became something of a simple mantra for me: watch it, catch it, tuck it. I would repeat that all the time. I remember concentrating so hard at doing those drills that even when I caught the pass and threw it back, I would be watching the ball all the way. John Hadl used to say I was the worst throw-back guy in the world. I told him that was because I was concentrating on watching the ball so much. (Over his career Alworth threw six passes and completed three of them.) On the days before games, I shortened it to "watch it, snatch it." Just remember, the most important thought is to watch yourself tuck the ball into your arms or body. Then nobody can get it!

Bobby Bell, linebacker, Kansas City Chiefs

Alworth would catch everything in sight. One game I just kept telling [Coach Hank] Stram that we had to slow him down somehow. Next thing I know I was covering him as part of a double team. Lance came out and said, "What are you doing out here?" I got up tight on him at the line and when he came off the line, I hit him so hard

I think I dazed him for a while. I didn't know how else to stop him.

Art Powell, split end, Oakland Raiders
Lance really challenged me to be better. I would watch him all the time. He was so good that he made me step up my game every time we played them.

Bobby Hunt, safety, Kansas City Chiefs
Alworth was the best I ever faced. He was fast and quick and could really jump. Things were different back then. There was more man coverage. We never tried bump and run against him because that would mean that if he got by the corner he'd be all alone to go deep. He was so quick that if the cornerback tried to jam him and didn't, you could forget him, he was gone.

Teams would try to do whatever they could to stop Alworth, with little success; everything from double-teaming to holding, knocking around, and even intimidating him, with all to no avail. He was such a focused receiver that he never let anyone get into his head.

Lance Alworth
The guy who would try to get to me the most was Johnny Sample of the Jets. He had just come over from the NFL. In his first game against us, I was running across the field on a crossing pattern and got in front of him. After the play was over, he came up from behind and nailed me. I went sprawling on my face and he looked down at me and said, "Welcome to the 'N'FL." It really ticked me off

but I just got up and went back to the huddle. Later in the game, after another play, our positions were reversed and I laid him out from behind just like he had done to me. He got up with a big smile on his face and looked over at me and said, "Okay, truce." And that was it. From then on, he never gave me a cheap shot again.

The Chargers first visit to Boston's Fenway Park was probably Alworth's best game of his career—at the very least, his best of 1963. Played on a sloshy field with constant rain, Lance was thrown to 18 times—catching 13 of them—to tie an AFL record, and accounted for 210 of the Chargers 258 receiving yards. His first quarter touchdown was the Chargers only score of the day, and turned out to be the game winner.

In an interview with *Sport* magazine, Alworth acknowledged that he loved playing in the rain but didn't know why he had so much success in it. Only that the defensive backs couldn't respond as quickly in the rain and that he could get away with things on a wet field that he wouldn't try on a dry one.

In 1963, he would be thrown to 103 times, making 61 catches (60 percent of those thrown to him) for 1,205 yards and 11 touchdowns, reaching a career high for receptions in the game against the Patriots on November 10.

In the evolution of Lance Alworth's Hall of Fame career, he went from being described as:

- having moves that were not terribly clever
- not running patterns very well
- running away from the defenders with moves that were not terribly deceptive

- not expected to do much blocking
- to becoming one of the best at running precise pass patterns
- and probably *the* best blocking flanker in pro football

Sid Gillman would say that he had more ability than anyone he ever coached. In the early days of his career, he would rely on his speed and quickness to find openings in the defense, using his speed to blow by defenders and force teams to cover him with more than one back. As he developed as a player, Gillman said he became the most complete receiver in football.

When he was traded to the Dallas Cowboys in 1971, he was told by Coach Tom Landry that he traded for him because he could block.

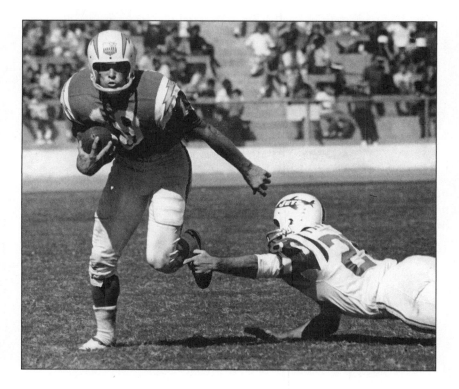

Lance Alworth

I flew to Dallas to join the team and found my way to the Cowboys offices and went to see Coach Landry. He had just a small, plain office. I went in and introduced myself and he said, "I know who you are, come with me." We went to another small room and sat down. He looked at me and said, "I traded for you because you can block. If you block for us we'll win the Super Bowl this year." I said, "Okay, I can block for you." He looked back at me and said "Good," then got up and walked out. We beat Miami in the Super Bowl that year, but the '63 Chargers are still the best team I ever played for.

Game 10: Just Enough

@ Buffalo Bills
Sunday, November 17, 1963, at Buffalo
War Memorial Stadium
Attendance: 38,592

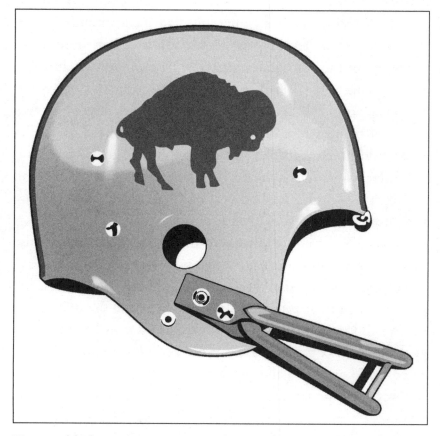

You could always count on two things when the Chargers visited Buffalo's War Memorial Stadium: The sky would be grey and the weather would be cold. You could also add, in most cases, a big crowd and a low scoring contest. All four were present for the team's late November match-up.

THE UNCROWNED CHAMPS

On opening day, the Chargers took the first step on their road back to the championship game by holding off the Bills, who were without the services of their leading rusher Cookie Gilchrist, 14–10. This time, although still not at full strength, Cookie was in the lineup and looking to carry the surging Bills further up the standings. In their rise up the ladder, Buffalo had won five of their last six games and had most recently beaten Boston and then Denver twice, to move from fourth to third and now into second place in the Eastern Division, only a half-game behind Houston.

Outside of the Chargers blowout in New York, these final two games of their eastern swing were classic and exhaustive battles that could have torpedoed their season and dropped them into a deadlock with Oakland had they not met the tests in Boston and Buffalo. In meeting and beating those teams, their defense gallantly took the lead and shut down the two powerful teams from the Northeast while their usually high-octane offense managed again to score just enough points to sweep the series.

This game belonged to the Chargers' defense again, just as every game on their three game road trip did. They held the Bills to just one touchdown and yielded only two touchdowns and four field goals in the three game win streak, holding New York and Boston to 13 total points and allowing the Bills just 13 more.

Over their previous six games, the Bills had been winning in unspectacular, yet steady style. A sub-par Gilchrist had run for 332 yards during their streak, but broke the century mark only once in ten games. On defense, except for shutting out the Raiders, 12–0, the Bills had given up an average of 25.2 points a game throughout their other nine contests. There was no room for a letdown by either squad in this game, as both teams entered the final push to the top of their respective divisions . . . and both teams needed to win.

What was supposed to be a tightly contested match looked like anything but from the outset. The first time they had the ball, Buffalo let Cookie lead the way to the end zone. Running as if he was still the leading ball carrier in the league, Gilchrist ran over the left side of the Chargers defense four times for 23, 4, 23, and then a 1-yard blast for a touchdown. If this was any indication of how the rest of the day was going to go, the Chargers were going to be in for a bruising afternoon. When San Diego took their first possession at their own 24-yard line, they used runs of 23 yards by Paul Lowe and a 54-yard sprint by Keith Lincoln on an inside trap to quickly tie the score. On their second possession, the Chargers scored again, starting with a 24-yard pass play to Lincoln and then picking up 18 more as Lincoln snuck through the Bill's defense on a draw play. After the drive stalled, George Blair kicked a 39-yard field goal. Through the first six minutes of the game the pace seemed almost un-AFL like, but as the game wore on both teams appeared to be working out the kinks in their game.

After their initial scoring drive, Buffalo had to punt twice after absorbing third down sacks by Earl Faison for five yards and Emil Karas for 16 yards. To his credit, Buffalo punter Daryle Lamonica kept San Diego deep in their own territory with his punts, causing the Chargers offense to play cautiously throughout the second quarter. All three Charger possessions produced only one first down, and each ended with Maguire punting the ball back to the Bills. The Bills finally tied the back-and-forth battle with less than three minutes to play in the first half on an eight-play drive that started at the Buffalo 44 and was spearheaded by the running and receiving of their all-purpose back, Ed Rutkowski. Mack Yoho finished off the half with a 27-yard field goal to send the teams into the locker rooms even at 10–10.

At this point in the game, the Bills were controlling the pace of play as well as the time of possession. Keeping the ball for 32 plays, Buffalo balanced their offense with 15 runs for 87 yards and 13 completions for 125 yards. The Chargers snapped the ball only 19 times in the half, gaining 93 yards on the ground and tallied only a disappointing 36 yards through the air, and needed to employ Paul Maguire's punting on every possession in the second quarter after successfully putting up points on their first two drives in the opening quarter. The game was turning into another chess match, with both teams vying for field position. With the Chargers offense being smothered by the Bills defense, Maguire was continually punting from deep inside of his own end, and his kicks were giving Buffalo field position beyond their own 40-yard line each time. Buffalo had been able to move the ball in the first half by picking up yardage in small chunks, tallying 13 first downs. But each time they looked like they would penetrate Chargers territory for a score, the San Diego defense resisted, using three sacks to halt the Bills advances. Offensively, in the first half, Keith Lincoln paced San Diego by rushing for 81 yards and catching three of Tobin Rote's four pass completions.

The second half started as furiously as the first half had. After Lance Alworth gained 22 yards on a reverse to give the Chargers a first down at the Buffalo 45-yard line, Rote tried to catch the Bills secondary flat-footed by throwing long for Alworth, but Willie West stepped up with an interception at the Buffalo 1-yard line to stop the Chargers momentum. The Chargers fortunes changed for the better when their defense held the Bills to 4 yards on the next three downs and Daryle Lamonica set up to punt from the Buffalo end zone. At the snap of the ball, rookie Walt Sweeney stormed in to block the punt and gave the Chargers the opportunity they had been waiting for. Starting their drive at the Bills 20-yard line after the block, Rote looked to atone for throwing an interception moments earlier as he went right back to Alworth to challenge Willie West, finding his flanker in the end zone for a 17-yard touchdown and a 7-point lead. It was exactly the kind of leadership and moxie that Gillman had hoped Rote would bring to his team when he won the rights for the veteran quarterback back in February. The dividends through two-thirds of the season were obviously producing huge benefits.

No stranger to adversity, Jack Kemp brought the Bills right back to answer the Chargers points by marching his team from their own 29 to the San Diego 2 by mixing Gilchrist runs with short passes. The key play of this drive had Elbert Dubenion catching a quick 6-yard slant at the Buffalo 45 and outracing Dick Westmoreland to the shadows of the Chargers goal post at the 5-yard line. On 3rd down and goal from the 4, Kemp connected with Dubenion on a slant at the two, where Dick Harris and Chuck Allen brought him to the ground, short of the end zone. The Bills settled for a 9-yard field goal to stay within four points of the Charger lead.

Again, the Chargers defense tightened when it had to, which kept them ahead 17–13 after 3 quarters.

Not only did their defense keep the Bills offense out of the end zone, but they were pressuring Kemp into throws that he would like to have taken back. Three times in the last 16 minutes, Dick

Harris intercepted Kemp to kill potential Buffalo rallies. His first came right after Buffalo's George Saimes intercepted Rote at Bills 8-yard line. Harris' pick gave the ball back to the Chargers at the Buffalo 31 and gave George Blair the opportunity to extend the Charger lead to 20–13. But his 47-yard kick was wide and put the ball back in Kemp's hands.

The Bills next drive took them from their own 20 to the San Diego 46, but again ended in the waiting arms of Harris, who pulled in his second Kemp miscue at the 30 and frustrated his former teammate again. After Rote and Alworth teamed up for a 54-yard gain on first down that placed the ball at the Buffalo 16, Blair found his range to split the uprights and give the Chargers a 7-point lead, 20–13, with nine minutes left in the game.

Never known for their razzle-dazzle plays, Buffalo caught the Chargers by surprise when they pulled out a little used "catch and toss" play that had Ed Rutkowski catching a short pass and then lateraling the ball to split end Bill Miller crossing behind him to pick up 20 yards for a first down at their own 47. Then when Faison sacked Kemp for a 7-yard loss on third down, Lamonica avoided a fourth down disaster by getting his punt away after a bad snap had him retreating to his 20-yard line to pick it up before booting it out of trouble.

The Chargers now went into their slow-down mode, running the ball seven times in a row and moving into field goal range. Blair gave the Chargers a 10-point lead by knocking another three-pointer through the goal post from 41 yards away. San Diego was now ahead 23–13, with 2:30 minutes remaining.

On Buffalo's last drive, Harris made his third interception on Kemp's desperation throw to end another Buffalo drive and the game, giving San Diego their eighth win in ten games.

Holding off Kemp and Gilchrist was a big undertaking for the Chargers, as both Bills players had productive afternoons—but not enough to carry their team to victory. Gilchrist gained 95 yards and averaged 5.6 a carry, while Kemp completed 23 of 36 passes. Had it not been for Dick Harris intercepting three passes late in the game, the outcome could very well have been different. Instead, he sealed the Bills doom and kept them in a second place tie with Boston with 5–5–1 records behind Houston's 6–4.

Dick Harris

Kemp and I were still good friends from our three years together with the Chargers before he left for Buffalo. Years after we both retired, Kemp was in California for some political event and I met with him and joked about the game in '63 when I intercepted three of his passes. Funny thing, though, Kemp said he didn't remember and denied any knowledge of the game.

The Chargers defense was at its smothering best for most of the game at War Memorial. Earl Faison's two sacks and Karas' blitz that dropped Kemp for a 16-yard loss came at the perfect time to stop Buffalo's drives on third downs, and Walt Sweeney's blocked punt deep in Buffalo territory led to the Chargers second touchdown. Time-and-again it was the defense, special teams, and offense all jelling at the right time to make a sweep of their east coast trip after losing all three games a year ago. It was completely gratifying to say the least. With a two-game lead on Oakland, the Chargers would return home to host the Eastern-Division-leading Houston Oilers the following week.

THE UNCROWNED CHAMPS

San Diego Chargers	10	0	7	6	-	23
Buffalo Bills	7	3	3	0	-	13

Buf-Gilchrist, 1 run (Yoho kick)
SD-Lincoln, 54 run (Blair kick)
SD-FG, Blair 39
Buf-FG, Yoho 27
SD -Alworth, 17 pass from Rote (Blair kick)
Buf-FG, Yoho 9
SD -FG, Blair 15
SD -FG, Blair 41

Charger Statistics:

Player	Rush Att	Yds	Avg	TD	Long	
Keith Lincoln	10	101	10.1	1	54	
Paul Lowe	14	65	4.6	0	27	
Lance Alworth	1	21	21	0	21	
	Pass Att	Cmp	Yds	TD	Int	Long
Tobin Rote	22	10	156	1	2	54
	Rec	Yds	TD	Long		
Lance Alworth	4	79	1	54		
Keith Lincoln	3	31	0	24		
Don Norton	2	20	0	11		
Dave Kocourek	1	26	0	26		

Interceptions: Harris (3)

Around the AFL: New York won their first game in six weeks by knocking off Denver, who had now gone six weeks without a victory, 14–9. Boston stayed at .500 by playing Kansas City even to a 24–24 tie, but also moved into a second place tie with Buffalo (5–5–1) after the Bills lost to San Diego (8–2). Oakland (6–4) and Houston (6–4) had the week off.

EAST		WEST	
	W–L–T		W–L–T
Houston	6–4–0	San Diego	8–2–0
Buffalo	5–5–1	Oakland	6–4–0
Boston	5–5–1	Kansas City	2–6–2
New York	4–5–1	Denver	2–7–1

Dick Harris

Successful teams realize that to stay on top, they need to continually turn some of their personnel over to keep improving. They also understand that in order to maintain a cohesive unit, they need to seamlessly mesh the old with the new. From their origins in 1960 to their championship season in 1963, the Chargers turned over eight of their defensive starters who played in their first championship game and also saw fit to embrace three constants who seemed to stabilize the unit, as well as keep them headed in the right direction. One of those three constants was defensive back Dick Harris.

Chris Burford, split end, Kansas City Chiefs
Harris was a real good cover guy. He was one of the best corners in the league. He usually covered me and I remember him well; he was real feisty.

Describing himself as a free spirit, the young Californian had a love for football and having fun. He was one of Sid Gillman's favorite sons and also one of his most piercing thorns. No matter his role on the team, the San Diego Chargers defensive back was a fearless and confident pro who walked off the streets of Los Angeles to win a starting spot when Gillman put out an APB for recruits to try out for his new football club. Cast as a cornerback, Harris won All-League honors in both 1960 and 1961, and was one of the noted Seven Pirates in '61 who set a pro football record for interceptions with 49, helping his team to a #1 team defense ranking, #1 pass defense, and #2 rushing defensive. He also gained All-League 2nd Team honors in '62 and '63 when he led the Chargers in interceptions with a career high 8. In leading the Chargers in interceptions twice in four years, he pulled in a total of 25, returning five of them for touchdowns.

Dick Harris
Our front four really made our passing defense much better because of the pressure they put on opposing quarterbacks. It made it easier to cover guys because they usually weren't able to get to the spot they needed to because the ball was coming sooner than planned. This allowed us to play more aggressively in the secondary.

We had really good defensive coaches with the Chargers, first with Jack Faulkner and then Chuck Noll. Jack was my motivator. I really like playing for him. He was a really good guy and sort of made it easier for me to play because I had that devil-may-care attitude. In those days, a lot of coaches didn't like that kind of attitude. Things were a lot stricter about behavior and everything. They didn't put up with too much, but Jack was good to me and for me.

I wasn't a big guy (5'11", 185 lbs.), but I was fast so when I had to cover guys like Don Maynard or Art Powell and Chris Burford, I had to press them more. They were all good possession receivers and three of the best. You know, I found that the better the receiver was, the better I played, because I had to concentrate more. Out there on the corner, you were all alone so you couldn't be intimidated by anyone. One time I remember being a little too aggressive, though, against Powell. He ran a slant into the end zone and I dove in front of him and intercepted it. But when I hit the ground the ball popped out and right into his hands for a touchdown.

We played almost all single man coverage, too, so when I got a guy like Lionel Taylor, who was a great pattern runner but not too fast, I had to really pay attention because they would run him on a lot of crossing routes to try to get the linebackers in the way of our coverage, kind of like screening for him.

There were two things that really helped our defenders. The first was scrimmaging against our offense. Gillman knew everything there was to know about passing and had an incredible passing system. I had to go against Lance Alworth every day in practice and he made me better. Having to cover the best guy in the league gave me confidence against all the other receivers I had to go against in games.

The other thing that helped us was having Al Davis in those early years. He was the receivers coach and was always complaining about us. If we were closing down his receivers in practice, he'd be all over us. That got us all pumped up because we figured if he wasn't complaining about us pushing his guys around or knocking down passes in practice then we weren't playing well.

Back in the early days I played a bump and run coverage against Houston in the championship game. Nobody taught it to me, and it didn't have a name then, but if I'd see a receiver go down in a 3-point stance and look in at the quarterback, I'd sneak up to the line and jam him before he could react.

My favorite season as a player was definitely 1963. I guess winning does that to you. We were all together that year. Rough Acres brought us closer together because it was like being in the Army out there. We all became a family.

Sunday, November 24, 1963
AFL Postpones All Games
Nation Mourns Death of JFK

AFL Commissioner Joe Foss directed all games scheduled for Sunday, November 24, in the aftermath of President Kennedy's assassination on Friday, postponed as the nation mourned his death.

Games scheduled for the weekend were moved back one week, to December 1, with the only exception being Oakland and Denver, who would play on November 28, Thanksgiving Day.

As a result, the remaining games on the AFL schedule were adjusted accordingly.

Games scheduled for November 28 and December 1, would be played on December 8, with the exception of Buffalo at New York, which was moved to December 14.

Games scheduled for December 8 were moved to December 22, except the New York at Buffalo game, which remained scheduled for December 8. The Boston at Kansas City game was moved to December 14. Games originally scheduled for December 15 stayed as scheduled, with the New York at Kansas City game changed from December 14 to December 22.

The AFL Championship Game, scheduled for December 22 and hosted by the Western Division champion (if there is no divisional playoff necessary), would now be played on Sunday, December 29. If a divisional playoff were necessary, it would be played on Saturday, December 28, with the Championship Game moved back to January 5, 1964.

As the season played out, Boston and Buffalo tied for first place in the Eastern Division and met for a playoff game in Buffalo on December 28. That necessitated the AFL Championship Game to be moved back one week and played on January 5, 1964. It became only the second game in pro football history to be played after the New Year. (The first game to be played after the New Year was the AFL's first Championship Game, which was played on January 1, 1961.)

In response to Foss' decision to forego the November 24 games, writer Jerry Magee of the *San Diego Union-Tribune* wrote, "In my thinking, and in other people's thinking, that had more to do than anything with impressing of the American populace that these AFL people were a people of substance. That probably did more to establish the AFL, which began in 1960, than anything the AFL ever did."

Game 11: Sending a Message

Houston Oilers
Sunday, December 1, 1963, at San Diego
Balboa Stadium
Attendance: 31,713

THE UNCROWNED CHAMPS

The Chargers two-game lead over the Oakland Raiders seemed insurmountable compared to what was going on in the East. A slim margin of one and a half games separated all four teams, with the Oilers 6–4 record leading the way. Boston and Buffalo were both breathing down Houston's neck with records of 5–5–1, and New York, the last-place team, was still alive at 4–5–1. Houston looked like they had the roughest road to travel in the season's last month, having to play San Diego twice, along with Boston and Oakland, who were both still contenders. Boston had only three games left, including Buffalo at home this week, and then ending on the road against Houston and Kansas City. After traveling to Boston, Buffalo would finish their season with home and away meetings against New York. Both Boston and Buffalo would be off on the last Sunday of the season. The Jets, playing at home against the Chiefs, would finish in Kansas City after meeting the Bills twice. Knowing they still had to play first-place Houston twice, along with the two teams they had already lost to (Oakland and Denver), the Chargers knew that the rest of the schedule would be anything but a cakewalk. Now was the time to use the momentum they created on their East Coast trip to elevate their game and pave their way to the title. The Raiders, whose game against the Broncos was moved up three days to play on Thanksgiving Day, would finish their season with three games at home against the Chargers, Broncos, and Oilers; two of whom they had already beaten. The table for the last month of the season was now set and all that was needed was for everyone to start rolling the dice.

To get into the top spot, Houston had alternated losing and then winning over their first six games, then beat Buffalo and Kansas City before getting beaten badly by Boston. They then rebounded with a win against New York. Over their first three seasons, the Oilers had been the cause of a lot of frustration for the Chargers, appearing to have San Diego's number by winning four of their six regular season games and then knocking them off twice in successive championship games. The Oilers in this meeting were without halfback Billy Cannon, the MVP in both title games. Cannon carried the ball only 13 times in 1963 while nursing an ailing back. The rest of the Oilers offense was still fueled by George Blanda's passing, Charlie Hennigan's catching, and Charlie Tolar's running. Still a pass-first team, Houston led the league in that department, but without Cannon, dropped from fourth to seventh in rushing. Defensively they dropped from second to sixth overall, but their secondary was still the best in the league, led by safety Freddie Glick, who was at the top of the interception list with twelve. For the season, Houston had intercepted more passes than every other AFL team. Gillman was not one to shy away from the challenge of dealing with the Houston pass defense, but was aware that teams were rushing for more than 123 yards against them in each contest, with only New York giving up more ground yardage. Offensive line coach Joe Madro was still irritated at the Oilers lack of respect for his troops from years ago, and every game against Houston was another chance for Ernie Wright, Sam DeLuca, Don Rogers, Pat Shea, and Ron Mix to take them to the woodshed. Having the number one rushing team in the AFL was no accident, either.

Madro was considered one of the best line coaches in the league, and everyone knew that the success of Lincoln and Lowe—both in the top four among AFL runners—was the by-product of a line that could handle the big bodies in front of them. Keeping the Oilers guessing was one of their offensive keys to winning. Teams

Offensive line coach, Joe Madro.

were always off balance when playing the Chargers because of their ability to score quickly through the air and on the ground with any one of their many weapons. Whether it was the run setting up the pass or vice versa, it was common knowledge that stopping the Chargers juggernaut offensive was usually only a temporary achievement.

Coming off their eastern swing and giving up a total of 26 points against Houston's three division mates, Chuck Noll's defense was also at the top of the league's stats and looking to make it a clean sweep of the Eastern Division by beating the

Oilers. After spending the last three weeks playing under cloudy skies, rainy weather, and 40 degree temperatures, the Chargers welcomed the perfect San Diego weather of 69 degrees and mild 6-mph breeze under sunny skies as they lined up to receive the opening kickoff.

After stopping the Chargers on the game's opening series, Houston got the ball at their own 22-yard line. In an attempt to shake things up, George Blanda called for runs on 8 of their first 9 plays. When faced with a 4th down and 2 from the San Diego 41, Blanda's field-goal attempt was blocked by Paul Maguire and put the Chargers on track for their first scoring drive. Alworth started things off with a 19-yard reception and then Keith Lincoln followed guard Pat Shea and tackle Ron Mix for 7 yards off the right side. Lincoln picked up 13 more yards by sweeping the left side for a first down at Houston's 15 and then, as the Oilers rushed Rote as he dropped back to pass on 2nd and 10, Lincoln took a delayed handoff and slipped by the defense on a draw play, depositing it in the end zone four minutes into the game.

San Diego's next score, a field goal, was set up by moving the ball with short yardage pickups. Lowe ran for 3, Norton's catch gained 6, Lowe ran again for gains of 6 and 8 yards, and Lincoln took off on another draw play for 14 yards. Blair then kicked a 42-yard field goal for a 10–0 lead nine minutes into the second period.

The ensuing kickoff gave the ball right back to the San Diego offense when Oilers kick returner Freddie Glick (brother of the Chargers Gary Glick) fumbled and the Chargers recovered at Houston 35-yard line. After three incomplete passes, Blair trotted onto the field again for another 42-yard attempt. The Chargers then caught the Oilers by surprise with a bit of well-disguised trickery, as holder Tobin Rote took the long snap from Don Rogers. Just before Blair swung his leg into the ball, Rote pulled the ball up for a fake and threw to his left, finding Dave Kocourek for 14 yards and a first down at the Oilers 21-yard line. Three plays later, Houston safety Tony Banfield tripped Kocourek for a pass interference call at the 1-yard line and Paul Lowe finished the drive off with the Chargers second touchdown and a 17–0 lead.

The Charger defense held the Oilers scoreless on their first six possessions in the first half. Then, when Lincoln, on his way to his fourth 100-yard game of the year, and Lowe, combined to run for 41 yards right before the second quarter ended, Blair converted for a 20-yard field goal to give San Diego a 20–0 halftime lead.

Blanda was mixing his calls in an attempt to keep the Chargers off balance. He used 15 passes and 13 runs through two quarters

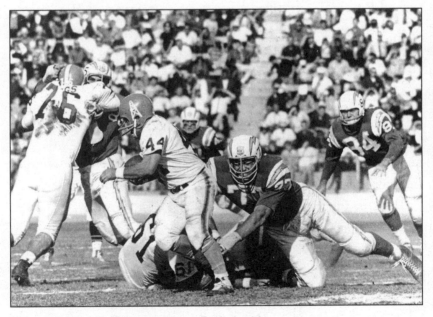

Houston's Charlie Tolar runs past Ernie Ladd.

with minimal results and zero points. Rote, on the other hand, was penetrating the Oilers with 22 runs, even though he squandered a scoring opportunity near the end of the half. After Emil Karas intercepted a pass at the Houston 10 to give the Chargers solid field position, he was intercepted in the end zone by Tony Banfield three plays later.

Staying mostly on the ground, Rote was leaving it to his offensive line to dictate play, enabling Lincoln to pick up 86 yards and Lowe another 45 through the first half. As running mates, it was rare that both Lincoln and Lowe were able to have simultaneous big games. Usually opposing defenses were able to stop one but not the other. Today, however, they were both kicking up their heels at the Oilers defenders, giving Rote the opportunity to use his arm sparingly and hand off almost twice as many times as he threw.

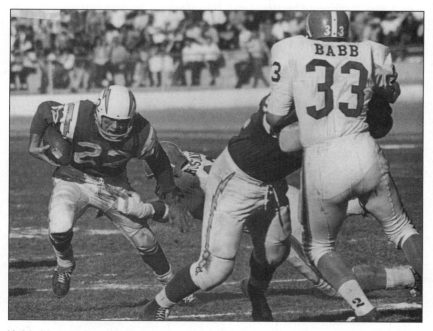

Keith Lincoln breaks Ed Husmann's tackle.

Paul Lowe is stopped by Houston's Mike Dukes (30) and Jim Norton (43).

In the scoreless third quarter, both teams struggled to navigate into scoring range, although Blanda did have some success using fullback Charlie Tolar on passing routes and running him into the teeth of the Chargers front line. But the few times Houston was able to get a first down, their attempt to move farther down field was choked off by the Chargers defense and forced kicker Jim Norton to punt the ball away. Just as the third quarter was about to end, the Chargers blocked another field goal attempt and turned it into the game's last score, with Lance Alworth pulling down a 22-yard touchdown pass as the final period began.

In watching the Chargers win their ninth game of the season, San Diego's largest crowd of the year also witnessed the first time in 45 games that the Oilers had been shutout. They also saw another stellar performance by the Chargers defense that had

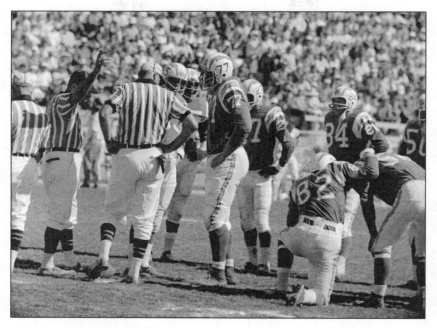

The Chargers defense takes a breather.

now given up only two touchdowns in their last sixteen quarters, while holding the teams from the East to a total of 26 points in their last four games against them.

In getting by Houston, the Chargers, now 9–2, had sent the message that they were on the verge of winning the division and needed only to beat the Raiders the following week when they traveled north to Oakland.

Houston Oilers	0	0	0	0	-	0
San Diego Chargers	7	13	0	7	-	27
SD-Lincoln, 15 run (Blair kick)						
SD-FG, Blair 42						
SD-Lowe, 2 run (Blair kick)						
SD-FG, Blair 20						
SD-Alworth, 22 pass from Rote (Blair kick)						

THE UNCROWNED CHAMPS

Charger Statistics:						
Player	**Rush Att**	**Yds**	**Avg**	**TD**	**Long**	
Keith Lincoln	13	102	7.8	1	16	
Paul Lowe	21	92	4.4	1	14	
Gerry McDougall	1	16	16	0	16	
Bob Jackson	1	11	11	0	11	
	Pass Att	**Cmp**	**Yds**	**TD**	**Int**	**Long**
Tobin Rote	24	13	134	1	2	22
John Hadl	7	0	0	0	2	0
Don Norton	1	1	15	0	0	15
	Rec	**Yds**	**TD**	**Long**		
Lance Alworth	4	56	1	22		
Don Norton	2	16	0	10		
Keith Lincoln	1	5	0	5		
Paul Lowe	3	25	0	10		
Don Kocourek	3	40	0	15		
Interceptions: Gary Glick, Emil Karas, Bob Mitinger **Fumble recovery:** Paul Maguire, Bob Petrich, Bob Jackson **Tackles:** Maguire 7, Westmoreland 6, Allen 5, Mitinger 5						

Around the AFL: New York gave themselves a huge boost by recording their franchise's first shut-out, beating Kansas City 17–0 to move up in the standings. Boston stayed close to the top and returned Buffalo to the Eastern Division basement with a 17–7 victory. Oakland won its fifth game in a row by winning on Thanksgiving Day in Denver, 26–10.

EAST		WEST	
	W–L–T		**W–L–T**
Houston	6–5–0	San Diego	9–2–0
Boston	6–5–1	Oakland	7–4–0
New York	5–5–1	Kansas City	2–7–2
Buffalo	5–6–1	Denver	2–8–1

Offensive Line

Chuck Allen

Our sweeps on offense were really unique. The coaches knew what they had with their personnel and what each of them could do and what would work. Most times they had the tackle or tight end sealing off to the inside and pull the whole rest of the line. Coach Madro and Gillman knew what they were doing and everyone had confidence in the plans they devised.

Playing on the offensive line for some was a badge of honor; a fraternity of men who fired out on their blocks to open holes that sprung fullbacks and halfbacks to the promise land. They guarded quarterbacks with quick feet and strong arms to hold off charging defensive linemen and blitzing linebackers, giving them the three, four, or five seconds needed to complete their passes to the so-called *skill* players. And all of this was done in quiet anonymity, for smaller salaries and a lot of one-on-one punishment without an ounce of glory and very little notoriety. In the San Diego locker room, it was no secret as to why the Chargers offense was so successful. It was the front line of Ernie Wright, Sam DeLuca and Sam Gruneisen, Don Rogers, Pat Shea and Ron Mix, which made the Chargers go. Their pass protection was so good that they allowed less than two sacks per game and their downfield blocking so precise that it enabled their runners to average over five yards a carry and accumulate over 2,200 yards rushing.

Ernie Wright, left tackle

An original Charger, Ernie was selected to the Western Division All-Star team three times and was a starting left tackle for eight straight years. One of only ten players to play in all ten AFL seasons, he also started in five championship games. Solid and mobile even after two knee surgeries, Ernie and Ron Mix were the best tackle tandem in league history. The 6' 4", 270-pound Wright was an accomplished technician whose strength was pass blocking.

Sam DeLuca, San Diego left guard
Prior to joining the Chargers in 1960, Sam played in Toronto for two seasons. He had an explosive charge off the line and was a good lead blocker on sweeps, as

well as being a hard-nosed hitter. He was a left guard starter in 1960 and 1961 before voluntarily sitting out in 1962.[7] Coaxed out of retirement by Gillman as insurance after several lineman were injured, he rejoined the team in Rough Acres for the 1963 season. He then moved into the starting left guard slot at mid-season when Sam Gruneisen fractured his arm.

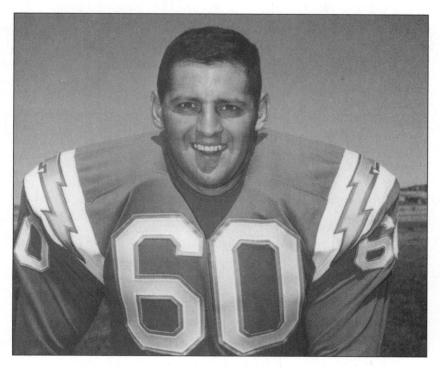

Sam Gruneisen, San Diego left guard
Injuries sidelined Gruneisen at midseason after starting out as the number-one left guard. Along with Pat Shea, Sam was a monster of a player on special teams in 1962.

7   DeLuca and Gillman could not agree on a contract, so he went back to Queens, New York, to teach high school.

He was given a chance to start after all the injuries in '62 necessitated some shuffling on the offensive line. He would go on to play eleven seasons with the Chargers and became one of the best centers in pro football history. During his time in the game, he was considered to have been the most intelligent center in the league.

Don Rogers, San Diego center
Another original Charger, Don was a starter in '60 and '61, and then temporarily lost his starting job to Wayne Frazier after he was sidelined with an injury in 1962. He

then moved back into the starting role when Frazier was also injured. From there, he solidified his hold in the middle as the offensive line's leader. He made the 2nd All-AFL Team in 1963 and was known for his constant hustle on the field. Don also did all the long snapping for extra points and field goals.

Pat Shea, San Diego right guard

Originally a defensive tackle, Pat was a weight-lifting enthusiast and the resident California beach boy of the team. After a stellar 1962 season on special teams, he earned a chance to start at right guard in training camp and held the position for five seasons. He was the first San Diego native to play for the Chargers and started in three straight championship games.

John Hadl

Pat was a wild man, California all the way, and had a nasty streak on the field. I never saw a guy who wanted to win more than he did.

Lance Alworth

Shea came out of nowhere in '63. He played so great on special teams in '62 that they had to give him a chance to start and he made the most of it right away. He was a California surfer and was always looking for a fight everywhere we went. He scared a lot of people and was a rough and tough football player.

Ron Mix, San Diego right tackle

Ron was an All-League tackle in 1960 and '61, then was switched to guard in 1962 when the team suffered a

multitude of injuries. He made All-League there as well. Moved back to his natural tackle position in '63, he continued his string as an All-League selection through 1968.

Chargers line coach Joe Madro said Mix was an excellent fire-out blocker and a great stick blocker, staying with his man until the whistle blew. He was often seen making a key block 20 yards down field after he threw an initial block at the line of scrimmage. He was an excellent pass blocker, too. Ernie Ladd said that he liked going up against Mix in practice drills because if he beat him, he felt like he'd accomplished something.

Bobby Bell, Kansas City Chiefs Hall of Fame linebacker
The Chargers had a great line, and Mix was unbelievable at tackle. He was quick and smart. He'd analyze things so quickly and so well that it was hard to get by him. With his pass blocking, he didn't give anything away as to what he was going to do, run or pass. He always played the same way. A lot of guys would give things away with the way they lined up or shifted their feet or looked around. But other guys weren't like Ron Mix. He gave no secrets away so you couldn't capitalize on anything he did. When he would post up on sweeps, Mix would keep his opponent contained by sealing them off for the guards coming around to lead. He could take a hit, too. He was fast, smart, and strong, you just couldn't get around him.

Game 12: Fourth Quarter Letdown

@ Oakland Raiders
Sunday, December 8, 1963, at Oakland
Frank Youell Field
Attendance: 20,249

When the Chargers boarded Flight 119 to San Francisco on the anniversary of Pearl Harbor, they had one collective thought on their mind: Win tomorrow, and the division is ours.

Al Davis and his Oakland Raiders had other thoughts in mind and looked to narrow the gap to a single game by winning their sixth in a row. If they beat the Chargers, the Raiders would also set a franchise record by winning their eighth game of the season. Although there was always a friendly respect and a congenial atmosphere surrounding the teams when Gillman and Davis met head-to-head, it was understood that both teams would like nothing more than to take it to the other and send them home dragging their tail between their legs.

The temperature at game time was a cool 48 degrees as Mike Mercer kicked off to Keith Lincoln. Taking the ball at the 13, Lincoln hit a seam through the forward wedge and gave his offense great field position at the Charger 40-yard line for their first play from scrimmage. Looking to strike quickly and dictate the tone of the game, Rote passed to Lincoln coming out of the backfield on first down and picked up 34 yards right out of the chute. Three plays later, he connected with Don Norton for a 32-yard touchdown and the Chargers had given notice that they were going to come fast and furious at the Raiders defense by scoring 1:53 seconds into the game. The defense also made a statement on the Raiders first possession, as Ladd, Faison, and Petrich all met at the quarterback to drop Tom Flores for a 12-yard loss on 3rd and 10.

Both teams found it much harder to move the ball for the rest of the quarter until Clem Daniels took a page out of the Chargers playbook with a halfback pass to Art Powell for 10 yards. The completion set up Mike Mercer's 37-yard field goal to put Oakland on the scoreboard. On the next play after the kickoff, Keith Lincoln, who was coming off two consecutive 100-yard games, took a handoff for a 5-yard pick-up but ended up injuring his calf muscle, which would sideline him for the rest of the game after only two carries. Lincoln had been a consistent catalyst for the Chargers offense with his running and receiving, and kept the defensive spotlight off Paul Lowe for much of the season. As the first quarter ended, the Chargers had only one first down to their name while Oakland tallied five, though they trailed 7–3.

Early in the second quarter, the Charger offense came alive, moving 89 yards on six plays. It all started with Alworth beating Fred Williamson for a 54-yard reception to the Raider 35-yard line. From there, a pass to Kocourek picked up 9 yards and Rote ran for 5 yards and a first down. Then Norton caught a 7-yard pass to the Raider 14. In Lincoln's absence, Bob Jackson filled in at fullback and powered up the middle for final 14 yards and a touchdown. With the new Al Davis system of pride and poise—in all circumstances the Raiders rally cry—they came roaring back, and matched the Chargers touchdown with Art Powell scoring from 45 yards away, making the score 14–10 in San Diego's favor.

The Chargers game plan from day one had been to keep the heat on defenses by forcing them to cover the entire field with their fleet of offensive stars. On their next drive, after the Raiders scored, Oakland may have been looking to stop Alworth and Kocourek a little too closely, taking their eye off Don Norton and leaving him isolated on the left side. The split end was able to beat Claude Gibson first for 21 yards to the Raider 39, and then again for 36 yards to the Raider 3.

Working from a double tight-end set, Rote then split the defense with a 3-yard toss to Jacque MacKinnon to put the Chargers ahead, 20–10. Then, just as he had in their first matchup, George Blair missed the extra point. In that game, the miss was the margin of victory for the Raiders 34–33 win. Both team's defenses were tying up the running game and forcing the other to move the ball through the air. The Chargers had held

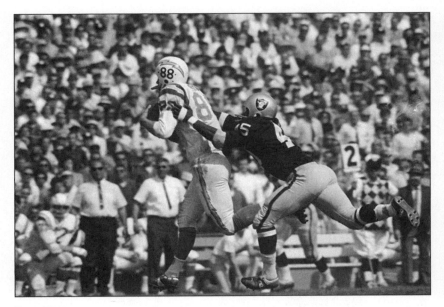

Don Norton

Daniels to 22 yards thus far, giving Oakland only 27 yards on the ground for the half. Oakland had tied up the Charger runners as well by holding them to only 30 yards. The leaders were Bob Jackson, who picked up 18 yards on two carries, and Tobin Rote, who scrambled for 12 yards. Still, leading by 10 points at halftime was an acceptable lead for Gillman and his players.

In the third quarter, the Raiders put together two time consuming drives of seven and nine plays, but failed to turn either of them into points. The Chargers, although having the ball only twice in the quarter, had to wait until their second possession to finally get rolling. With only 1:57 left in the quarter, Rote hooked up with Lance Alworth for a 15-yard touchdown pass which gave the Chargers the illusion that they had the Raiders right where they wanted them, ahead by three scores, 27–10, with fifteen minutes to play.

In their last nineteen quarters, the Chargers defense had given up only 36 points. Using their strength and agility that started being developed back at Rough Acres Ranch, they had put together an extraordinary string of tightfistedness by shutting down their opponents in a way they had not done since 1961. As the team's changed sides for the last time, it appeared that the Oakland faithful were out of hope and had seen enough. It seemed as though nearly half of the 20,000 fans in attendance were heading to the exits so that they could beat the rush to the highway that sat behind the stadium.

But as quickly as you could describe Murphy's Law to a man on the street, the Chargers fourth quarter began to unravel, and everything that could go wrong for them, did. Five plays into the quarter, Bob Jackson took a screen pass at the Charger 15 and ran it up to the 39, where he was hit and fumbled. The ball was recovered by Raiders safety, Tom Morrow. Then Clem Daniels shot through the line on a quick-hitter, picking up 35 yards right up the middle to the Charger 4-yard line. The defense tightened, though, and Earl Faison sacked Cotton Davidson for a 6-yard loss. But Oakland still had momentum, and scored on 3rd and goal to cut the Chargers lead to 10. Suddenly it was as though the Raiders had completed their transformation from being a disorganized franchise to one that was now a primetime force. They were like a boulder rolling down a mountain, gaining momentum and speed with every bit of motion. There was still 12:48 left on the game clock as the Chargers tried to hold onto the lead.

On the second play of their next possession, Paul Lowe picked up 3 yards on a draw play, but was stripped of the ball for another Charger fumble. Oakland recovered the ball again, this time at San Diego's 20. As the Raiders offense jogged back out to the huddle, you could hear the screeching of tires out on the highway as the cars that had just left the parking lot were stopping beyond the stands of Youell Field. The fans that had left the game early were still listening to the game on their car radios and were now trying to head back to the parking lot to see if the Raiders could pull off a seemingly impossible comeback.

Art Powell, split end, Oakland Raiders

That game against San Diego in Oakland was crazy. I never saw anything like it. We were behind 27–10 at the start of the fourth quarter and the Chargers were thumping on us pretty good and fans started leaving the stadium. You could see the highway from the field in Youell Stadium packed with cars driving home.

Photo courtesy of the Oakland Raiders

Aerial view of Frank Youell Field.

Then we recovered a fumble at their 30-yard line and scored a quick touchdown, but we were still ten points behind. We then recovered another fumble around the 20 right away after the kickoff and kicked a field goal. That got us to within a touchdown, and we were only three and a half minutes into the period. It was hysterical what was happening. You could see all these cars stopping and pulling off the highway. They must have all had their radios on because a lot of them were even turning around to come back to the stadium or just parking on the highway to see if they could watch the game from there. It was really funny to watch it all happening while the game was going on and we were just scoring points on Charger gifts to us.

The Chargers defense again had their backs against the wall and was being asked to shut down another opponent's scoring opportunity after their offense turned the ball over deep in their territory. From the 20-yard line, Cotton Davidson tried three straight passes that could not penetrate the tight Chargers coverage and Mercer came in to kick a 30-yard field goal. With 11:36 remaining in the game, the Chargers lead had shrunk from 17 to only 7 points.

San Diego was now back in attack mode, and instead of sitting on the ball to run down the clock, Gillman gave the word to press forward and score, hoping to take the Raiders momentum away and at the same time run away from them on the scoreboard. Rote went back to the air looking for Don Norton, but Claude Gibson broke up his pass on first down. He then threw an incomplete to Alworth, but Williamson was flagged for pass interference, giving the Chargers a first down at their 33. When the drive stalled on their own 38, Paul Maguire came in to punt and put some distance between the Chargers end zone and the Oakland offense. As he set up and called for the ball, Rogers mishandled the snap and it skidded back to him, rolling around the field like a scared squirrel. Maguire had to strike at the ball while it was rolling on the ground and was just able to give it a soccer-style kick before the Raiders got to him. Naturally, it was his worst punt of the year and gave the Raiders the ball inside Charger territory at the 43-yard line. Maguire's punt traveled only five yards. On their three possessions in the final quarter, San Diego had fumbled to the Raiders twice and muffed a punt that gave Oakland a shortened field to negotiate for more points.

The Raiders were back on the move and picking up even more momentum as the Chargers defense was on their heels and feeling the pressure of having to hold the lead. On 3rd and 1, the Chargers defense had Davidson pinned in the pocket and his receivers blanketed, but somehow the Raider quarterback was able to escape, avoid the rush, and scramble downfield for a 12-yard gain to the Chargers 22. On their next play, Daniels moved the ball to the 9, and then Davidson dropped back looking to pass on what was actually a well-designed quarterback draw against the Chargers spread defense. Davidson ran into the end zone for another Oakland touchdown. Within eight minutes of the fourth quarter, the Raiders had capitalized on three Chargers mistakes to pick up 17 points and tie the score at 27–27.

Still unable to move against the pumped-up Raiders defense, Maguire again punted from his own 25-yard line. The kick took punt returner Claude Gibson back to his own 40, where he picked up only 5 yards on the return. Another 15 yards was added on to the Oakland advance when the Chargers were flagged for grabbing Gibson's facemask. The Raiders now had the ball at the San Diego 40-yard line with a chance to take the lead.

It took them only three plays to do what nine minutes earlier was thought to be the impossible. A 40-yard touchdown pass to Art Powell and the extra point that followed gave the Raiders their 24th point of the fourth quarter and the lead, 34–27. It was bedlam in Frank Youell Field as the Raiders teed the ball up to kickoff yet again.

Gillman now put the Chargers' hopes of winning on the shoulders of young John Hadl, relieving Rote at quarterback with 5:30 left to get the lead back. A pass to Norton got them a quick first down at Oakland's 38-yard line, but the three incompletions that followed had them facing a crucial decision on 4th and 10: punt for field position and hope the defense can get the ball back, or push the envelope and go for the touchdown. It was do-or-die time for Gillman and the Chargers. Gillman decided to go for it on fourth down. Hadl called for a swing pass and faded back to toss it toward the sideline, but it was intercepted by linebacker Clancy Osborne, who ran it all the way down to the Chargers 12-yard line, almost insuring the Raiders of at least a field goal and a 10-point lead. The Raiders had come up with their fourth break of the quarter, and for the fourth time in a row took advantage of the gift and scored another touchdown, and their 31st point of the period. Their incredible comeback had Oakland leading 41–27 with only a minute left to play.

Davis then went for the kill and added a huge dose of salt to the Chargers wounds. On the ensuing kickoff, his Raiders successfully pulled off an onside kick and held the ball until the final gun sounded.

In one quarter, the Raiders had scored more points on the Chargers than they had allowed in their previous four games combined. By virtue of two fumbles, a punting miscue, and an interception, Oakland scored on every possession in the quarter and on every mistake that San Diego committed. It was by far San Diego's worst quarter of the year and a big letdown in their quest to win the division. Now, instead of flying back to San Diego as the division champions, they were faced with a one-game lead and an all-important trip to Houston, which was still trying to win in the East. The champagne was put on ice for at least another week as the Chargers faced the biggest test of the year on their road to a title; the test of resiliency.

| San Diego Chargers | 7 | 13 | 7 | 0 | - | 27 |
| Oakland Raiders | 3 | 7 | 0 | 31 | - | 41 |

SD-Norton, 32 pass from Rote (Blair kick)
Oak-FG, Mercer 37
SD-Jackson, 14 run (Blair kick)
Oak-Powell, 44 pass from Flores (Mercer kick)
SD-MacKinnon, 5 pass from Rote (kick blocked)
SD-Alworth, 15 pass from Rote (Blair kick)
Oak-Powell, 10 pass from Davidson (Mercer kick)
Oak-FG, Mercer 30
Oak-Davidson, 9 run (Mercer kick)
Oak-Powell, 41 pass from Davidson (Mercer kick)
Oak-Miller, 2 run (Mercer kick)

Charger Statistics:

Player	Rush Att	Yds	Avg	TD	Long	
Keith Lincoln	2	0	0	0	0	
Paul Lowe	6	5	0.8	0	3	

Bob Jackson	5	33	6.6	1	14	
	Pass Att	**Cmp**	**Yds**	**TD**	**Int**	
Tobin Rote	25	17	284	3	0	
John Hadl	6	2	20	0	1	
	Rec	**Yds**	**TD**			
Lance Alworth	3	71	1			
Don Norton	6	119	1			
Dave Kocourek	4	34	0			
Keith Lincoln	1	34	0			
Bob Jackson	2	29	0			
Paul Lowe	2	12	0			
Jacque MacKinnon	1	5	1			

Around the AFL: By beating San Diego (9–3), Oakland (8–4) closed the gap that now separated the two teams by one game and extended their win streak to six. As they did in September to open the season, Kansas City (3–7–2) crushed Denver (2–9–1) again, 52–21, bringing their two game total with the Broncos to 111–28 and winning for the first time in two months. In the topsy-turvy East, it was Boston's (7–5–1) turn to play king of the hill by knocking Houston (6–6) from the top spot, 46–28, giving them the chance to wrap up the division next week with a win in Kansas City. Buffalo (6–6–1) kept pace by exploding on New York (5–6–1), 45–14.

Significant Others
Hank Schmidt, San Diego defensive lineman
Hank was the fifth man on the defensive line and saw time as a starter and substitute at all four positions. Hank preferred the

defensive tackle position over defensive end, as he could maneuver quicker on the inside and didn't get cut at the knees as often as he did on the outside. Known to his teammates as the "wedge buster," Hank earned his nickname for his efficiency and tenacity while knocking out blockers on kickoff returns.

Bob Petrich

It was tradition that the veterans would not befriend rookies in camp because it was so hard to get to know them and then have to see them be cut. We had a whole bunch of rookies who were drafted in 1963 and only a few were going to make the squad, so the vets made it an unwritten policy not to hang out with us. But one of them broke the tradition with me. Hank Schmidt helped me out a lot, even though he knew I was trying to beat him out for a roster spot on the front four. He was a marine boxer and arrived at camp early. He was a tough guy but had a big heart. I can honestly say that I would not have made the team without his help and him staying with me after practice to work on things. He was a great guy. One time he came in after practice complaining of a headache. Well, back then the trainers were not too sophisticated and didn't want to deal with stuff like that, so he told Hank to just go over and turn on the whirlpool and stick his head in it. Wouldn't you know it, old Hank turns right around and walks over to the whirlpool, and next thing we know he's got his head in it and the jets are just beating him up. He was some kind of player, tough as nails, and became the best wedge buster on kickoff teams in the league.

Hank Schmidt

I can tell you I cracked a lot of helmets on those kick returns busting up wedges. And I'm still around to talk about it without any side effects.

Charlie McNeil, San Diego safety

Described as a savage and sure tackler, McNeil came back from knee surgery after being limited to only four games in 1962. He returned to his free safety position in 1963 and intercepted four passes. An All-AFL defender in 1961, he intercepted 9 passes and returned them for a league high 349 yards and scored two

touchdowns. Right side cornerback Dick Westmoreland credited McNeil with taking him under his wing and helping adjust to the pros his rookie year. Dick Harris said he and McNeil would always communicate and cover for each when taking chances to make interceptions.

Emil Karas, San Diego linebacker

An All-Star starter from 1961–1963, Karas was a hard-hitting linebacker with quickness and lateral speed on the left side of the Chargers defense. Voted by his teammates as the Most Inspira-

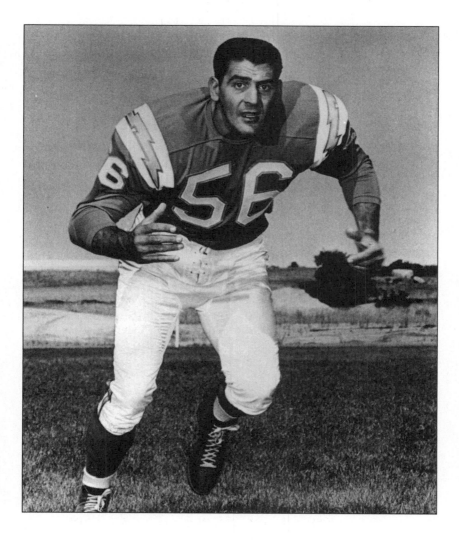

tional Player in 1962, he was one of two team captains in 1963. Emil made the AFL 2nd Team All-League in 1962.

George Blair
Karas was a big guy and a strong tackler who could run, too. He was really good at dropping off the line in

pass coverage, usually taking a back coming out of the backfield. We didn't blitz much but when we did he went at it all out to get to the quarterback.

Paul Maguire, San Diego linebacker and punter
Paul was a rare combination of right outside linebacker and punter. He was a four-year starter and brought experience and tenacity to the Chargers defense. Not to mention his devil-may-care approach to the game. He intercepted four passes in '63 and averaged 38.6 yards on his 58 punts, the lowest average of his eleven years as a pro. His longest kick of 1963 sailed 60 yards. Maguire led the league in punting in 1960 and played in the 1963 All-Star Game.

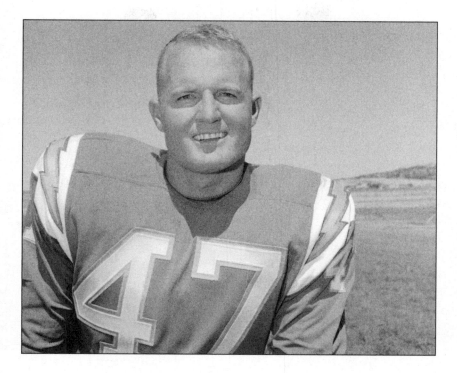

Bud Whitehead, San Diego defensive back

Bud was the Chargers super-sub in the secondary. He started at left cornerback until Dick Harris returned and then at free safety when Charlie McNeil was injured. Versatile and fast, Bud was as dependable as they come. He became a starter at safety in 1964 and remained a first-team Charger through 1967.

George Blair

Bud was my roommate on the road and was really valuable to the defense because he could play anywhere in the secondary. He started at left cornerback for Harris when Dick was injured and then played right safety when McNeil got hurt. He was also a backup flanker when we needed him and played on the special teams.

Don Norton, San Diego split end

There was at least one San Diego player that left Rough Acres Ranch in August who was not a fan of Alvin Roy and his weight-lifting regiment, and that man was Don Norton. One morning, while going through Roy's strength routine, Norton felt a twinge in his back and the next thing he knew he was on the injury list and missed the first seven games of the season. It wasn't until the Chargers flew to New York in November that he would be activated and start a game in 1963. In half a season he caught 21 passes, which put him on pace to equal his usual average of 40+ pass receptions. Norton led the Chargers in receptions 1962 when he pulled down 48 passes after hauling in 47 in 1961, numbers that put him on the Western Division All-Star team both years.

Lance Alworth

Don was a smart receiver and in our system, you had to know what everybody else was doing. Everyone was a main receiver. Don ran very precise patterns and knew how to play split end from his days as an All-American at Iowa. He didn't have great speed but he had great hands and great eye-hand coordination.

John Hadl

Norton was a good possession receiver. Sid wanted to attack the whole defense so we needed two wide receivers who could be on the same page on patterns, and Don was always where he needed to be and on time. He was reliable for sure.

Jerry Robinson, San Diego split end

As the starting flanker in the Chargers last 10 games in 1962, Jerry caught 21 passes for 391 yards. Nicknamed "Ghost" and "Smiles" by his teammates, Robinson replaced Lance Alworth as flanker in '62 and split end Don Norton for the first seven games in 1963, when he caught 18 passes. Robinson was one of

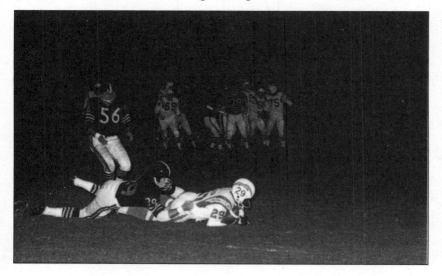

the fastest players on the Chargers, having run a 9.4 hundred at Grambling. A raw talent, Jerry was noted for his explosiveness after catching a pass. He was second in AFL in kickoff returns and kickoff return yardage in 1962.

Lance Alworth

Jerry was a fabulous athlete and I was always competing with him for a job. He was really fast. He pushed me to be better and I was really glad he was on the team because he always made me feel like I had to keep improving. He could have started on a lot of teams.

Game 13: One Step Closer
@ Houston Oilers
Sunday, December 15, 1963, at Houston
Jeppesen Stadium
Attendance: 18,540

After sitting on top of the Eastern Division for six weeks, Houston was in a tailspin and no longer in control of their own destiny after losing two games in a row.

Sitting a half game behind Boston (7–5–1) with a 6–6 record, the Oilers task at hand was clear: Win or be eliminated. Boston was playing their final game of the season and was the only team that could dicate their own outcome. A win or tie in Kansas City would bring their first title to New England. What was also clear was that every team in the East still had a mathematical chance at the title as well, but they all needed help to move forward.

The tightness of the races presented both divisions with the possibility of needing a playoff to determine the winner with only two weeks to go. Coming off their fourth quarter disaster in Oakland, the Chargers needed a win to insure themselves of at least a tie for the Western crown. If Oakland won their last two games and San Diego split their last two, they would need to meet for the third time in a playoff game to break the tie. The East, with a multitude of scenarios, could produce a similar showdown.

The Chargers needed to win out to secure their fourth division championship, and were hoping it was a lucky omen when they checked in the Shamrock Hotel in downtown Houston on Friday morning to prepare for the Oilers.

For the second week in a row, Keith Lincoln would not be available to the Chargers offense. The injury that ended his afternoon after two carries in Oakland kept him on the sidelines again against the Oilers. Gerry McDougall started in his stead.

Two weeks earlier, the Chargers were able to close down the Oilers offense and shut them out, 27–0. In doing so, the defense kept Blanda in check and allowed him only nine completions and intercepted him twice. Passing had always fueled the Oilers offense, so repeating their performance of two weeks ago was at the center of their game plan. Offensively, the ground game that the Oilers were unable to stop in San Diego had the Chargers run up over 200 yards with Lincoln and Lowe enjoying their best afternoon together. And any time Gillman could deploy his runners for that kind of result he was going to be looking to do it over and over until someone showed that they could stop them. Tobin Rote also liked to use his runners as a first option to enable his receivers to manuever in single coverage and to make the linebackers think *run* first, giving his backs an advantage to gain a step or two coming out of the backfield for passes.

The temperature in Houston, ten days before Christmas, was a chilly 42 degrees at game time and whipped up winds of 12 mph that affected passes early on. Both teams started slowly, like two prize fighters feeling each other out in the opening rounds, looking for a weakness. The Chargers mixed six runs with six passes on their first two possessions to get a feel for the Houston defense. Paul Lowe ran the ball on the Chargers' first four downs and then Rote took to the air four straight times, completing two for 20 yards and picking up three first downs the second time they had the ball. They advanced from their own 34 to the Oilers 24-yard line where the drive came to a halt when Lowe fumbled and the Oilers recovered. Houston, starting Jacky Lee at quarterback instead of George Blanda, started in similar fashion, running seven times and passing seven times with only two first downs to their credit in the scoreless opening quarter. Houston's deepest penetration ended at the Chargers 28-yard line where Blanda missed a 35-yard field goal attempt on their third and final drive of the quarter.

It was not until Houston's first play of the second quarter that the Chargers got their first break and picked up a little momentum. Emil Karas stepped in front of Lee's pass to Charlie Henningan for an interception at the Chargers' 39-yard line and Tobin Rote wasted no time in taking advantage of the turnover. Lowe took an inside handoff on first down and shot through a

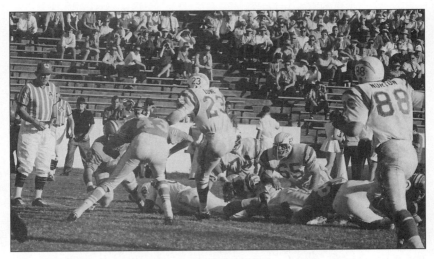

Photo courtesy of the Houston Oilers/Tennessee Titans.

Paul Lowe high steps through the Oilers defense for 59 yards.

hole between Shea and Mix on the right side and sprinted 59 yards to the Oilers 2-yard line.

Bob Jackson picked up one of those yards and then Rote finished off the drive with a sneak for the touchdown and the lead, 7–0.

There was no time for the Oilers to test the waters with Lee any longer after the Chargers scored, and sent the veteran Blanda in to relieve Lee behind center on the team's next posssession. The result, however, was more of the same. Chuck Allen picked off Blanda's second pass attempt and the Chargers were back on offense at the Oilers 30. Two runs by Lowe for 9 and 7 yards, and a 9-yard pass to Alworth had the Chargers primed to take advantage of their second turnover. The honors this time went to their battering-ram specialist, Bob Jackson, who barreled in on a 1-yard plunge to give them a 14–0 lead.

Before the Chargers could celebrate, though, Blanda came back with a vengeance, needing only two plays—a 27-yard pass to

tight end Bob McLeod and a 24-yard pass to Willard Dewveall—
to move his team 51 yards and put 7 points on the board.

The gloves in this fight were now off, and the one-two punch
combinations intensified. On the next Chargers drive, Rote
threw his sixteenth interception of the year, but two plays later
Paul Maguire intercepted Blanda and the Chargers had their
third turnover and the ball at the Oilers 24. Capitalizing for
the third time on their three takaways, George Blair gave the
Chargers their 17th point of the quarter with a 22-yard field goal
and a half time lead of 17–7.

The Chargers defense was dominating the Oilers offense in
every category, and gave up only four first downs in the half
while holding their running offense to an abysmal 19 yards
rushing. Houston's total yards gained for the half was less than
100 yards. Paul Lowe was having another stellar day running in
Lincoln's absence, and posted 92 yards in the first half, equaling
his total day's output when the two last met.

The third quarter was all San Diego, as they ran 19 plays to
Houston's 8 and controlled the line of scrimmage from both sides,
as well as the clock and the scoreboard. The Chargers picked up
their fourth takeaway on Houston's first possession of the second
half when Allen recovered Charlie Tolar's fumble at the Oilers 30.
And for the fourth time in the game, they seized the opportunity
to turn a Houston error into points. This time they did it the
hard way. On 4th and 3 from Houston's 23, George Blair kicked
a 30-yard field goal, but Houston was flagged for offsides. Rather
than taking the points, Gillman elected to try for more. With
a first down on the penalty, the Chargers successfully moved
down to the Houston 3-yard line but had to settle for another 3
pointer. The third quarter ended with San Diego ahead, 20–7.

The question now was whether the Chargers 13-point lead would be enough to get them their 10th win of the season after their 17-point lead wasn't enough the week before.

But more good fortune would come the Chargers' way as the fourth quarter started. After Blair's field goal and Freddie Glick's 32-yard kickoff return, Blanda mounted an eight-play drive, using four straight completions to pick up 66 yards and drove the Oilers down to the Chargers 9-yard line where they went for the touchdown on fourth down. But Blanda's completion to Dewveall ended a yard short of the goal line, and a turnover on downs.

Taking their time and moving conservatively after the possession change, Rote called for runs on six of the next seven downs and took three minutes off the clock before they had to give up the ball.

Photo courtesy of the Houston Oilers/Tennessee Titans.

Chargers Lane (57), MacKinnon (38), and Jackson (40) in hot pursuit of Freddie Glick.

Blanda then went back to work with a sense of urgency, moving Houston 64 yards on eight plays, culminating with halfback Bo Dickinson diving across the goal line for a touchdown, cutting San Diego's lead to six points, 20–14. But the drive ate up five more minutes of precious time.

Six and a half minutes remained when the Chargers got ball back with a feeling of déjà vu. Rote sent Gerry McDougall up the middle on first down where he was separated from the ball, but the eyes of Texas must have been looking in the Chargers direction this day, as the ball bounced right back to McDougall. When the Chargers punted back to Houston, Blanda moved under center at his own 17-yard line with four minutes to work with and needing six points to even the score. Three incompletions then called for punter Jim Norton to punt again. Unable to run out the clock with less than two minues left, the Chargers had to give the ball to the Oilers for one more try at the end zone. Ninety seconds remained as Houston started their final possession 89 yards away from victory. On first down in their hurry-up offense, Blanda threw incomplete to Dave Smith coming out of the backfield. Then, using his backs exclusively on pass routes, he picked up 9 yards on a completion to Dickinson and Smith for 5 yards on 4th down and 1 to keep the Oilers moving. Dickinson pulled in two more passes for 2 and 18 yards to put the ball at the San Diego 44-yard line with only a few ticks left on the clock. Blanda's next toss fell incomplete. Facing what was probably the last play of the game, Blanda gave it the old college try and connected with flanker Charlie Frazier on the sideline where he was brought down after 9 yards, but before he was able to get out of bounds to stop the clock. The Oilers' season ended 35 yards from paydirt as time ran out, clinching at least a tie for the Western Division title for the Chargers with their 10th win.

THE UNCROWNED CHAMPS

It was another spectacular display of defensive strength by the Chargers and the fifth time that they allowed fewer than 100 yards rushing in the season.

The Chargers, running twice as often as they passed today, picked up 162 rushing with Lowe accounting for 96 of them.

Finally able to take a brief sigh of relief, the Chargers flew back to San Diego a bit more relaxed knowing that by defeating the 2–10–1 Broncos the following week at home, they could be hosting the AFL's fourth championship game in January.

San Diego Chargers	0	17	3	0	-	20
Houston Oilers	0	7	0	7	-	14

SD-Rote, 1 run (Blair kick)
SD-Jackson, 1 run (Blair kick)
Hou-Dewveall, 24 pass from Blanda (Blanda kick)
SD-FG, Blair 22
SD-FG, Blair 10
Hou-Dickinson, 1 run (Blanda kick)

Charger Statistics:

Player	Rush Att	Yds	Avg	TD	Long	
Paul Lowe	19	96	5.1	0	59	
Gerry McDougall	15	56	3.7	0	22	
Bob Jackson	2	2	1	1	1	
Tobin Rote	3	8	0	1		
	Pass Att	Cmp	Yds	TD	Int	
Tobin Rote	17	9	81	0	1	
John Hadl	1	1	4	0	0	
	Rec	Yds	TD			
Lance Alworth	3	28	0			
Dave Kocourek	1	13	0			
Paul Lowe	3	21	0			
Gerry McDougall	3	23	0			

Interceptions: Karas, Allen, Maguire
Fumble recoveries: Allen

Around the AFL: With a chance to win the Eastern Division title, Boston (7–6–1) imploded and lost 35–3 to Kansas City (4–7–2), forcing a playoff game with Buffalo at the end of the season, as both teams had byes on the last weekend. The Bills (7–6–1) found themselves in first place for the first time in the season after eliminating the Jets (5–7–1), 19–10. Oakland (9–4) won their seventh in a row and kept San Diego from celebrating, by holding off Denver (2–10–1), 35–31. The Broncos were now winless for nine straight weeks.

Role Players

"They also serve who sit and wait."

The old adage stresses the importance and role of every player on a team. The good teams know that no one makes it through a championship season without ready-and-able reserves to pick up the slack and provide quality minutes while filling in as substitutes when needed. The Chargers were no exception.

Gerry McDougall, San Diego fullback

Gerry forged his reputation with the Hamilton Tiger Cats as one of the CFL's best runners and helped them win the 1957 Grey Cup. He gained over 1,000 yards in each of his first three seasons in Canada and averaged over 5 yards per carry. He joined the Chargers during the 1962 season and played a key role in their championship season as a powerful short yardage blocker and runner. As the third running back, he played both fullback and halfback, gaining 199 yards and averaging 5.2 yards per carry. He also caught 10 passes for an 11.5-yard average. Having played in Toronto with Tobin Rote in 1962 before coming to San Diego, he was a key liaison in Rote's decision to sign with the Chargers

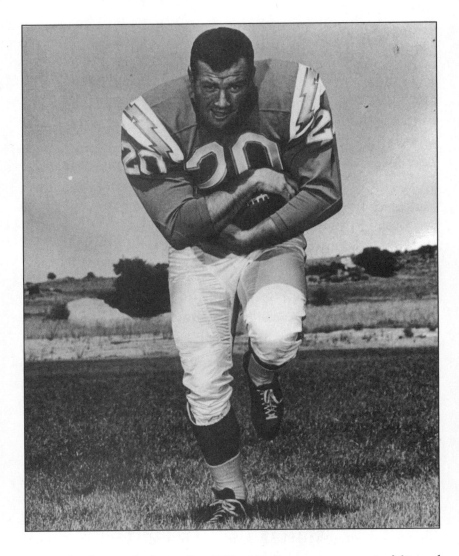

instead of retiring from the CFL. He threw one pass in '63 and completed it for a touchdown.

Bob Jackson, San Deigo fullback

A punishing runner and blocker, Bob was often called upon to be the lead blocking back on third downs and also drive himself

over the goal line for short yardage touchdowns. He scored nine touchdowns in two years and had four in 1963 on only 18 carries. As a rookie starter at fullback in 1962, he gained 411 yards on 106 carries. He was also a valuable part of the special teams as a strong blocker and deft tackler. A sure-handed runner, he fumbled only one time in over 100 carries between 1962 and 1963.

Jacque MacKinnon, San Diego tight end

Known as "Baby Huey" to his teammates for his youthful looks and large stature, Mac was a jack-of-all-trades for the Chargers, playing halfback, fullback, tight end, offensive tackle, and on special teams. At 6'4" and 240 pounds, he was a decathlete at Colgate University and ran a 10-second hundred-yard dash. After toiling as an understudy early in his career, he came into his own in the late sixties, making the All-Star team in '66 and

'68. Of his 11 pass receptions in '63, four were for touchdowns, with two going for over 50 yards.

Frank Buncom, San Diego linebacker

Frank joined the Chargers in 1962 out of USC and became an instant hit with four interceptions as a rookie linebacker. As the first sub off the bench, he was one of the best pass coverage linebackers on the team and would often come in on passing downs as the fourth linebacker. Playing mostly on the right side, Frank was the fastest of San Diego's linebackers, as well as a strong tackler. He became a starter in 1964, played in three consecutive championship games, and made the Western Division All-Star team in '64, '65, and '67.

Bob Mitinger, San Diego linebacker
Bob logged plenty of minutes on the field in 1963, filling in for several players at different positions throughout the year. The valuable swingman on defense was able to move between all three linebacking spots and also played several games at defensive end. At 6' 2" and 245 pounds, he had the perfect size and speed to stop sweeps, cover passes, and penetrate on pass rushes. He was the Chargers Defensive Rookie of the Year in 1962.

Walt Sweeney, San Diego tackle/defensive lineman

Walt was an All-American college player at Syracuse, playing defensive end, offensive end, tackle, and guard with equal efficiency. He started the season as a backup defensive end, and spent time as a backup guard and tackle as well. He made his mark as a

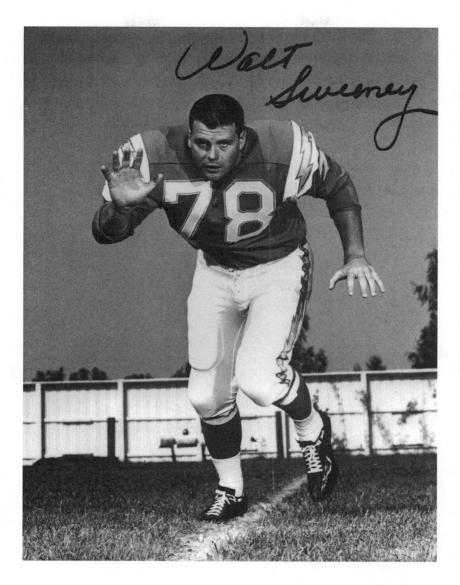

fierce special teams player in '63. Walt hit his stride in 1964 and made the All-Star team every year from 1964 through 1972. He was selected to the All-Time AFL 2nd Team as the right guard.

Game 14: Winning the West
Denver Broncos
Sunday, December 22, 1963, at San Diego
Balboa Stadium
Attendance: 31,312

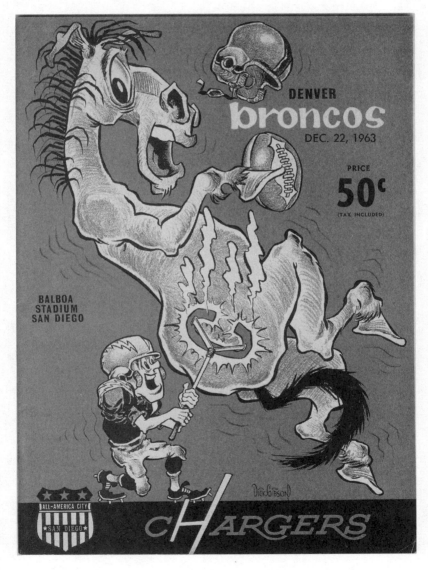

All that stood between San Diego and their third championship game was the Denver Broncos, the team that stampeded over them for 50 points and handed them their first loss of the season back on October 6. Unfortunately for the Broncos, they had not won a game since.

As both teams warmed up for the 1:30 kickoff, all eyes were glued to Northern California, where the Raiders were hosting the Houston Oilers in a must-win game for Oakland. If they lost to Houston, whatever happened in Balboa Stadium would be irrelevant. The Chargers would win the West with a Raider loss.

Already in the second quarter, the Raiders had come back from a 21–7 deficit to tie the game at 21–21. Then, just before George Blair put his foot onto the ball to start the game against Denver, it was announced that the Oilers had retaken the lead. The entire crowd let out a mighty roar in support of the Houston touchdown and set the tone for an afternoon of scoreboard watching and Charger rooting.

Right from the outset, the Broncos tried to catch the Chargers napping. Taking a hand-off from quarterback Don Breaux, halfback Gene Mingo swept to his right and fired a pass to tight end Gene Prebola that fell harmlessly incomplete. But it gave notice that Denver was going to pull out all the stops to prevent the Chargers from winning the title outright.

Perhaps it was the tone set by Jack Faulkner or maybe it was the residue of the determination that was entrenched in the players way back at Rough Acres, but on the second play from scrimmage, after Mingo caught a swing pass to the right and started around end, he was hit by Emil Karas and fumbled. Johnny-on-the-spot, George Gross hustled to recover the ball and gave the Charger offense a chance to strike from the Denver 14-yard line. In

Houston the week before, the Chargers converted all four Oiler turnovers into the points they needed to win, 20–14. Now they had another break handed to them by a defense that continued their run of spectacular play that started back in New York. After two handoffs to Paul Lowe, the Chargers led, 7–0. A glance at the out-of-town scoreboard showed that Houston was now leading Oakland 35–28 in the second quarter as the Chargers pressed on.

Broncos fullback Billy Joe tied the game on Denver's next drive that took them 68 yards on 11 plays. The Chargers quickly answered back from their own 22-yard line with Keith Lincoln, back after sitting out the previous two games, starting the next drive with a 12-yard gain off a draw play. Paul Lowe followed Lincoln's run by sprinting 13 more yards around right end and,

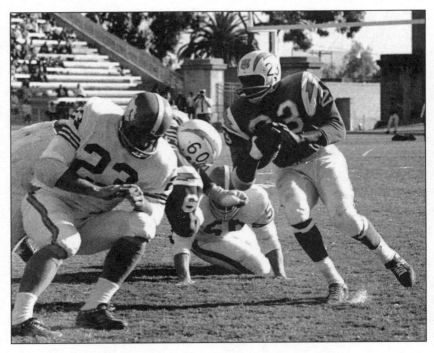

Paul Lowe ran of 183 yards against the Broncos.

after Alworth was interfered with at the Denver 14, the drive ended with a field goal and a 10–7 lead.

After Blair's extra point conversion, the Balboa Stadium PA announcer informed the crowd that the halftime score in Oakland had the Raiders and Oilers tied at 35–35.

With three minutes left in the second quarter, the Chargers seized another opportunity deep in Denver territory. Linebacker Bob Mitinger picked off Breaux's pass intended for Lionel Taylor and returned it 18 yards to the Broncos 30. The Chargers then pulled off another bit of Gillman deception, catching the Broncos by surprise. Lincoln took a hand-off and starting running to his left, but then stopped and pitched the ball back to Tobin Rote who threw to Don Norton for a 29-yard completion that gave the Chargers the ball at the Denver 4. It was then time for Bob

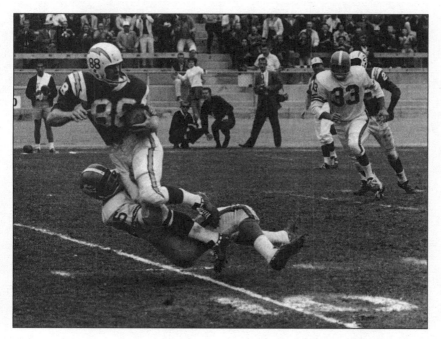

Don Norton's 29-yard reception set up the Chargers' second touchdown.

Jackson to do his thing: power the ball into the end zone. He gave the Chargers a 17–7 advantage, making the last six Charger scores the beneficiary of defensive takeaways.

A determined Denver squad came right back with another tally on their next possession to close the gap to 17–14. Gillman and Faulkner were engaging in all out warfare, matching play for play and score for score. The Chargers struck again with a completion to Dave Kocourek for a 26-yard touchdown to increase their lead to nine points, 23–14.

The news from Northern California now had Oakland taking the lead 42–35 in the third quarter.

A 12-yard Denver field goal kept the game close as halftime neared and Rote's offense returned to the field. Aided by a

Lowe runs for 22 yards.

22-yard run that took Paul Lowe zig-zagging through Denver tacklers, the Chargers put 3 more points up to take a 26–17 lead into the locker room.

During the intermission, the Raiders and Oilers continued to trade scores, going from Oakland leading 42–35, to Houston tying, and then taking the lead, 49–42. Early in the fourth quarter, the Raiders had re-tied the score, 49–49.

The third quarter in Balboa was uneventful until late in the quarter, when Paul Lowe made the move that separated the Chargers from Denver for good by taking a pitchout around left end for a 66-yard touchdown.

The run put him over 100 yards for the day and within 60 of breaking 1,000 for the season. The touchdown also increased San Diego's lead to sixteen points, 33–17, and essentially gave the Chargers the game. There was no stopping them from that point. Even the scoreboard watchers appeared disinterested when the Raiders final score appeared with Oakland winning, 52–49. The Chargers had taken control of the game and their fate, and were now looking to keep their foot on the gas pedal and pour it onto the Broncos. Before the third quarter was over, the Chargers had another interception and another turnover conversion of 3 points.

As the fourth quarter began, the Chargers were not about to sit on their 36–20 lead, either. Remembering that Faulkner's team had embarrassed them by running the score up to 50 points in their first meeting, Gillman wanted to return the favor. The deluge continued as Faison recovered another Denver fumble and Lincoln scored on a 29-yard run. Moments later, Chuck Allen made it nine scores on their last nine takeaways by running 42 yards for a touchdown with a fumble recovery, flooding the scoreboard with a 50–20 score. Still intent on not letting up against their former coach, the defense created another fumble midway through the quarter and gave Lowe the chance he had been waiting for.

Itching to break into the elite class of 1,000-yard rushers since sitting out all of last season, Lowe was not going to be denied. On his last carry of the day, he capped off his 183-yard afternoon by taking another sweep 21 yards and finishing off his season with 1,010 yards.

Even though Lowe was done for the day, Gillman seemed adamant to play Scrooge to Denver and his former assistant three days before Christmas. Not only did John Hadl and Jacque MacKinnon team up to score a last-second touchdown with six ticks left in the game, but Gillman went for and made a 2-point conversion with a pass to Earl Faison, running the score up to 58–20. And, just to remind the Broncos coach who the master was, Gillman ordered an onside kick in the aftermath. Though

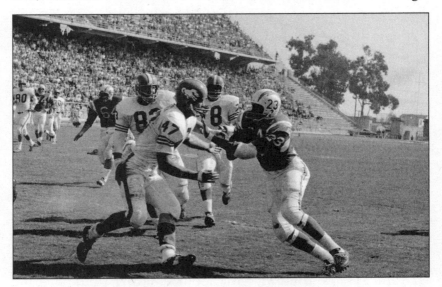

On his final carry of the day, Paul Lowe went over 1,000 rushing yards for the season.

Denver recovered the ball, the play was called back for illegal procedure. With one second left in their season, Sid ordered another onside kick. This time it was successful. It was just that kind of season.

For the third time in four years the San Diego Chargers were the Champions of the Western Division, just as Sid had vowed they would be after winning the coin flip for Tobin Rote back in February. They would now have a week off while Boston and Buffalo battled to determine who the winner of the East would be in a one-game playoff. The Chargers would host the AFL Championship game the following week, on January 5, 1964, in Balboa Stadium.

Denver Broncos	7	10	3	0	-	20
San Diego Chargers	10	16	10	22	-	58

SD-Lowe, 10 run (Blair kick)
Den-Joe, 1 run (Mingo kick)
SD-FG, Blair 17
SD-Jackson, 2 run (Blair kick)
Den-Stone, 10 pass from Breaux (Mingo kick)
SD-Kocourek, 26 pass from Rote (kick failed)
Den-FG, Mingo 12
SD-FG, Blair 28
SD-Lowe, 66 run (Blair kick)
Den-FG, Mingo 15
SD-FG, Blair 13
SD-Lincoln, 29 run (Blair kick)
SD-Allen, 42 fumble run (Blair kick)
SD-MacKinnon, 6 pass from Hadl (Faison pass from Rote)

Charger Statistics:

Player	Rush Att	Yds	Avg	TD	Long	
Paul Lowe	17	183	10.8	2	66	
Keith Lincoln	10	66	6.6	1	29	
Gerry McDougall	2	21	10.5	0	21	
Bob Jackson	2	3	1.5	1	2	

	Pass Att	Cmp	Yds	TD	Int	Long
Tobin Rote	17	7	109	1	1	30
John Hadl	7	5	88	1	1	35
	Rec	Yds	TD			
Don Norton	3	48	0			
Lance Alworth	1	4	0			
Dave Kocourek	1	26	1			
Paul Lowe	1	12	0			
Keith Lincoln	1	19	0			
Gerry McDougall	1	2	0			
Jerry Robinson	2	45	0			
Jacque MacKinnon	2	41	1			

Interceptions: Mitinger, Harris
Fumble recoveries: Gross (2), Allen, Faison
Tackles: Mitinger 7, Allen 5, Petrich 5, Glick 4, Schmidt 4, Ladd 4, Gross 4

Around the AFL: In the only other game besides Oakland (10–4) edging Houston (6–8) and the Chargers (11–3) win over Denver (2–11–1), Kansas City (5–7–2) ended their season as strongly as it began and won their third in a row, shutting out New York, 48–0. In their three game winning streak to close out the season, the Chiefs outscored the opposition 135–24.

FINAL STANDINGS			
EAST		WEST	
	W–L–T		W–L–T
Boston*	7–6–1	San Diego	11–3–0
Buffalo	7–6–1	Oakland	10–4–0
Houston	6–8–0	Kansas City	5–7–2
New York	5–8–1	Denver	2–11–1

*Boston defeated Buffalo 26–8 in a playoff game on December 28 to win the Eastern Division title.

Paul Lowe

For many AFL fans, their vision of Paul Lowe was one of him sprinting down the sidelines with sun gleaming off those lightning bolts on his helmet, his high galloping knees churning up yardage and opposing defenders several yards behind him in pursuit. Since 1960, Lowe created that same image year after year while leading the Chargers to five division titles.

After missing his chance with the 49ers and working in the mailroom of Carte Blanche to make ends meet, Lowe was in the

right place at the right time when the AFL opened for business and his employer owned one the original franchises. He caught on with the LA Chargers, who signed him to an $800 bonus in the league's first year, and the first time he ever touched the ball in a game he gave everyone a taste of his breakaway brilliance by returning a kickoff 105 yards for a touchdown. After making the team as its fifth running back, he was used sparingly at first and carried the ball only 16 times through the Chargers first five games. Given the chance to start in the absence of injured fullback Charlie Flowers, Lowe took off and never looked back as he outran defenders consistently during his eight years with the Chargers. In that first season, he led the league in yards per carry (6.3), and finished the year as the second-leading runner. He followed his rookie season up in 1961 as the league's fourth best ball carrier and also led the league in rushing touchdowns, had the longest run from scrimmage (for 87 yards), and played in his second consecutive championship game.

Over the next few seasons, he became known as one of the best breakaway runners in pro football. After sitting out the entire year with an injury in 1962, he returned to the lineup in 1963 and continued his spectacular running by becoming the AFL's fifth back to break 1,000 yards rushing, and outgained all but one other AFL runner. His 5.7 yards per carry was second in the league behind only his Chargers running mate Keith Lincoln. He also finished second in rushing touchdowns and average yards per game.

Following his pulling guards and tackles in the intricate San Diego blocking scheme, Lowe became a sweep and pitchout specialist who was especially adept at finding seams to run through and past defenders as well as high stepping over perspective tacklers.

Bobby Bell, Kansas City Hall of Fame linebacker

The first time I saw Paul Lowe, I was a rookie defensive end. Tackle Buck Buchanan and I thought he was so fast that we had a hard time getting a hand on him. He hit the line so fast that we couldn't figure out what to do to stop him. He was really quick.

Two games during the Chargers 1963 championship season were particularly memorable for Lowe. One was his standout performance against the Jets, where he gained 161 yards and had two runs for over 30 yards. The other was his career high 183 yards that put him over 1,000 yards rushing for the season against Denver.

Billy Joe, Denver Broncos

Lowe was tough and not a particularly small runner. He was as big as Lincoln and had good height and was a strong, speedy runner. He didn't run inside too often but he had a lot of power and drive when he did.

After a sub-par, injury riddled season in 1964, Lowe bounced back in 1965 to gain 1,121 yards and lead the AFL in rushing. He was also the league leader in rushing touchdowns and yards per carry and the first AFL back to run for over 1,000 yards in a season twice. In 1966, he slipped to seventh in rushing, but still managed to average 4.4 yards per carry.

Lowe, however, was not just a running back. Sid Gillman often complimented him on his work ethic and ability to block and catch passes, even though he wanted to run the ball on every play. He took pride in the not-so-glamorous parts of the game that don't often make it to the highlight reels.

His quick bursts past the line of scrimmage became his trademark and he was the type of runner who could change speeds in an instant. His running style was more of a straight up-and-down motion with high-stepping knees that he developed as a hurdler in high school and college. He seemed to prance rather than run.

John Hadl

Lowe always felt underutilized. He would be moaning and groaning about everything, but that was just him. He just wanted to do well and be recognized. We were all young and that goes with the territory. He and Lincoln both loved to carry the ball, and that also made them better blockers, because if one didn't block for the other, then they would have to worry about not getting blocking when they carried the ball. Blocking's the part of the game nobody likes to do, but they all knew it had to be done. If they didn't block, they also knew they wouldn't get the ball.

Because of the high-profile treatment some of his teammates received, Lowe often felt unappreciated by his team and the fans, but his performance never suffered in spite of his disappointment. "I've come a long way," Lowe told *Sport* magazine. "It hasn't come easy, either. But now that I'm here, where am I? We have a lot of great players on the team, but I feel I am as important to the team as any one of them. Yet, no one else does, not my bosses, not the fans, and not even the writers. For all I have done, I am just another guy."

In eight seasons with the Chargers, Paul Lowe picked up 4,972 yards, led the team in rushing five times, and was named AFL

Player of the Year in 1965. He was emblazoned on the AFL's All-Time Team as the best halfback to ever have played in the AFL, and is the second leading rusher in league history. He holds the league's best per carry average at 4.87 over its ten years.

It may have been his perception that he was unappreciated, but in the eyes of his coaches and teammates, his value to the Chargers and their success was unparalleled. And the gratification he gave the fans who watched him play was unmeasurable.

THE UNCROWNED CHAMPS

Third Time's a Charm
AFL Championship Game
vs. Boston Patriots
January 5, 1964, at San Diego
Attendance 30,127

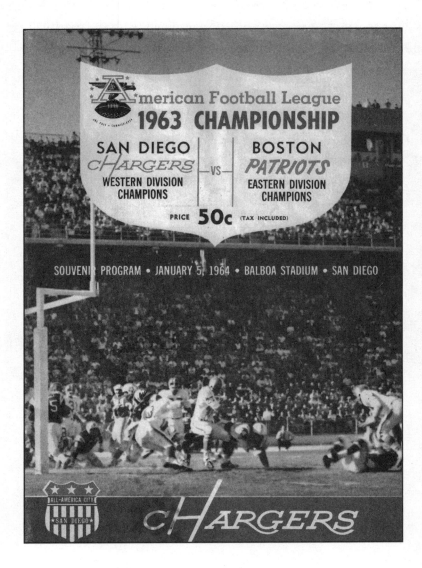

It goes without saying that all great football teams start with a great defense. And those who know a little about defense will tell you that the great ones start with a strong front line. The ability to keep opponents off the scoreboard is paramount to winning football games, and in that regard the two combatants in the 1963 Championship Game had what it took to win. In their two previous meetings of the season, the Chargers defense had held the Patriots to one touchdown and four field goals. In return, the Patriots defense held the Chargers to three touchdowns and one field goal. In all, only 43 points were scored. It no longer mattered that San Diego won both games by only five points. Nor that no team had ever beaten an AFL opponent three times in one season. All that mattered on January 5 was whether the Chargers could win *this* game. This game would also be a historic one, in that it was only the second time a professional football game was being played in January, with this one being the latest ever played.

This, too, would be Sid Gillman's finest hour as a coach, and probably his most memorable. Three times before, he had taken teams to the championship game: In 1955 with the Rams, and in 1960 and '61 with the Chargers. His teams had come up short each time. As he worked tirelessly in preparation throughout the winter and spring, through the Rough Acres summer camp and the sixteen-week AFL season, he had one objective on his mind. One singular goal that had eluded him through his legendary career that drove him to this moment: Winning their first AFL Championship.

With that thought continually motivating and driving him, Gillman came up with his most masterful game plan. In a move that was almost Hank Stram–like, he planned to attack Boston in their most impenetrable spot by using misdirection plays and distractions to take the Patriots off their game.

The speculation was that the best defensive team against the run—but the worst against the pass—would figure the Chargers would attack their weakest link by attacking through the air. So Gillman believed Boston would prepare to stop the pass and concentrate on pressuring Rote with blitzes at random. His thought was also that the Pats, the most blitz-minded team in the AFL, would send their entire front seven early and often to interrupt the San Diego offensive flow and rush Rote into quick passes and disrupt his timing, hoping to harass him into interceptions and sacks. Gillman's plan was to deter their blitzing by using backfield motion, double and triple wide set ups with Norton and Alworth wide on the same side, and even

Chargers captains Emil Karas (56) and Ron Mix (74) meet with Boston's Tom Addison for the pre-game coin flip.

splitting and flip-flopping Dave Kocourek wide from his tight end position. At times, he would also send Lowe and Lincoln in opposite directions on flair patterns at the same time, forcing the linebackers to scrap their blitz intentions to cover the five-man pass routes. He also wanted to get the Boston cornerbacks isolated on Norton and Alworth and out of reach of their safeties, or cause big gaps in their zone coverages by taking the linebackers out of the middle of the field. With his innovative strategy in place, the Chargers were ready take on the Patriots.

Following a perfectly designed game plan dubbed "Feast or Famine" by Sid Gillman to neutralize the Patriots' defense, the Chargers scored the first time they had the ball and continued their onslaught during the entire game. Tobin Rote was at his play calling best, and became the only quarterback to win a championship in both the NFL and AFL.[8]

His go-to guy against Boston was Keith Lincoln, who appeared to pick up yardage at will, gaining 206 yards on the ground and another 123 on seven pass receptions. He also scored two touchdowns and further etched his performance among the best in football history by completing a 20-yard pass. In all, the Chargers scored all but three times they had possession.

In their previous two meetings, the Patriots stopped the Chargers running game to the tune of 108 total yards. Today, the first two times Lincoln carried the ball, he eclipsed that total with runs of 56 and 67 yards.

---

8   His teams also ran up over 50 points in both title games, 59 with Detroit in 1957 and 51 with San Diego. In the two championship games, he directed from behind center and his teams outscored the opposition, 110–24.

On the second play of the game, Lincoln and Lowe were split left and right with Rote behind Rogers at center. Alworth, who had always lined up on the right side, was now wide on the left with Norton . . . a look that Boston immediately needed to adjust to. When Lowe started in motion to the left, it drew the two Boston linebackers offsides. Rote then spun right and gave an inside handoff to Lincoln on a counter play and he was off to the races through the vacated hole. Lincoln scampered 56 yards to the Boston 4-yard line and Rote finished the drive off with a 2-yard keeper moments later.

Using Paul Lowe initially as a decoy in motion, Lincoln experienced gaping holes on traps and misdirection plays that caught the Patriots in transitions they never thought they would have to make, and were obviously unprepared for.

Lance Alworth

The Patriots were prepared to stop everybody . . . except our fullback. Once Lincoln started picking up a lot of yardage, the rest of the stuff started working out because they didn't know what we were going to do next or who to focus on.

Ninety seconds into the game the Chargers already had a 7–0 lead. It had been common knowledge that the Chargers' meal ticket was sending Lowe wide on sweeps. So putting him in motion early in the game gave the Boston staff an unexpected dilemma. If they left Lowe alone, it opened him up for quick pitches that would have him turning the corner yards ahead of his nearest tackler. By moving *with* him, they suppressed their greatest strength, the blitz, and letting the cornerback pick Lowe up made their safeties vulnerable to passes in front of them.

On their second possession, after Rote was sacked for an 8-yard loss, he came right back with another sleight of hand. Moving out to his right, Rote faked a handoff to Lowe and pitched wide to Lincoln, who scooted around the left end for a 67-yard touchdown.

Keith Lincoln runs for a 67-yard touchdown.

Desperate to keep pace, on the Patriots' next possession Babe Parilli and Gino Cappelletti teamed up for a 49-yard gain and Larry Garron scored the Patriots' lone touchdown of the day with a 7-yard run two plays later.

Dick Harris

That play to Cappelletti should never have happened. It was mistake. We were in a cover six, which was a zone pass defense and I had the short route with the wide receiver and then any back coming out on my side. Charlie McNeil and I just miscommunicated on that play. I thought he would

> pick Cappelletti up and he thought I was going to take him
> all the way. That was the only time we screwed up all day.

Rote and the Chargers were not about to leave any door open for the Patriots, and slammed it shut on their very next series. This time it was Paul Lowe's turn to break free as the Pats turned their focus on stopping Lincoln. Lowe outraced the Boston defense for 58 yards and scored another touchdown. Three touchdowns on their first three possessions gave the Chargers a 21–7 lead at the end of the first quarter, and the backfield duo of Lincoln and Lowe had already rushed for 137 and 67 yards, respectively.

There was no stopping Lincoln or the Chargers that afternoon. The first time they got the ball in the second quarter, Lincoln took off again up the middle through the proverbial hole you could drive a truck through, for 44 more yards. Blair added another field goal at the end of the drive to balloon the lead to 24–7.

Before the half was over, Lincoln's 24-yard pass reception and a defensive pass interference call set up the Chargers fourth touchdown, a 14-yard screen pass to Don Norton making the score 31–10 at intermission.

The "Feast or Famine" game plan had taken its toll on the Patriots and thoroughly disoriented their defense. Historically the most difficult team to run against, Boston, who had given up more than 117 yards rushing only one time during their entire season and more than 240 only once in 56 games (57 including the playoff game with Buffalo), had already been torched for 247 yards rushing in just the first half. While the Patriots defense struggled, the Chargers' defense was having their way with the Pats offense. Ladd and Faison had already sacked Parilli three times for minus 27 yards, while the entire defense shut down their running game, giving up a meager 28 yards in the first two quarters.

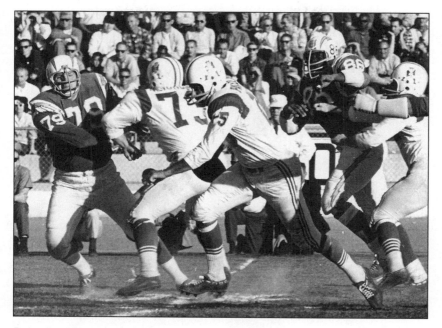

Babe Parilli tries to avoid the Chargers pass rush.

There are those who like to preach that the best offense is a good defense, and that may be the case for many teams. But in Sid Gillman's way of thinking, a good defense *was* a powerful and potent offense. And there was not a better example of that philosophy than the Chargers offensive display on this day.

San Diego continued to pour it on in the second half. Early in the third quarter they went the distance again, with their three offense icons combining to hit paydirt on an 80-yard drive. Paul Lowe got it started with an 8-yard sweep and Keith Lincoln added to his record-setting total with a 32-yard pass reception. Lance Alworth then completed the drive by out-leaping Bob Suci and stealing the ball from his hands at the 15-yard line and running the ball in for a 48-yard touchdown. The offensive onslaught had opened up a 38–10 lead with a full quarter left to play.

Lance Alworth out-jumps Boston's Bob Suci for a touchdown.

Gillman now handed the game off to John Hadl to finish off the fourth quarter with instructions to keep pressing forward. Following his coach's orders, Hadl drove the Chargers 70 yards, which culminated in another trip into the end zone—this time for Keith Lincoln—who was at the receiving end of a 25-yard pass. San Diego now led Boston 44–10.

Throughout the second half, the Patriots tried to move on the Charger defense, but could only pick up yardage in small pieces.

They were able to get out of their own end only twice, and made it to the San Diego 30-yard line once. It was all Chargers offensively and defensively, and was most definitely their finest performance of the year. Fittingly, the last time the Chargers had the ball, Hadl took them on another long drive that covered 80 yards. Finally, with 1:20 left in the game, Hadl scored for the last time on a 1-yard plunge to make the San Diego Chargers the 1963 AFL Champions with a 51–10 dismantling of the Boston Patriots.

As expected, Keith Lincoln was voted the game's Most Valuable Player for his record-setting performance of 329 yards of total offense (206 yards rushing and 123 receiving). All in all, the "Feast or Famine" game plan had worked flawlessly, producing 318 yards on the ground and another 292 through the air, amassing a franchise record of 610 yards of total offense.

Keith Lincoln was voted the game's MVP for his record-setting performance.

THE UNCROWNED CHAMPS

Paul Lowe

Let's put it this way: We were all well-coached, and we had the game plan to win anything. And after we won, we made sure we gave a little champagne toast to Coach [Gillman] for getting us there.

Boston Patriots	7	3	0	0	-	10
San Diego Chargers	21	10	7	13	-	51

SD-Rote 2 run (Blair kick)
SD-Lincoln 67 run (Blair kick)
Bos-Garron 7 run (Cappelletti kick)
SD-Lowe 58 run (Blair kick)
SD-FG Blair 11
Bos-FG Cappelletti 15
SD-Norton 14 pass from Rote (Blair kick)
SD-Alworth 48 pass from Rote (Blair kick)
SD-Lincoln 25 pass from Hadl (pass failed)
SD-Hadl 1 run (Blair kick)

TEAM STATISTICS	BOS	SD
First Downs	14	21
Rushing	6	11
Passing	8	9
Penalty	0	1
Total Yardage	261	610
Net rushing yardage	75	318
Net passing yardage	186	292
Passes att-comp-int	37-17-2	26-17-0

RUSHING

San Diego: Lincoln 13 for 206, 1 TD; Lowe 12 for 94, 1 TD; Rote 4 for 15, 1 TD; McDougall 1 for 2; Hadl 1 for 1, 1 TD; Jackson 1 for 0.

Boston: Crump 7 for 18; Garron 3 for 15, 1 TD; Lott 3 for 15; Yewcic 1 for 14; Parilli 1 for 10; Burton 1 for 3.

PASSING

San Diego: Rote 10 of 15 for 173, 2 TDs; Hadl 6 of 10 for 112, 1 TD; Lincoln 1 of 1 for 20.

Boston: Parilli 14 of 29 for 189, 1 int.; Yewcic 3 of 8 for 39, 1 int.

RECEIVING

San Diego: Lincoln 7 for 123, 1 TD; Alworth 4 for 77, 1 TD; Norton 2 for 44, 1 TD; MacKinnon 2 for 52; Kocourek 1 for 5; McDougall 1 for 4.

Boston: Burton 4 for 12; Colclough 3 for 26; Cappelletti 2 for 72; Graham 2 for 68; Crump 2 for 28; Lott 2 for 16; Garron 2 for 6.

Keith Lincoln

He was the consummate multipurpose back and the AFL's answer to Paul Hornung of the Green Bay Packers as the "do-it-all" player. He ran with speed and power, caught passes out of the backfield, threw passes, defended passes, returned punts and kickoffs, and even did some field-goal kicking. He also had a very identifiable look that set him apart from other AFL players at the time. Denver's Lionel Taylor was often identified for not having a tail on the bronco on the sides of his helmet, Boston's Jess Richardson played without a facemask, and Jim Otto of Oakland always wore a helmet that needed a new paint job. Keith Lincoln was the player known for having the top of his hip pads sticking out of his pants on the outside of his jersey.

After leaving Washington State as their all-time leading rusher, Lincoln got his big break on offense as a result of Paul Lowe breaking his arm in a 1962 exhibition game. Described by some as too slow to play halfback, too small to play fullback, and not accurate enough to play quarterback, Keith was a part-time offensive and defensive back during his rookie season in

1961. As a full-time halfback in 1962, he gained 574 yards and averaged 4.9 yards per carry for the year. In 1963, it was Gillman's plan to take advantage of having two halfbacks of nearly equal talent by using both Lincoln and Lowe in the backfield at the same time. Lincoln balked at the suggestion, feeling that he was not big or bulky enough to play fullback, but understood that playing anywhere on the field was better than sitting on the bench. Together, the tandem of Lincoln and Lowe became the most dangerous backfield in the AFL. They combined to have the best rushing average in AFL history in 1963 as Lowe (second in the league in rushing) logged over 1,000 yards with a 5.7 average and Lincoln (fourth in the league in rushing) checked in with 826 yards and a 6.5 per carry average. (Lincoln was injured in the first quarter after only 2 carries against Oakland and did not see action the next week against Houston.) Jets' coach Weeb Ewbank, who also coached a backfield of Lenny Moore and Alan Ameche with the NFL Champion Baltimore Colts, said that Lincoln and Lowe gave San Diego the best backfield in football.

What Lincoln is most remembered for is his record-setting performance against the Boston Patriots in the AFL Championship Game when he tallied over 300 yards of total offense He was a 1st Team All-AFL selection in both 1963 and

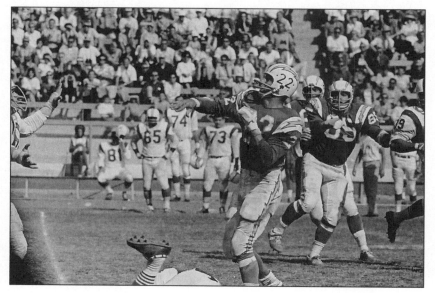

1964, and also won the All-Star Game MVP Award in both years. Keith was especially adept at hitting the line quickly and getting through the hole on trap plays and draws so fast that he often shot past linebackers and safeties for long gains. Once he had a defender beaten on a pass route, he was rarely caught.

In the championship game, he netted 176 rushing by halftime. Filling out the scorecard, he also had a 20-yard pass completion and seven receptions.

After the game, Boston Coach Mike Holovak said, "I don't know how a back could be better than Lincoln." While defensive end Bob Dee said, "Lincoln is the best back in league, bar none." The praise for Lincoln was so high that New York Jets' owner Sonny Werblin even offered Gillman anything he wanted if he would trade him to New York.

Already a favorite son in San Diego, Lincoln suddenly became a household name across the country as the AFL's glamour boy. Sid Gillman said, "Keith is much more powerful than he appears. He breaks tackles like a fullback. Burst through the middle like a fullback. Blocks like a fullback. That makes him ideal for the position. And as an extra, he has the speed of a good outside runner. There isn't a better all-around player in pro football." Forty years later, when asked about Lincoln again, Gillman hadn't changed his opinion, replying "Has there ever been a better all-around back than Keith Lincoln?"

5

WHAT WOULD HAVE HAPPENED IF THERE WERE A GAME BETWEEN THE TWO LEAGUES?

It wasn't until after the merger, following the 1966 season, that teams from the AFL and NFL would meet and play in their first-ever championship game. Then, beginning in the 1967, interleague games were played in the preseason only, and continued until they were included in the 1970 regular season schedule. At that point, the ten-team American Football League was absorbed into the NFL and became known as the American Football Conference (AFC). Through most of the sixties, the NFL was flaunted as superior to the AFL in every way and boasted that there was no way any team from the AFL could hold their own against the NFL powerhouse.

The measuring stick for most of this belief was Vince Lombardi's Green Bay Packers, who had situated themselves above the rest of their league, separating themselves from the "pack" as the best team in football. The Packers participated in NFL championship games from 1960–62 and 1965–67, winning all but one (1960). They were rightfully crowned the team of the sixties with five NFL titles. There was little doubt in the early sixties that the AFL champion Houston Oilers or Dallas Texans would fall well short of matching the quality of the Packers performance in a head-to-head matchup.

But all that changed in 1963. The Packers lost twice during the regular season to the Chicago Bears, who beat them out by a half game for the Western Division title. Powered by their league-leading defense and an offense that had just enough talent and moxie to stay ahead of the rest of the league, the Bears took an 11–1–2 record into the championship game where they beat the New York Giants, 14–10.

The San Diego Chargers, who finished with an 11–3 record, ran away from the Boston Patriots, 51–10, to win the AFL title with an explosive offense and the best defense in the league. As AFL supporters were clamoring about their Chargers being the best team in pro football, there was suggestion that an AFL vs. NFL championship game should be played to determine a true champion. NFL supporters were quick to pull the trigger and shoot holes in the claim as being whimsical and repudiated the suggestion, citing the notion that no AFL team led by a castoff quarterback and an inferior roster could touch the best defensive team the NFL had seen in years.

This would be the same rhetoric that would surface prior to January 12, 1969, when the Baltimore Colts brought their "best ever" NFL defense to Super Bowl III and were favored to win by 17 points over the New York Jets. As we all know of "Broadway" Joe Namath's famous promise, the Jets would be victorious, 16–7. It would be echoed again the following year prior to Super

Bowl IV when the newly anointed "best defensive team of all-time," the Minnesota Vikings, were favored to win by 12 points over the AFL Kansas City Chiefs. They lost to the Kansas City Chiefs, 23–7.

The AFL's claim was also fired upon because NFL supporters discounted the AFL's championship quarterbacks (George Blanda, Len Dawson, Tobin Rote, and Jack Kemp), who they labeled as unwanted players who were retreads that couldn't make it in the NFL and were only successful because they played in an inferior league. While it was true that it took the AFL until 1967 to have a quarterback win a championship without prior NFL experience (Daryle Lamonica with Oakland), those who were dissenters neglected to recall that over the AFL's time period, eight of the ten quarterbacks to appear in the NFL's championship games (Norm Van Brocklin, Y. A. Tittle, Bill Wade, Frank Ryan, Johnny Unitas, Earl Morrall, Bill Nelsen, and Joe Kapp) were themselves unwanted castoffs. The only difference was that some (the AFL quarterbacks) made the most out of the opportunity to relocate outside of the NFL and took a chance with a new league. While others (the NFL quarterbacks) merely moved to another team before their talents were appreciated and they became successful.

In a time when most football fans around the country rarely saw a team outside of their local market and had to rely mostly on the print media to get their information, it is easy to see how a reader could be influenced to think that every opinion—in each story about the NFL or AFL—was factual. This was in part (or mainly) because most sports writers at the time were mostly NFL supporters who themselves had no interest or respect for the new AFL, and rarely made time to even view the games.

Another criticism that NFL supporters circulated was that the AFL was little more than a game of "basketball on cleats," depending on the pass too often instead of adhering to the NFL mantra that "the running game is what pro football is all about," which was chanted by Vince Lombardi and his disciples. To their credit and foresight, the AFL did not want to offer more of the same game that the NFL played. What the AFL had was wide-open, long-distance offenses that attracted a new generation of fans. As a result, AFL games were more exciting to watch, with the anticipation of a possible score on every play. So it was by design that the AFL passed and ran in a more wide-open style. As many will testify, the new league survived and flourished because of this. When analyzed, the real numbers do not support the accusation of excessive passing.

As can be seen in the chart on the next page, the differential of passing to running plays was never more than four more runs per game between the two leagues over the course of a season. Overall statistics and the passing attempts per game through the first four years dropped from seven more AFL throws in their first year to five the second, less than four in the third year, and in 1963, AFL team's passes declined to a mere four more times per game than the NFL. So the claim that the AFL was less of a league because they relied too heavily on passing was simply not true. It was also debatable how anyone could arrive at the conclusion that one league was superior to the other when the information that was disseminated appeared to be just more slanted propaganda that was similar to the facetious passing claim.

Sports Illustrated, in December of 1963, endorsed the championship game when it published a letter written by AFL

NFL-YEAR	ATTEMPTS RUNNING	AVERAGE	ATTEMPTS PASSING	AVERAGE	TEAMS
1960	5091	32.6	4114	26.4	13
1961	6106	31.2	5292	27	14
1962	6064	30.9	5356	27.3	14
1963	6112	31.2	5415	27.6	14

AFL-YEAR	ATTEMPTS RUNNING	AVERAGE	ATTEMPTS PASSING	AVERAGE	TEAMS
1960	3391	30.3	3699	33	8
1961	3218	28.7	3630	32.4	8
1962	3285	29.3	3456	30.9	8
1963	3066	27.4	3539	31.6	8

commissioner Joe Foss to NFL commissioner Pete Rozelle, proposing a "World Series" game between the two leagues, which Rozelle politely declined. Even though it was felt that fans were excited by the prospect, the speculation for the rejection was that the NFL was already holding most of the cards and had nothing to gain by playing such a game. If the NFL won, people would claim that it was because they should have, according to *SI* writer Tex Maule, who predicted a six-touchdown margin of victory for the NFL. And if the AFL won, the NFL would have to admit they were not the superior league, which they had no interest in doing.

While the AFL was signing over one hundred top college players who were also drafted by the NFL, in their first four years, the new league had gone from having former NFL players make up 50 percent of their rosters in 1960 to having less than 25 percent on their current squads. The numbers proved that the AFL was not a league made up of unwanted players, since all of those hundred college draft picks who signed with an AFL team were wanted by the NFL. Ultimately, what the NFL did not want to acknowledge was that league parity was on the horizon. And they did not want to admit that the horizon was not as far away as they wanted it to be.

As soon as the Jets beat the Colts in Super Bowl III, the immediate reaction from NFL people was that it would never happen again. It was a fluke. And right after the Chiefs defeated the Vikings in Super Bowl IV, it was opined that the Chiefs were lucky and caught Minnesota on an off day. Surely if they played the games again the following week, the outcomes would have been reversed (as said by the NFL). Curiously, one has to wonder why we never heard those same claims after Super Bowl I or II, won by Green Bay, suggesting that the AFL teams might be able to change the outcome a week later. Privately, if you talk to any Kansas City or Oakland player after their loss to Green Bay or any AFL supporter for that matter, we probably should have. But those who suggested as much were immediately dismissed by the media.

As we all know, a championship game is a one-and-done event to be won by the best team on that day. There is no going back to appeal for a "do over," so you must bring your "A" game on game day!

In 1963, there was no opportunity for the teams to settle the debate as to who was that year's best team in professional football. But through the use of computer technology, crunching numbers and statistics, using a myriad of facts, figures, trends, and tendencies to analyze the strengths and weaknesses of the Bears and Chargers and then develop objective game plans for each team, a mythical championship game was staged to determine what *would* have happened. In the next chapter, the opportunity that did not materialize over fifty years ago presents itself in a one-and-done simulation event. The San Diego Chargers and the Chicago Bears of 1963 will finally meet. Enjoy the game!

6

SCOUTING THE BEARS AND CHARGERS

THE BEARS are a rugged, cold-weather team built to withstand the elements of the Windy City and play with the grit needed for the frigid northern venues of Green Bay, Detroit, and Minnesota. Ten of their fourteen games were played in these colder cities, as well as a late season 35-degree game in Pittsburgh, reinforcing the Bears offensive strategy to patiently control and protect the ball. Bears Coach George Halas liked to use his backs with power runs between the tackles and short passes to their all-pro tight end, slants to their flanker, and screens to their backs. Their defense was designed to out-muscle the opposition with their front seven and pinch in on receivers with their stingy secondary. The defense boasted four All-NFL players. In their first ten games, the Bears played once

THE CHARGERS are a warm-weather team built for speed and quickness. With half of their games played in the mild temperatures of Southern California, Sid Gillman liked to utilize his arsenal of speedy weapons with outside sweeps and long passes to stretch defenses and take advantage of his offensive strength to score from anywhere on the field. Their offense boasted four all-AFL players. On defense he had a front four that was large, strong, and mobile and could control the line of scrimmage as well as applying ferocious pass pressure. His ball-hawking back seven was as quick and dangerous as the offenses the AFL style of play endorsed. Through the Chargers season they played four games that were over 70 degrees, four in the 60s, two in the 50s, three in the 40s. Their coldest in 70-degree weather, three times in the 60s, four times in the 50s, and twice in the 40s. Of their final four games, three were in the 30s while their last one was a single digit above zero.

The title game played in Chicago on December 29 was played in an icy 4 degrees.

game was played in Houston on December 15 when it was 38 degrees.

The AFL championship game was played in San Diego on January 5 in a mild 57 degrees.

RECORD: 11–1–2
at 5–0: Lost 20–14 @ 49ers (0-5)
at 9–1: Tied 17–17 @ Pittsburgh (6–3–1)
at 9–1–1: Tied 17–17 vs. Minnesota (4–7)

RECORD: 11–3
at 3–0: Lost 50–34 @ Broncos (1–2)
at 5–1: Lost 34–33 vs. Raiders (3–4) at 9–2: Lost 41–27 @ Raiders (7–4)

OFFENSIVE STATISTICS
301 POINTS SCORED
21.5 POINTS/GAME
157 POINT DIFFERENTIAL (3rd)
10th in total offense
4.6 yards/play (12th)
8th in rushing
8th in passing

OFFENSIVE STATISTICS
399 POINTS SCORED
28.5 POINTS PER GAME
144 POINT DIFFERENTIAL (1st)
1st in total offense
6.7 yards/play (1st)
1st in rushing
3rd in passing

RUSHING OFFENSE
119.9 yards rushing/game
487 attempts (54.7% of offense)
3.4 yard/carry average (13th tied)
15 touchdowns (4th tied)
16 fumbles (1st fewest)
1679 total yards rushing (8th)

RUSHING OFFENSE
157.2 yards rushing/game
395 attempts (52.5% of offense)
5.6 yard/carry average (1st)
20 touchdowns (2nd)
16 fumbles (1st fewest)
2201 total yards rushing (1st)

BEARS PASSING OFFENSE
178.1 yards/game
404 attempts passing (45.3% of offense)

CHARGERS PASSING OFFENSE
210.3 yards/game
357 attempts passing (47.5% of offense)

12.1 yard avg. catch
54.7% comp.
18 TDs
14 INTs
2493 TOTAL YARDS PASSING

DEFENSIVE STATISTICS
144 POINTS GIVEN UP (10.3 AVG.)
1st in total defense
1st vs. pass
1st vs. rush
1st against kickoff and punt returns
gave up 4.0 yds./play (1st)
gave up 17 total touchdowns (1st)

RUSHING DEFENSE
412 rushes against for 1,442 yards
3.5 yard rush avg. (1st)
7 rushing touchdowns (1st)
103 yards/game rushing (1st)

PASSING DEFENSE
353 passes thrown against
164 completions for 1,734 yards
46.5% completion (1st)
124 yards/game (1st)
12.5 yards per catch (1st)
10 TD's allowed (2nd)
36 interceptions (1st)
4 interception returns for TD

KICKING
Green: 46.5 punting avg. (64 punts)
LeClerc: 13 for 23 FGs (56.5%)
Jencks: 35 of 37 PAT (94.6%)

15.5 yard avg. catch
56.6% comp.
28 TDs
24 INTs
2944 TOTAL YARDS PASSING

DEFENSIVE STATISTICS
255 POINTS GIVEN UP (18.2 AVG.)
1st in total defense
5th vs. pass
3rd vs. rush
2nd against kickoff and punt returns
gave up 4.7 yds./play (2nd tied)
gave up 27 total touchdowns (1st)

RUSHING DEFENSE
378 rushes against for 1,468 yards
3.9 yard rush avg. (2nd)
10 rushing touchdowns (1st)
104.9 yards/game rushing (3rd)

PASSING DEFENSE
472 passes thrown against
231 completions for 2,679 yards
48.9% completion (5th)
191.4 yards/game (4th)
12.9 yd. per catch (1st)
17 TD's allowed (1st)
29 interceptions (3rd tied)
1 interception return for TD

KICKING
Maguire: 38.6 punting avg. (58 punts)
Blair: 17 of 28 FGs - 60.7%
44 of 48 PAT (91.7)

COACH: GEORGE HALAS

Both Halas and Gillman wear the same two hats as the head coach and general manager. The founder of the NFL has always liked defense but was the first to introduce the pro-T formation. Staunch, stingy, and as dominant a figure as you'll find in football.

TOP ASSISTANT: GEORGE ALLEN

Second year as defensive coordinator after taking over for Clark Shaughnessy. Was once on the Rams staff until Gillman took over in 1955. A brilliant defensive mind, he helped create the Bears BUZ defensive system.

OFFENSIVE LINE

Viewed as an average line— experienced and adequate with Mike Pyle as the quality leader and best of the group.

Left Tackle: **Herman Lee**
Seven years of experience, six with Bears after coming from Pittsburgh. At 6'4", 244 pounds, he holds his own moving and protecting.

COACH: SID GILLMAN

His teams have won the West in three of the AFL's four seasons. The Patriarch of the passing game advocates stretching the field and forcing the defense to cover every yard on the gridiron. An innovator and motivator, he is one of the best head coaches in the game.

TOP ASSISTANT: CHUCK NOLL

Took over as defensive coordinator in '62 and convinced his players of his different style defensive schemes. They responded by becoming the best in the league. A tireless student of watching game film.

OFFENSIVE LINE

As a group they are underrated and underappreciated. Many felt that they were the strength of this year's team.

Left Tackle: **Ernie Wright**
One of the top four tackles in the AFL, he is often over looked as a top tackle because of Mix's greatness. Wright would be the best tackle on at least six AFL teams. Fast enough to lead sweeps.

Left Guard: **Ted Karras**
Lesser known than his brother, Alex, he is a steady blocker. Six years of experience, four with Bears. He is a steady if not stellar performer.

Center: **Mike Pyle**
This center from Yale is the line leader and a standout, very dependable and hasn't missed a start in 42 straight games. Made 2nd Team All-NFL.

Right Guard: **Roger Davis**
Another experienced and adequate lineman who toils in anonymity but performs well.

Right Tackle: **Bob Wetoska**
His strength is in his preparation and desire to be the best. He's a good one.

Tight End: **Mike Ditka**
Is the best in the pros. Made All-NFL Team for third consecutive year in '63. The Bears passing attack goes through him. Caught 56 or more passes each of his three pro years.

Split End: **John Farrington**
Not as consistent as Halas would

Left Guard: **Sam DeLuca**
A very good fire-out blocker, he returned to San Diego after a one-year trial retirement to help stabilize the line.

Center: **Don Rogers**
Had his best season this year and made 2nd Team All-League. Originally a reluctant pro, Rogers made himself into an All-Star center.

Right Guard: **Pat Shea**
Underrated, he is one of the strongest Chargers. Lifts weights as a hobby and plays with a wild California swagger.

Right Tackle: **Ron Mix**
Best offensive lineman in the AFL, he has been All-League at tackle and guard every year. Great pass blocker and fast enough to lead on screens and sweeps, he is a great student of the game.

Tight End: **Dave Kocourek**
Voted 2nd Team All-League, is fast enough to play wide and at 245 pounds and can handle blocking inside as well. Considered one of the top tight ends in the pros.

Split End: **Don Norton**
Very fast and elusive he runs

like and is known to occasionally drop passes.

Flanker: **Johnny Morris**
Capable and consistent, he is helped by all the attention Ditka draws in coverage. Has good speed and is the primary deep threat on passes.

Fullback: **Joe Marconi**
Had his best season in '63. Led Bears in rushing with 446 yards, but ranked only 20th in NFL. Undervalued in Los Angeles, he found a home and a starting role in Chicago.

Halfback: **Ronnie Bull**
The 1962 Rookie of the Year and second-leading Bears rusher with 404 yards. Has sprinter speed but likes to run between tackles. His strength is running like a fullback. Good blocker and above-average pass catcher.

Quarterback: **Bill Wade**
Ranked 8 of 14 NFL starters in passing. His average yard per pass was NFL's lowest among starters.

precise patterns. Missed several games with injury. Good possession receiver.

Flanker: **Lance Alworth**
Possibly the best deep receiver in pro football, if not the most dangerous. Led team in receptions and selected as All-AFL in his first full season. Exceptionally fast he averages nearly 20 yards per catch.

Fullback: **Keith Lincoln**
An All-League triple threat, Lincoln had 349 yards of total offense in AFL championship game. Gained 826 during season and led league in yards per carry at 6.5. A good blocker when called upon, he is an above-average pass catcher.

Halfback: **Paul Lowe**
Back with a vengeance after missing all of 1962, Lowe was second in AFL with 1,010 yards and 5.7 per carry average. Not only has sprinter speed but is also strong moving straight ahead. Has great change of pace that allows him to follow blockers through a hole and then shift into high gear instantly.

Quarterback: **Tobin Rote**
All-AFL after leading the league with 59.4% completion. Won NFL championship in '57.

Is still dangerous when running out of the pocket while his veteran maturity has helped his decision making. Rarely panics when hurried. His strengths are throwing short darts on look-ins and slants and his leadership.

DEFENSIVE ROSTER
Had 52 takeaways—36 interceptions and 16 fumble recoveries for a +27.

Lead NFL in 10 defensive categories. Cut their average run yield from 4.7 in '62 to 3.4 in '63.

Left Defensive End: **Ed O'Bradovich**
The second-year year man is young and mean. Missed the first half of the season with an injury and is still learning his position tactically. Good straight ahead pass rusher.

Left Defensive Tackle: **Stan Jones**
Former All-Star guard has moved across the line, uses his NCAA weight-lifting champion skills to fend off blockers.

Right Defensive Tackle: **Fred Williams** Has a dozen years of

Doesn't run any more, but his leadership and accurate passing is what makes the Chargers go. Excellent play caller with great ability at calling audible.

DEFENSIVE ROSTER
AFL's top rated team, they allowed the fewest points and touchdowns both rushing and passing.

Left Defensive End: **Earl Faison**
His 6'5" frame can be deceiving. He plays much bigger and has speed to catch runners on sweeps. Ferocious pass rusher, he was rookie of the year in '62 and All-League this year. Requires two blockers on most plays. Has Hall-of-Fame ability.

Left Defensive Tackle: **Ernie Ladd**
At 6'9" and 321 pounds is known as the Big Cat with a nasty temperament. Has learned how to finesse blockers as well as being able to throw them around at will. Has great lateral pursuit and superior straight ahead charge.

Right Defensive Tackle: **George Gross** Has enormous strength, experience and is best used as a situational player and as a straight ahead pass rusher.

the rookie teamed with Petrich to make an All-Rookie right side. Very good pass rusher with 6'3" frame, he's the smallest of the front four.

Right Defensive End: **Doug Atkins** At 6'8" he is big, strong, tough, and punishing. One of the best in the NFL, he combines size and quickness to pressure passers. All-NFL and one of the top two in the NFL at his position.

Right Defensive End: **Bob Petrich** The rookie is considered a fast learner. His progress early enabled Gillman to trade former starter Ron Nery.

Left Linebacker: **Joe Fortunato** Consistent and intelligence is his game. Rarely makes mistakes and is very opportunistic. Great anticipation, will not over-commit, but has limited pass coverage. Always around the action. Voted 1st team All-NFL.

Left Linebacker: **Emil Karas** A solid backer, he is the strong man that shreds blockers on sweeps.

Middle Linebacker: **Bill George** All-NFL, he invented the middle linebacker position. Had career best season in '63. One of the hardest hitters in football he will never be out prepared or out played.

Middle Linebacker: **Chuck Allen** Good leader in the middle; he stabilizes the second layer of the defense. Hard hitter with good instincts.

Right Linebacker: **Larry Morris** Tenacious blitzer and strong in pursuit. Made 2nd Team All-NFL.

Right Linebacker: **Paul Maguire** Is smart and adequate against both runs and passes.

This is the best trio of linebackers in football.

Left Cornerback: Bennie McRae
Has great reaction skills and excellent speed. Picked off six passes in '63. Former Big 10 hurdling champion.

Left Cornerback: Dick Harris
Was 1st Team All-League in '60 and '61, and was 2nd Team All-League in '62. The teams "wild child," he may be the Chargers best cover man.

Right Cornerback: Dave Whitsell
Steady player with experience and speed. Has made himself an effective open field tackler.

Right Cornerback: Dick Westmoreland Free agent was runner-up for ROY Award in '63 and made 2nd Team All-League. Very fast and has quick feet that keep him close to receivers.

Free Safety: Rosey Taylor
Led the league with nine interceptions. Has freedom to roam and plays with the idea that every pass thrown his way is up for grabs. An All-NFL player, he is part of the best set of safeties in the pros.

Free Safety: Charlie McNeil
All-League safety when healthy. Excellent and aggressive tackler in the open field.

Strong Safety: Richie Petitbon
The other half of the best set of safeties, he is All-NFL and a strong and superior tackler. The best strong safety in football.

Strong Safety: George Blair
A strong tackler and team kicker, made 2nd Team All-AFL. His specialty is zone coverage and ability to pick through shifts.

7

THE GAME: CHARGERS VS. BEARS IN THE FIRST SUPER BOWL

AFL vs. NFL Championship Game
January 12, 1964
Tempe, Arizona
Sun Devil Stadium, on the campus of Arizona State University

Good afternoon, ladies and gentlemen, and welcome to this historic event: the first World Championship of Professional Football between the American and National Football Leagues, featuring the NFL champion Chicago Bears against the AFL champion San Diego Chargers.

Since the AFL began playing in 1960, the debate has gone back and forth as to how good this new league was and how it would fare against the NFL's best. Today, for the first time, we will get that answer as the father of the NFL, "Papa Bear" George Halas and his big bad Bears take on Sid Gillman and his explosive Chargers. Gillman is no stranger to championship games, as he took his 1955 Los Angeles Rams to the NFL title game in his first season as the team's coach, and followed that up by taking the Chargers to three of the first four AFL title games.

The temperature is an arid 71 degrees under bright clear skies with no wind; overall a perfect day for football.

Halas' Bears earned entrance to this game by defeating the New York Giants, 14–10, on December 29 in the Windy City. The Bears defense, under the direction of George Allen, set up both Chicago touchdowns, influencing the tempo of the game just as they had done all season long. Now they take on offensive team that is unlike any in the NFL.

Halas's offense is guided by the steady hand of veteran Bill Wade, who likes to control the ball while consuming the clock. The Chargers are a very balanced and quick striking offensive team. They led the AFL in total offense and rushing offense, and were also the league's best defensive team. So on paper it looks like an even match-up, and it's likely that the team that creates turnovers, stays away from penalties, and stays healthy will have the advantage.

The Bears, a charter member of the NFL, are wearing their white jerseys with dark navy stripes. Their pants are also white with navy and orange stripes down the sides. Their helmets are navy with a white Chicago "C" on each side.

The Chargers are wearing their powder blue jerseys with the familiar lightning bolts on the shoulders, accented with white numbers with a gold outline. They have white pants with a gold lightning bolt down each side. Their helmets are white with two gold lightning bolts and their jersey number on each side. On some helmets you will notice a small shield in the front middle—honoring the city of San Diego for its national award designating it as an All-American city. They earned their way to this game by overwhelming the Boston Patriots, 51–10, in the AFL Championship Game.

The Chargers George Blair is teeing the ball up and we are about to get underway. Ronnie Bull and Willie Galimore are deep for the Bears.

And here we go!

* * *

Blair kicks it high and straight. Bull receives the ball at the five and moves up the middle to the 15, where he is tackled by Emil Karas at the 21.

Wade brings the Bears to the line; he's looking over the Charger defense that is in a standard 4-3 set. The ball is snapped and he drops back and fires over the middle—complete to tight end Mike Ditka for 8 yards. Ditka was well covered by Blair, but Wade was on target and the Bears have opened up with a quick look-in pass to their top receiver. It's now 2nd and 2.

Wade comes to the line, drops back to pass again . . . he's looking wide and throws out to Ditka again, complete, as he muscles to the 39-yard line and the Bears have a first down. Ditka again was covered by Blair, but Wade fired a frozen rope to the sidelines, giving Ditka his second catch. This could be the Bears strategy, to isolate Ditka and keep throwing to him until the Chargers prove they can stop him. The Bears have another first down on their own 39-yard line.

Galimore checks into the Chicago backfield for Ronnie Bull. With the snap, Wade turns, hands to Galimore who is running wide to the right, and he is stopped cold by Bob Petrich near the line of scrimmage. The ball is placed at the 40. Great play by Petrich, who fought off Lee's block and hit Galimore before he could turn the corner.

It's 2nd and 9, Wade drops back, he's looking down field but now dumps it off to Marconi on a screen. He's over the 45 and is brought down by Chuck Allen on the Chicago 48-yard line. That time Ditka had two men on him with Karas dropping off to help Blair with underneath coverage. Ditka is the best tight end in football, and if the Chargers are going to go toe-to-toe with the Bears, they will have to keep him in check.

The Bears come to the line on 3rd and 1, with the Chargers staying in a standard 4-3 defense. Here's a pitchout to Marconi, he's got the 1 yard he needed and is hit by big Earl Faison, who reached out and wrestled him to the ground for the stop. First down, Chicago.

Wade comes to the line, calling signals. Ditka is being played tightly on the line by Karas, with Morris split wide right. Wade spins and gives the ball to Ronnie Bull on a trap right over George Gross, and the rookie defensive tackle has him after 4 yards. Gross is one of three rookie defensive starters for Sid Gillman, and all three have lived up to his expectations and earned the coach's confidence, as well as that of their teammates. Petrich and Westmoreland are the other two first year starters.

Nearly four minutes have gone by with the Bears now across midfield. On 2nd and 6, Wade steps back to pass and finds Ditka over the middle; Ditka breaks away from Blair, runs past Karas, and he is off! He's at the 20, to the 10, and finally dragged down by Dick Harris inside the 10 at around the 7-yard line. And the Bears have the first scoring chance of the day! Ditka just bulldozed his way past the initial coverage and headed untouched to the 7. That's a 40-yarder from Wade to Ditka, and his third catch of the drive. San Diego is going to have to figure out what to do with Ditka. I think Chuck Noll is going to have to try and hit the big tight end at the line to hold him up and then designate two defenders to guard him, or Iron Mike is going to have a big day. Those quick strikes by Wade are also getting the ball away before the big Chargers front line can even get to him.

Rick Casares, the veteran Bears fullback, now joins Marconi in the backfield. Casares, the old pro, is a hard runner and strong blocker, and when he can see pay dirt he's even tougher. Here's a give to Casares who dives ahead to the 5-yard line. It's 2nd and goal.

Wade fakes to Casares this time and throws short, looking for Morris on a slant, but the ball falls incomplete, just missed him for six. Harris had inside positioning that time and Wade had to fire high, but the ball was out of Morris's reach. It's now 3rd and goal.

The Chargers line is stacked tight with a five-man front, and the corners are right up on the line in front of Morris and Farrington. Karas is right on Ditka's nose. Wade fakes to Marconi and drops back. He throws to the corner and . . . COMPLETE TO CASARES FOR A TOUCHDOWN! And Chicago gets on the board as they took the opening kickoff the length of the field for the game's first score.

Bobby Jencks, one of two Bears kickers, comes on to attempt the extra point. It's up . . . it's good. Time-out is taken on the field with the Chicago Bears leading, 7–0. That drive consisted of eight plays and took 4:20 off the clock.

Bobby Jencks, also a reserve tight end, tees it up to kickoff. Lincoln is the deep man for San Diego, and is flanked by Alworth and Westmoreland about 10 yards in front of him. The kick goes to Keith Lincoln a yard deep in the end zone. He's bringing it out. He's to the 10, the 15, the 20, and hit by Larry Morris at the 24. A 25-yard return for Lincoln and the Chargers will have the ball from their own 24-yard line.

San Diego comes to the line for their first play from scrimmage. Quarterback Tobin Rote hands the ball to halfback Paul Lowe on a sweep to the left side, and he's brought down by Doug Atkins for a one yard gain.

On 2nd down, Rote snaps the ball and steps back to pass. He looks to Lowe on a screen and it's incomplete, making it a 3rd and 10 from the Chargers 25.

Tobin Rote will have to be at his championship game best today as he goes against the best defensive secondary in the league. The Bears defensive backs have given up less than one touchdown pass a game and held the opposition to completing less than 50 percent of their passes.

Rote steps up to the line. He has Alworth in the slot with Norton wide left. The Chargers used this set up last week against Boston to confuse them and overload the coverage on one side. Rote fades and throws over the middle . . . and it's complete to Paul Lowe on a quick slant pattern for 11 yards, giving the Chargers a first down on their own 36-yard line. Lowe ran a circle pattern and got a step on Fortunato, and Rote just led him up field for the first down. That time the safety and cornerback were tied up with Norton and Alworth, isolating Fortunato one-on-one with Lowe, who got a quick step on the linebacker.

Rote steps back to pass again. He has Alworth on a short out . . . and Alworth has it and side-steps McRae, he's over mid-field and is pushed out of bounds by Petitbon after a gain of 20 yards. Another first down for the Chargers, who are now in Chicago territory.

Rote has been on target hitting his receivers, who have so far been just out of the reach of the Bear defenders. The old pro may have a weaker arm than the last time he played against an NFL team, but what he lacks in zip, he more than makes up for in knowledge of game situations. He's done it all year as the leader of this San Diego offensive. On that one you saw the quickness and speed of one of the AFL's brightest stars, as Alworth pulled in the short pass and picked up an additional 15 yards after the catch.

First down, and Rote drops back to throw . . . incomplete to Lincoln, but there's a flag on the play. Let's see . . . it's on Chicago. O'Bradovich was offside, and that will advance the ball 5 yards and give the Chargers a 1st and 5 from the Bear 39.

Rote sends Lowe in motion, he fakes a handoff to Lincoln and is looking long for Alworth . . . he's got McRae beat and . . . CAUGHT! HE HAS IT AT THE 10 AND RUNS IT IN FOR A CHARGERS TOUCHDOWN! Wow, 76 yards on five plays, capped off by a 39-yard touchdown to Lance Alworth who accounted for 59 of the 76 yards on the drive, and that was just a straight "go long and out-run the defender" play. As good as McRae is—and he's a good one—I don't think the Bears have seen a receiver in the NFL as quick and fast as Alworth. At least it looked like that on these last two plays. Alworth has that extra burst that he can turn on when he gets a step on defenders and that time he just flat outran McRae. Knowing this Bear defense, I don't expect that we will see that happen again, as they're known for making key in-game adjustments.

Here's Blair for the extra point . . . it's good. And with 6:09 remaining in the opening quarter, we have 7–7 tie as both teams drove downfield on their opening possession for touchdowns. This looks like it has all the makings of real classic.

San Diego is set to kickoff. Blair boots it to Billy Martin at the two. He's to the 15, now 20, and tackled up at the 34 by Dick Westmoreland for a 28-yard return. It's 1st and 10 for the Bears from their own 34.

Wade is at the line. The snap, Wade drops back and throws a short out to Ditka . . . incomplete. Again, Ditka had two men on him and they are knocking him around from the second the ball is snapped. They'll have to be careful with that strategy, as Ditka can be quick to give a couple shots of his own. Right now he is fighting off the defenders, but that is also changing Wade's timing as his tight end finds some open space.

Wade drops back again, deeper this time, he throws a screen to Bull . . . it's incomplete. Wade had to adjust that pass over the outstretched arms of Ernie Ladd, which may have caused the ball to be a bit higher than it needed to be.

The Chargers are showing blitz from the corners with Karas and Maguire. Here's another screen, this time to Marconi . . . and he has it at the 32 with blockers in front. He's to the 40, across the 50, to the 45-yard line for a 21-yard pick-up before he's brought down by McNeil and Harris. The Bears have another first down at the Chargers 45-yard line. The Chargers got caught on that one and probably thought that Wade would not call two screens in a row. But that is what Wade brings to the Bears offense: a cagey sense of the game. They also know that Wade is a runner, so that is probably why they sent the outside linebackers; to box him in and also hurry his throw. Wade caught them that time.

From the 45 it's Marconi on a trap to the left side and Schmidt and Petrich are there to meet him. He maybe got a yard, but nothing more. It will be 2nd and 9.

THE GAME: CHARGERS VS. BEARS IN THE FIRST SUPER BOWL

Wade takes the snap and hands it off to Ronnie Bull who cuts to his left. He's by Petrich and met by Maguire after picking up 6 yards, bringing up a 3rd and 3. The Chargers bring their corners up, almost challenging Morris and Farrington to go deep. Wade on a long count and there's a flag; I think somebody on the Bears line moved . . .

. . . and that is it. I think it was Herman Lee, the tackle, and the Bears will move back 5 yards to their 38, where it will now be 3rd and 8.

Wade comes to the line, he's looking to throw, but the Chargers are blitzing again. Wade throws and finds Ditka at the 43, and that will be enough for a first down at the San Diego 33, with Chuck Allen and George Blair on the stop.

The Bears are staying with what has worked all year long, and are having the same success today by using screens and their running game to open up the middle for Ditka. Ditka now has 4 catches for 68 yards. I'm not sure the Chargers are going to be able to single cover him like that when they are sending their linebackers on blitzes, as Wade seems to be able to sense it and checks off to call Ditka's number. Noll is going to have to go with one plan: stop Ditka. Otherwise, by blitzing, he will give Wade an open path on quick look-ins. The Chargers are not really a blitzing team, so they may just be trying to see what kind of success they can have early before settling in.

From the 33 the Bears step up to the line. Wade fakes to Marconi and looks down field . . . he's got Johnny Morris on a slant for 14 more yards to the 19-yard line. The Bears are knocking on the door again with another great drive. This has been the Bears way, and Wade is showing why his offense may not be as explosive as the Chargers or other NFL teams, but as long as the Bears have the ball, they have control of the game.

It's now 1st and 10 at the San Diego 19. Here's Marconi taking a handoff, off tackle. He fights forward and gets 3 yards on pure desire. Ernie Ladd met him at the line and spun him down.

To the line again, it's Bull to the other side of the line for 3 more, making it 3rd and 4 from the Chargers 13.

Wade calling signals—there's a flag thrown. It looks like Ernie Ladd this time. Yep, the Chargers are offsides for a 5-yard penalty and that will give Wade and the Bears a first down at the San Diego 8-yard line.

With 1:52 left in the quarter, Wade hands to Bull who runs right into the Big Cat. Ernie Ladd just devoured him before he could take a step. It's a 1-yard loss and sets up a 2nd and goal from the 9.

Wade steps back to pass—it's to Ditka over the middle but the throw's a little behind him and incomplete. That play has been working for Chicago all day, and Wade was looking for it to be his bread-and-butter one more time, but was a bit underthrown.

The Chargers bring in Bud Whitehead as an extra defensive back, now feeling that the Bears would be stretched to run the ball in from here. Wade looks over the defense, Galimore and Bull are in the backfield. Wade takes the snap and drops back . . . he's got Farrington on a crossing pattern in the back of the end zone for a TOUCHDOWN! And the Bears have taken the lead back with their second touchdown of the quarter, as John Farrington beat the rookie Dick Westmoreland, who appeared to be either screened or confused by the crossing route.

Jencks lines up for the point after try and . . . it's good. Chicago takes a 14–7 lead.

So far Chicago has been able to make two sustained and time-consuming drives down the field on the Chargers defense. This last drive used up nearly six minutes on 12 plays, as the Bears worked runs in and out, screens, and short passes to keep the Chargers defense from digging in. Even when they tried to blitz Wade, he was equal to the task. Chicago has run 22 plays and Wade has hit on 9 of his 13 passes to five different receivers while mixing in nine runs using four backs. It is somewhat uncharacteristic of the Bears to be throwing more than they run, but they are controlled, high percentage passes and are doing what they set out to do by controlling the ball and eating up the clock, as well as keeping the Chargers' defense guessing.

Jencks is ready to kickoff. He kicks it high and deep to the 1-yard line, taken by Alworth who brings it to the 10, 15, and is knocked to the ground at the Chargers 18 for a 17-yard return.

The Chargers break the huddle and move to the line for only their second possession of the game. From the 18, Rote is looking for Kocourek on a button-hook but it's knocked away by Petitbon.

It's second down, and Rote fades and throws out in the flat to Lincoln, but it's out of his reach for another incompletion, making it 3rd and 10. No need to panic at this stage of the game, as both teams appear to still be feeling each other out.

Rote drops back again, looking left . . . and he's got Don Norton on a slant and he's got some room to run. He's at the 30, and brought down by Dave Whitsell at the 36. It's an 18-yard pickup for Norton and the Chargers.

And with that, the first quarter comes to a close, as the Chicago Bears lead the San Diego Chargers, 14–7.

Second Quarter

As the second quarter begins, the Chargers have the ball at their own 36, as Rote steps back to pass. He's being rushed by Atkins, turns, and he's stripped of the ball, FUMBLE! Let's see who has it . . . and Chicago recovers! It's Fortunato with the recovery, and the Bears have the first turnover of the afternoon. Oh, what a big play that was, as Chicago now has possession in San Diego territory. Atkins came hard from the outside and when Rote turned to avoid him, he ran right into Fred Williams who knocked the ball out of his hand. This is what the "Monsters of the Midway" have done time and again this season, and now it is up to Wade's offense to capitalize on the Chargers' mistake.

Wade steps up to the line and checks out the defense. He hands off to Bull on the left side who is hit by Ladd and stopped for a 1-yard loss at the 43, where it will be 2nd and 11.

Wade moving deliberately, he looks out over the defense and takes the snap, fakes a pitch to Marconi, now turns and throws a screen pass to Galimore . . . he has it and follows a block by Karras to the 38 for a 5-yard gain. It will be 3rd and 6 for the Bears.

Wade drops back and has some time. He's looking for Ditka, he steps up in the pocket to avoid Faison and throws to the sideline . . . it's incomplete. Ditka could not get his hands on it and the Bears will be punting for their first time today.

This is a bit beyond LeClerc's field goal range, and it looks like Halas wants to pin the Chargers deep in their own end. Bobby Joe Green comes on for his first punt of the game. He gets it away and it's headed to the sideline. It hits down at the 10 and rolls out of bounds at the 4-yard line. A great punt by the veteran, and now the Chargers will start their drive from deep in their own end. You couldn't have asked for a better kick by Green, and Halas looks like a genius with that call.

The Chargers are at the line. Lincoln and Lowe are in the backfield, with Alworth split right and Norton to the left. Rote takes the snap. He's looking down field, now throws to the outside to Lincoln . . . AND IT'S PICKED OFF BY FORTUNATO! He's brought down immediately by Lincoln inside the Charger 10. The Bears defense has another turnover. Wow, what an ill-advised throw that was by Rote. That ball just kind of fluttered out there, and Fortunato was again the opportunist. I think maybe Leggett got a hand on it as Atkins and Leggett were really bringing the pressure. Rote was definitely hurried and may have been better off throwing it away or taking the sack. The Bears now have possession on the Chargers 9-yard line.

The Chargers are looking for the Bears to run and have stacked six men on the line. The corners are a few yards deep as Galimore takes a pitch out. He's running left, he's past Petrich, following Karras and Davis, he's past the 5 and IN FOR THE TOUCHDOWN! The Bears have just take a 20–7 lead early in the second quarter. Galimore found the seam as Davis sealed off Maguire and Harris, and he sprinted in for the rest. Interesting call from Wade, and he may have checked off at the line when he saw the Chargers stacking the line toward the middle. George Halas congratulates Galimore and Davis as they reach the sideline after putting the Bears up by two touchdowns.

Jencks readies for the extra point. It's up and . . . BLOCKED! I think Ernie Ladd or maybe Faison in the middle of the Chargers line got a hand on it. That's only the third time in forty tries that Jencks has failed to covert, and we'll have to see just how important that one will be. Halas is not happy, but he does have a 20–7 lead with 13:28 left in the first half.

Jencks kicks off to Lincoln at the goal line. He moves up field and is stormed under by a host of Bear tacklers at the 12. So the Chargers will have a long way to go and are down by 13 points and in need of a solid drive to regain their confidence. They have two turnovers already, so Rote needs to put something together on this possession.

Rote hands the ball to Lowe on a sweep to the left side. Paul Lowe turns the corner and is sprung with a great block by DeLuca. He's past the 20 to the 25 and a first down. Lowe picked up 13 yards on that carry and it was the halfback's quick burst that got him by Atkins and Fortunato before finally being brought down by Rosey Taylor with the help of Bill George.

From the 25, Rote hands to Lincoln on a quick trap. He breaks loose from George and is hit by Petitbon and brought down at the 34 for an 11-yard run and another San Diego first down. The Chargers runners are quick off the snap and equally as quick getting through the hole that was opened by Deluca and Rogers with some misdirection that time.

The Bears bring Taylor up close, looking to blitz on first down. Now he backs off as Lowe goes in motion left. Rote takes a short drop and throws long to Norton . . . it's incomplete, just off his hands and nearly intercepted again by Taylor who went for the deflection. Petitbon closes in on the line as the Bears again show blitz. Morris and George step up. They're coming this time, looking to rattle Rote. Rote fades and circles right, now looks back and floats a screen to Lowe . . . who pulls it in and heads up field to the 50 and turns it on until he's pulled down by Taylor who was in hot pursuit, but not until Lowe picked up 19 yards on the reception. Rote read that one perfectly and had just enough time to avoid the blitz by George and Morris.

The ball is at the Chicago 45. Rote sets to pass, throws a quick slant to Jerry Robinson, but it's out of his reach and incomplete, bringing up 2nd and 10. Norton returns for San Diego as Robinson goes to the sideline.

Rote gives to Lincoln sweeping right, he has some blocking and Lincoln is brought down after an 8-yard gain by Larry Morris. It's now 3rd and 2 for the Chargers.

This is a big play for the Chargers, who need to get points and—most importantly—keep this drive alive. Rote turns . . . and there's a whistle, blowing the play dead. It's on the Chargers for illegal procedure, and that will move the ball back to the 42-yard line and give the Chargers a 3rd and 7. Not what Sid Gillman wanted at this point in the drive—or any time for that matter.

The Chargers need to regroup as they go back to the huddle. Will the Bears bring pressure? They line up in their normal 4-3. Rote looks out over the Bears defense. He spins and gives to Lincoln on a sweep to the right side again, but this time he's met by O'Bradovich and Morris and stopped cold. He's down after a short 2-yard gain, bringing up fourth down for San Diego from the 40. Rote is staying away from Atkins and Leggett right now, so O'Bradovich needs to be ready for something to his side on every down, and he stood tall right there.

Let's see if Gillman will give Blair a chance to make a long one. This would be a 48-yard attempt, and the longest try of the season for the Chargers kicker. He did convert on two of his six attempts during the season from beyond the 40, but this one would push his limit. I don't see Maguire ready to come in either, so I'm not sure Gillman is looking to punt here.

It looks like Gillman is going to give his offense a chance to pick up the 7 yards they need on fourth down. Oh my, this is a gutsy move by Sid. And if they don't make it the Bears will have excellent field position near midfield. At least a missed field goal try would put the ball back to the 20 and would appear to be at least as good as a punt. Even letting Maguire kick to the sidelines to pin Chicago inside the 20 would be the more conservative move, but Gillman looks like his mind is made up. He may want his offense to push the envelope and force the Bears to make a play. He's going for it. Now that's confidence . . . I guess. Well, if they don't make it and the Bears convert it into some points, it's a decision that will be questioned for a long time. Huge play here for San Diego. The Bears look determined to get their offense the ball back. Now Rote brings his team to the line and looks over the set. Could he be looking to draw them offside and move the Chargers closer?

Rote takes the ball, fades, and is looking long for Alworth. Now he throws to his right to Lowe in the flat. Lowe brings it in, he's got Morris to beat, and he's by him. He's to the 30 and cuts back inside to the 20 where he sidesteps Petitbon. He's at the 15 and is hit from the side by Taylor and McRae, and is brought to a stop at the Bears 11-yard line. Great call by Gillman! Lowe has been the catalyst so far for the Chargers offense, and that little backfield pass netted 29 yards for San Diego. Good call to try and isolate the speedy Lowe on Morris and use his ability to accelerate to the outside. Again, the Chargers—and especially Lowe's speed—enabled him to get by the first flow of tacklers. I think those early long pass completions to Alworth and Norton have kept the Bear defensive backs on their heels to an extent, and Rote has seen that his backs can get a step on the Bears linebackers who are so good and stopping the run.

The Chargers now have a first down with the ball at the 11. Here's Lincoln into the line, but he won't get much. Well, he won't get anything as Leggett, George, and Atkins are all over him. Lincoln ran right into the teeth of the Bears defense, and that is what you can expect from Chicago. You are not going to move them out or run over them. Even though the Chargers have had a little success running, it has been mostly to the outside using their speed. Rote turns and fakes to Lincoln on a play action and he has Lowe on a short button-hook for 6 yards. He threaded that one—and he had to—because Fortunato and McRae were right there. It's now 3rd and 4 at the 5 for San Diego.

The Bears get set in a 4-3 defense. Norton is spread left along with Alworth, and Kocourek is tight to the right. Lowe goes in motion right. Rote takes the snap and drops to pass. He's looking, he fires . . . HE FINDS ALWORTH OVER THE MIDDLE FOR A CHARGER TOUCHDOWN! It's his second of the day, and the Chargers are back on the board with a 5-yard touchdown pass from Rote to Alworth. They sent four receivers into the end zone that time and appeared to have three of them crossing and using the goal posts as screens as Alworth waited for the clear-out before he broke to the middle, and it worked. Here's Blair to try for the extra point. It's up . . . AND HE MISSED IT! HE MISSED THE EXTRA POINT! No one got a hand on that one, he just shanked it. He'd hit on 44 of 48 attempts during the season, but this time he just missed it, which leaves the Chargers seven points short with 8:50 left in the half. Bears' lead is now cut to 20–13.

Bull and Galimore are deep for Chicago to return the kick. It's Bull at the 5, to the 15, and brought down at the 23 for an 18-yard return. At this point you would think that the Bears offense would look to control the ball and not give it back to the Chargers, who have shown that they can move it against the rugged Bears defense.

Wade gives to Marconi into the line. He's got a yard . . . and that's all, as Ernie Ladd and Chuck Allen come in on the stop.

Now second down, Wade takes a quick snap. He throws to Angelo Coia . . . incomplete. I'm not sure, but I wonder if that big front wall of the Chargers is influencing the Bears' play calling. Wade has already thrown 16 times in the first half, but Halas knows that the way to beat the Chargers is not by going after the front line. He's seen the film and knows that Hank Stram and others have tried to handle them to no avail. This will be the challenge for Chicago to move the ball on the ground the rest of the way. They averaged 28 throws per game, so they are a little ahead of that pace right now, but are moving the ball and are leading, so Halas's game plan is working.

Wade steps to the line. He drops back and finds Morris on a slant, and Johnny has the yards he needed for a first down. What a great route by Morris, who had to know exactly where the marker was. And an equally great throw from Wade, who continues to find the seams to his receivers. Ditka was double covered on that play, which left Morris in a one-on-one coverage and he made the most of it that time.

Wade steps back to pass again—his eighteenth of the half— and he hits Marconi on a screen for 5 yards. Marconi just bulled his way through Emil Karas and Faison as he made a play that should have been stopped into a hard-earned gain.

The Bears get set on second down. Ditka is tight right with Morris wide on the same side. Angelo Coia is split left, with Bull and Galimore in the backfield. The give is to Galimore running left, and he's pulled down by Petrich who was slanting in and beat the blocking. Marconi replaces Bull in the Bears backfield.

THE GAME: CHARGERS VS. BEARS IN THE FIRST SUPER BOWL

The line play on both sides has been pretty much even, with the Chargers' front four going nose-to-nose with the Chicago line, and even the somewhat underrated San Diego offensive line has been able to hold their own against the Bears' front four. Although we should not diminish the fact that three of the Chargers' linemen are either 1st or 2nd Team All-League, we just take them for granted sometimes with so many stars on offense.

Wade has started to slow down the pace and take his time. Now he steps back to pass. Ditka is doubled again, so he throws over the middle to Galimore who has circled in, but the ball's knocked down by Chuck Allen in the middle for an incomplete pass, leaving the Bears 4 yards short to bring up a fourth down on their own 39-yard line. The Chargers are really blanketing Ditka since his hot start, and Wade may be using him to decoy the defenders and open things up for his other receivers.

Bobby Joe Green comes onto the field to punt on fourth down, and, boy, he really got a hold of that one. A booming, towering kick that is headed to the end zone for a touchback, and the Chargers will take over at the 20-yard line.

Kocourek is set up tight on the left side alongside Ernie Wright. Norton and Alworth are both lined up on the left as well, putting all three receivers on the left side. Rote hands to Lincoln on an inside trap and he's got a seam between O'Bradovich and Morris and is past the 30 to the 33. Thirteen yards for Lincoln as Mix seals off the defense and DeLuca gave Lincoln a good route to the inside.

The ball is at the 33 with less than five minutes to go in the half. Here's a give to Lowe on a trap play for 2 yards. He was knocked to the ground by Bill George, who was not fooled on the play.

On 2nd and 8, Rote pitches to Lincoln. He's going wide around the left side, he's past the line and into the Bears secondary, cuts inside and eludes Taylor . . . one man to beat, but there's Petitbon on the tackle at the 50. A 15-yard run for Lincoln, and he's showing the same form he had a week ago against Boston when he ran for over 200 yards against the best running defense in the AFL. The Bears are going to need to tighten that up, as San Diego has the ball at midfield with just over four minutes to go.

The Chargers continue to challenge this Bears defense with their speed to the outside and so far they have shown that they can turn the corner and break off some big runs. The Bears will have to shore that up in the second half and, if I know George Allen and the number-one defense in the NFL, they will come up with something at half time.

Bobby Jackson checks in for Lowe in the Chargers backfield as Chicago is still in their standard 4-3 defense. Rote turns and fakes a handoff to Lincoln and looks up field to throw. He's got Bob Jackson coming out of the backfield, complete, and Jackson has Fortunato beat. He's by Petitbon and finally pulled down by Taylor at the Bears 25-yard line. A 25-yard pass and run by Jackson as Rote continues to have success with short passes, isolating his backs on the Chicago linebackers. They had two men on Alworth that time, and I think Lincoln is getting some extra attention from the Bears as well. But that time I think they just forgot about Jackson or maybe just relaxed a bit with Lowe on the sidelines. At any rate, the Bears are looking less than impenetrable right now.

Rote steps back to pass on first down. He spots Norton in the middle . . . but Bill George bats it down for an incompletion. Lincoln was drawing double coverage out of the backfield on that play and you can sense that the Bears are keying on him to make sure he doesn't sneak behind them.

It's now 2nd and 10, and Rote is taking his time at the line. He drops back and fakes a draw to Jackson, now looks wide where he hits Lincoln with a screen pass. Lincoln breaks one tackle and heads to the sidelines. He's past the 20 to the 15 and dragged down at the 14 by Joe Fortunato. An 11-yard gain for Lincoln as the clock shows under three minutes to go in the half.

Now on the Chicago 14-yard line, this drive has eaten up nearly four minutes as the Chargers have moved 66 yards downfield, still trailing 20–13.

Now it's Lincoln with a hand-off, but he's going nowhere, as Stan Jones has something to say about this one. Jones out muscled Pat Shea, which is not an easy task, as he's one of the strongest Chargers. But Jones won that battle!

Jacque MacKinnon gives Lincoln a rest on 2nd and 9, as Lowe checks in for Jackson.

Rote looks to hand to Lowe, now fakes it and throws out in the flat to MacKinnon, but it's behind him and falls to the ground, incomplete.

Chicago digs in as Rote comes to the line. Bill George is signaling to Fortunato for something as Alworth starts in motion and now stops. Here's the snap and here comes Fortunato on a blitz! Rote gets the pass away and finds Norton slanting toward the end zone and HE'S IN FOR A TOUCHDOWN! A 13-yard completion for Rote's third touchdown pass of the game, this one to Don Norton and San Diego can retie the game with the extra point. Norton had the inside on McRae and Taylor was a little too deep in the zone to help out. Norton just ran underneath and Rote was on target, hitting him at the 5-yard line as Norton went in untouched for the score.

Blair steps up for the extra point . . . it's good, and we have our second tie of the day at 20–20.

As the half comes closer to an end, Blair gets ready to kick off. It's a good kick, and taken at the 5 by Bull, who rushes down the right side past the 15 and 20 and is brought down by Bud Whitehead and Bob Mitinger at the 23. An 18-yard return for Bull and the Bears will see if they can put some more points on the board before halftime. As the offense gets set, Galimore and Marconi line up behind Wade for Chicago. Ditka splits about five yards to the outside with Morris wide right and Farrington split left. The Chargers show blitz, but now Maguire and Karas back away. Wade hands to Galimore, who's met by Ladd and Faison in the Bears backfield for a 2-yard loss and the Bears will take a time-out.

As the teams come back onto the field, it's now 2nd and 12 for the Bears with under two minutes left. Wade drops back and hands to Marconi on a draw play. Marconi moves ahead and picks up about 4 yards, giving the Bears a 3rd and 8 at their own 25.

Wade brings the Bears up to the line. The Charger safeties move a little deeper now, anticipating a pass. And . . . there's a flag. We haven't had many in this game, but this time San Diego jumped and that will move Chicago up to the 30.

Wade fakes to Marconi straight ahead and pitches wide to Galimore, but he can't turn the corner as Charlie McNeil moved in quickly to make the stop after a short gain, and the Bears will have to punt on 4th and 2.

Green gets it away and it's another booming kick, taking Alworth back to the 18. He sidesteps J. C. Caroline and picks up 9 yards on the return and the Chargers will have less than a minute to see if they can break the tie, starting at their own 27.

The Bears secondary is giving up the short yardage here as they move a little deeper than normal. They don't want to give up a big play now.

Rote fires a short curl to Alworth who pulls it down at the 29. He's got some room as he cuts to the middle of the field, past the 35 and gets to the 40-yard line where Taylor and Whitsell catch up with him. McRae gave him a little too much room to operate, and that quick little 2-yard curl gave him some running room. He's dangerous in the open field and picked up 13 yards on the play.

The ball is at the 40. Rote drops back and is looking for Norton down the left side, and now flips to Lowe on another screen pass. Lowe has it with Shea in front, and takes it to the 49 for a 9-yard pick-up. Again those screen passes are putting the pressure on the Bear linebackers. The Chargers have been able to spring their backs for some nice gains. The Chargers take a time-out.

The Bears are taking no chances of getting caught with under a minute to go as they keep Taylor and Petitbon deep. George drops a step or two deeper in the middle and Whitsell and McRae are also giving a step or two. It's Lowe on a trap and he's pulled down by Stan Jones and Earl Leggett after picking up 3 yards and a first down. The Chargers are moving again and now call a time-out to stop the clock at the Chicago 48-yard line.

I think Rote was hoping to catch the Bears in a prevent defense that time and was looking to spring one of his backs for a long gainer but the veteran Bears' tackles held their ground.

The Chargers hurry to the line with only a few seconds remaining, Rote takes the snap and now loses the ball! He recovers it and falls forward for a 2-yard gain. Rote pulled out a little too quickly and was lucky the ball bounced right back to him. And now the Chargers call their last time out.

It's 2nd and 8 with the ball on the Bears' 46 as Rote takes the snap and pump fakes to Kocourek. He finds Alworth on the outside for a completion—wait . . . it's incomplete. Alworth had the ball but bobbled it as he stepped out of bounds and the refs say he did not have possession. Only 11 seconds to go.

Rote drops again and throws to Norton, but it falls incomplete as the clock stops with two seconds left. It's now 4th and 8, and Gillman will probably just have Rote fall on the ball rather than risk a blocked punt here.

There's the snap and, yep, Rote just falls on the ball and the gun sounds. The first half of this historic championship game is in the books, and both teams have played to a standoff. They have both had their moments on offense and defense, and I don't think anyone can say they have not played well and up to their talented expectations. I think because of what this game may mean in pro-football history and because each team knows how talented the other is, that both teams have elevated their game.

Chicago scored on their first drive, as did the Chargers. And after the Bears took a 20–7 lead, the Chargers tenaciously came back with two scores to tie it at 20. Both teams have played well and we'll have to see who can make the better adjustments for the second half now that they have felt each other out.

The Bears have kept their passes short and taken advantage of some mismatches with Ditka, and also on throwing screens to Marconi and Galimore. Johnny Morris has taken advantage of some of the Ditka double-coverage as well.

THE GAME: CHARGERS VS. BEARS IN THE FIRST SUPER BOWL

For the Chargers, I think they have figured out that the Bears are waiting for the long ball to Alworth or Norton that proved successful early on and are using the speed of Lincoln and Lowe to run wide and catch screen passes to outrun the Bears and have been content moving the ball underneath the deep coverage.

Defensively the Chargers front four has neutralized the Bears running game, but Wade has adjusted by throwing more often. The Bears on the other hand have not been able to use their muscle that dominated the NFL offensive lines because of the Chargers quickness to the outside.

So George Halas and George Allen will have to come up with something defensively to slow San Diego down. I think Sid Gillman and company have to be pretty happy with how things are going so far for the AFL champs. It's been a good game for the first thirty minutes, so hang tight, fans, as we still have thirty more to go.

Now let's look at the first half statistics.

FIRST HALF STATISTICS									
	SD	**CHI**							
1st downs	16	11							
Rushes	14-78	16-33							
Passes	23-13-218	19-12-144							
Sacked	0	0							
Fumbles	1	0							
Turnovers	2	0							
Time of pos.	13:54	15:55							
3rd down	4-5	8-9							
4th down	1-1	0-0							
Net offense	296	177							
SAN DIEGO									
Passing	**Att**	**Cmp**	**%**	**Yds**	**Sk**	**Int**	**Td**	**Rate**	
Rote	23	13	56.5	218	0	1	3	113.3	

Rushing	Att	Yds	Avg	Td	Lg			
Lincoln	7	50	7.1	0	15			
Lowe	4	19	4.8	0	13			
Rote	3	9	4	0	6			
Receiving	Rec	Yds	Avg	Td	Lg			
Lowe	5	74	14.8	0	29			
Alworth	4	77	19.3	2	39			
Norton	2	31	15.5	1	18			
Lincoln	1	11	11	0	11			
Jackson	1	25	25	0	25			
CHICAGO								
Passing	Att	Cmp	%	Yds	Sk	Int	Td	Rate
Wade	19	12	63.1	144	0	0	2	121.4
Rushing	Att	Yds	Avg	Td	Lg			
Bull	5	11	2.2	0	6			
Marconi	5	10	2.0	0	4			
Galimore	5	10	2.0	1	9			
Casares	1	2	2	0	2			
Receiving	No	Yds	Avg	Td	Lg			
Ditka	4	68	17	0	40			
Marconi	3	34	11.3	0	21			
Morris	2	23	11.5	0	14			
Farrington	1	9	9	1	9			
Galimore	1	5	5	0	5			
Casares	1	5	5	1	5			
	1	2	Half					
SAN DIEGO	7	13	20					
CHICAGO	13	7	20					

Third Quarter

We are back and ready for the second half kickoff, and for all the hype this game has generated over the last week[9]—maybe

---

9   The AFL moved their season back one week from their original schedule when they suspended their games the week Kennedy was assassinated. They also pushed the championship back another week to accommodate the Eastern Division's need for a playoff game. The Bears would have had two weeks to prepare for this game, compared to one for the Chargers.

even all season as to which league will own the ultimate brag-
ging rights, this game thus far has delivered an even contest,
as each team has shown signs of a champion no matter which
league they are from. With the Chargers starting with the ball
to start the half, we'll see what the next thirty minutes of football brings.

The Bears are on the field and getting ready to kick off.
Lincoln and Alworth are the deep men for the Chargers. Here's
the kick—it's a long one. Lincoln catches the ball about four
yards deep and takes a look up field but decides to take a knee
for a touchback. The Bears had great coverage and Lincoln was
not going to force the issue.

The Chargers start out with Lowe and Gerry McDougall in
the backfield. Norton is split left, with Alworth wide out on the
right. Here's the snap, and the give is to McDougall off the right
side where he is met by Ed O'Bradovich and Stan Jones after a
short 3-yard pick-up. Pat Shea and Ron Mix are the guard and
tackle for the Chargers on the right side—which is considered
their strong side—but Jones got to the hole first and was assisted
by O'Bradovich.

Now second down and Rote drops back, he looks right, pumps,
and now throws a screen to the left side . . . look out! Rosey Taylor
shoots the gap and has an interception for Chicago. He's tackled
by Lincoln on the spot and the Bears have their first break of
the half and possession at the San Diego 23-yard line. The Bears
really played that one well, as that's their third takeaway of the
game. Taylor saw that one coming and that may be one of the
things Coach Allen drew their attention to at halftime.

The Bears get set; Ditka lines up on the left side with Angelo
Coia split wide. Wade looks to throw and hits Coia on a quick

out pass that's good for 8 yards. Wade avoided the Chargers blitz from Emil Karas to pick up some nice yardage to the 15.

I think Farrington may have been injured at some point in the first half because Coia has taken most of the snaps on the last couple possessions. We'll see if we can get some word from the Chicago bench.

The Bears are at the line, Wade turns and hands to Joe Marconi, who follows Mike Pyle through the center of the line and picks up the first down with a 2-yard dive. They chose to avoid Ernie Ladd that time and went to the right of Pyle and through George Gross. Sometimes it's better to let Ladd stand up and go right at him, but most times his brute strength will cause teams to go the other way. That time the Bears did and got another first down at the 13.

Now here's Marconi again over Herman Lee, and he's hit by Petrich after a 3-yard pick-up, making it 2nd and 7.

Marconi and Bull line up behind Wade. It's a give to Bull off the right side and he's drilled by Ladd, the big 6'9" defensive tackle out of Grambling in his third year with the Chargers. He stopped that play for no gain.

That will bring up a 3rd and 7 for Wade. Wade takes the snap and drops back, he's looking, looking, now tucks it away and takes off . . . he may score . . . he's hit and dives forward, but looks to be short of the goal line. He did pick up another first down, though. That was the Billy Wade of old right there. He was looking for Ditka and decided to just tuck and go, and it paid off. Charlie McNeil and Chuck Allen brought him down just short of the goal line, and the Bears have a 1st and goal inside the 1-yard line.

The Chargers put up a seven-man front with Schmidt, Buncom, and Mitinger in the down position—Allen and Karas are the linebackers with Whitehead and Westmoreland on the corners. The Bears come out with two tight ends. Wade gives to Marconi up the middle and he's hit hard and knocked back for a 1-yard loss. That was George Gross and Allen making the penetration to stop Marconi, and now the ball is a little short of 2 yards from the endzone. Let's call it at the one and a half.

Again the Bears show two tight ends with Morris split wide left as the flanker. Marconi and Bull are in the backfield. Wade on a long count gives to Bull . . . AND HE'S IN FOR A TOUCHDOWN! Ronnie Bull takes it in to give the Bears a six-point lead again, and Papa Bear is applauding his offense as they come off the field.

Jencks lines up for the extra point. He's had one blocked today so this is in no way a gimmie. Here's the kick, it's up . . . and it's good. Time-out on the field as the Chicago Bears have just retaken the lead, 27–20, on a 1-yard plunge by Ronnie Bull with 9:36 left in the third quarter after a Rosey Taylor interception.

Here's the kickoff to Lincoln at the goal line . . . he's heading right . . . he's at the 10, 20, and brought down by Dave Whitsell at the Chargers' 28-yard line.

So let's see what Rote will do on this possession after throwing his second interception of the game, with both coming deep in Charger territory.

The Chargers break the huddle. Rote is under center, he takes a two-step drop and throws, and Alworth has it for a short gainer, maybe 4 yards on a quick little hook in front of Whitsell, who was giving him a lot of room. They don't want to get into a track meet with Alworth, so they are playing him about 5 yards off the line.

Now 2nd and 6, Rote calling signals, turns and gives the ball to Lowe around right end and there's Bill George shooting the gap to bring him down for no gain. He's one of the best, and showed there why he's All-NFL in the middle. The Chargers have a 3rd and 6 on their hands now from their own 32.

Norton and Alworth both line up wide right. We saw this a time or two in the first half on the left side. Kocourek the tight end is split a few yards wide on the left side. Fortunato splits with him as the Bears overshift. Rote drops to pass. The Bears are blitzing with Morris and George—Rote's got Alworth deep and Norton over the middle, now he throws wide on a screen to Lowe which is complete, and Lowe has blocking in front of him and an open field with Mix and Shea as an escort. Lowe is to the 45 and over midfield; he's past the Bears 40 and brought down inside their 35-yard line for a huge pick-up of 32 yards. Alworth and Norton cleared the side by taking their coverage deep over the middle, which left Fortunato all alone underneath as the Bears sent two linebackers on a blitz. Mix and Shea sprung Lowe who has the sprinter's speed to take off, which is what we just saw him do.

It's now 1st and 10 for San Diego in Chicago territory. Rote fakes to Lowe this time and finds Lincoln in the flat on a swing pass. He's one-on-one again with George and he's by him with some open field in front. Lincoln is to the 20, to the 10, and tackled by Petitbon at the Chicago 9-yard line. What a back-and-forth contest this has been. Rote is working both sides of the Bears' defense and utilizing that dangerous Charger speed. We are seeing that this team really can accelerate.

Bob Jackson checks into the Chargers backfield, replacing Lowe. Jackson is their big blocker and has the body to handle the pass rush and blitzes. Rote gives to Lincoln behind Mix and he picks up about 4 yards, giving the Chargers a 2nd and goal from the 5.

THE GAME: CHARGERS VS. BEARS IN THE FIRST SUPER BOWL

Stan Jones checks back in on the Bears front line. They dig in. Lincoln goes in motion. Rote gives a quick pitch to Lincoln who's headed to the corner flag and is hit by McRae for only a yard gain. McRae came up hard and fast to catch Lincoln before he could get any momentum. Norton was a little slow on that block as the Chargers tried to isolate Lincoln without any blocking in front. Nice play by McRae to read that play to make the open field tackle.

Lowe checks back in for San Diego. Rote steps up to the line. He spins and hands to Lowe on a sweep behind DeLuca and Shea . . . AND HE'S IN! A 4-yard rushing touchdown by Paul Lowe brings the Chargers back for the third time today. After the turnover to start the half, it looked as though the Bears had taken control, but the Chargers have answered yet again. They are clearly staying away from Doug Atkins on the left side, and with Charger guards able to get outside and lead those sweeps, that strategy is looking pretty good.

George Blair is in to attempt the extra point. He missed one in the second quarter so he's taking his time setting this one up. It's up . . . it's good. The Chargers have tied the score at 27.

Just a tick under six minutes left in the third quarter as the Chargers get ready to kickoff. Galimore and Bull are deep as Blair tees it up.

It's a short kick, taken at the 7 by Bull. He's at the 15 and downed at the 20-yard line by Frank Buncom and Bob Mitinger.

Chicago has been conservative thus far with short passing routes and off-tackle runs, so let's see if Wade continues to be patient and let the game just materialize with their game plan. He hands to Marconi off left tackle and picks up 4 tough yards as Gross and Ladd converge on him.

Wade steps up to the line and again hands it to Marconi, who rushes off the left side for four more yards. Wade likes that match-up with Herman Lee, his left tackle going against the rookie Petrich. It's now 3rd and 2 for the Bears.

Bull gets the ball and heads off left tackle again and runs past the first down marker for 5 yards. Three consecutive runs off left tackle makes it look as if Wade is being very methodical on this drive. The Chargers sent Allen up the middle that time to plug the hole, but Bull slid to the side and picked up the yardage needed and then some.

Wade has another 1st and 10 at the Bears 33. Ditka is tight right with Coia still in for Farrington wide left and Morris split right. Wade drops to throw, and it's complete to Morris 15 yards down field. He breaks the first tackle and heads up-field, over midfield, gets a block from Ditka, and moves over the 40 before Charlie McNeil brings him down at the San Diego 33 for a 34-yard gain. The Chargers may have been looking run there but Morris ran a great curl route in front of Blair and was able to break away for a big gain. Chicago ball from the Charger 33 and the Bears are on the move with 3:03 to play in the third.

Wade hesitates to look over the defense, now steps up under Pyle. He takes the snap and pumps to Ditka, now throws complete to Ditka over the middle to the 25-yard line . . . but hold on, there's a flag back behind the line of scrimmage. Here's the call . . . and it's holding on the Bears. That will cost them 15 yards and take away the 8-yard completion, giving their offense a long 1st and 25. They place the ball back at the Charger 48.

Wade steps back to throw again, looks to Morris, now flips a screen to Marconi who has it and cuts back inside where he'll pick up about 9 yards before Paul Maguire pulls him down from behind. The Bears will have a 2nd and 16 from the San Diego 39-yard line. Wade gives to Ronnie Bull on a draw play but it's going nowhere as Ernie Ladd smothers him for a two yard loss. That will bring up a 3rd and 18. Tough call now for Wade, as the offense is pretty much out of field goal range for LeClerc. So if they can get close here we may see Halas give it a shot on fourth down.

Wade is looking long for Morris but Westmoreland has him step-for-step. Wade takes off and Faison has him after a 6-yard gain, bringing up 4th and 12. I guess Halas isn't comfortable with the distance of a 50-yard field goal, as Bobby Joe Green is heading out to kick it away and try to pin the Chargers up against the wall as he did in the first half.

Green takes the snap and . . . it will go into the end zone for a touchback. It went in and out of the end zone on a big bounce, so the Chargers will take over at the 20 with less than a minute to go in the third.

We are deadlocked at 27 as both teams have scored a touchdown this quarter. Rote hands the ball to Bob Jackson straight ahead, who breaks one tackle and is then dragged down by George and Atkins at the 28 for an 8-yard gain. Jackson is a big back and has been used primarily as a blocker for Lincoln and Lowe in short yardage situations, but he can carry it pretty well himself. He was a starter last year when Lowe was out with a broken arm, so he knows how to handle the ball. Now 2nd and 2, Rote steps back to pass looking for Norton . . . and he's nailed by Doug Atkins before he can get the pass off. It's a 3-yard loss as Atkins got by Ernie Wright. Wright and Atkins have been having quite a scrum today as they continue to trade off shots.

And that play brings an end to the third quarter, with the score tied up at 27. This should be a very entertaining final quarter.

Fourth Quarter

As the teams switch sides, the Chargers break the huddle on third down as Rote steps up to the line. He drops back and throws a screen to Kocourek with Wright in front, but it falls incomplete. I think he was trying to catch Atkins on a hard pass rush but he couldn't connect, and the Chargers will be forced to give the ball up as Maguire heads onto the field to punt it away.

Here's the punt, Morris is under it at the 41 and calls for a fair catch. Chicago's offense comes onto the field and huddles up. They break, with Bull and Galimore setting up in the backfield as Wade walks to the line. He turns and gives to Bull off the right side behind Wetoska where he finds a little room and fights for 4 yards. They went right at Faison to see if maybe they could catch him circling wide and Bull found an inside gap to get through. It's 2nd and 6 as Bull leaves and Marconi checks in.

Wade fakes a pitch to Galimore and looks over the middle to Marconi, complete inside San Diego territory to the 46-yard line and a Chicago first down. Can Wade engineer his patient offense on another time-consuming drive here in the fourth quarter to take the lead?

Wade moves up under Pyle and takes the snap, he dropped it! Wade falls on the ball and the Bears retain possession, but that was a close one, It looked like Wade never had a good grip as he came away and it's a 4-yard loss, giving Chicago a 2nd and 14 from midfield.

Casares and Galimore now check in for Chicago as Halas is working to keep his runners fresh and keep the Chargers from figuring out his offensive scheme. It's power and speed now behind Wade, with Morris s flanked wide left and Coia wide right. Here's a fake to Casares and another fake pitch to Galimore, Wade fires over the middle and finds Casares for another completion. He's hit and brought down by Chuck Allen but not until the big Bears fullback has a 10-yard gain to the Charger 40. Another few yards will get them into field-goal range.

It's now 3rd and 4 as Wade steps up to the line. He's looking over the defense. Whitehead is now in for McNeil at safety and he's creeping up to the line, but then backs away. Wade turns and gives to Galimore behind Ted Karras on a sweep and he runs into Bob Petrich who stops him after a yard gain, bringing up 4th and 3 at the 39. Halas did not want to try a field goal from a bit closer on the last possession, so we'll have to see what he wants to do this time, as there are only twelve minutes left in this contest.

Wade brings the Bears to the line and it appears that Halas is going for it. They step up to the line. Time is ticking off the play clock . . . and there's a whistle for delay of game. I guess they were just trying to see if they could draw the Chargers offsides, but they took too much time and the officials will move the ball back 5 yards to the Charger 44-yard line. And now Halas sends out his punter, so again he's going to try and pin San Diego deep and hope his defense can contain the explosive Chargers offense. Coach Allen knows the Chargers can strike quickly, so his defense should be well prepared to give some room and not get beaten deep. Green punts it away . . . it's deep . . . and Alworth is letting it bounce at the 8 as it keeps rolling right into the end zone for a touchback. Interesting that Halas didn't give LeClerc a shot at a field goal from the 39 that time. A miss would have put the Chargers at the same place they are now starting from. Perhaps he didn't want to risk a block by the big front line of the Chargers with Ladd and Faison in the middle of that line, which seems to be influencing some of the Bears' calls. At any rate it's San Diego's ball at their own 20.

Rote comes to the line and steps in under center. He turns and throws a screen to Keith Lincoln . . . he's got it and has some running room. He's up to the 33 for a San Diego first down. Rote has used his backs on screens a lot this afternoon while sending his wide receivers deep to take away the corners, and it's a 13-yard pick-up for Lincoln.

Rote sets to throw again, he's going deep . . . and Don Norton makes a great over-the-shoulder catch with McRae right on him at the 40 and takes it down to the Bears 46-yard line for a 31-yard catch, moving his Chargers into Chicago territory.

The Chargers are taking their time coming out of the huddle and to the line. Rote sets to throw again but Atkins is on him . . . Rote breaks free and is running, he's to the 42 and brought down by Larry Morris who was on him quickly to hold Rote to a 4-yard gain.

San Diego is looking very patient as we get down to crunch-time. Rote takes the snap and gives to Lincoln off left tackle, who slides inside and is met by George and Williams after picking up 8 yards for a first down at the Bears 34. This is close to Blair's range now and, as we mentioned before, he has hit on two of his six field-goal attempts between the 40 and 49 this year, so he's capable if need be. Right now it would be 41-yard attempt.

Rote drops back again, he's looking to throw, and he fires to Norton . . . IT'S PICKED OFF BY FORTUNATO! Rote's third interception of the game and Fortunato is now responsible for three turnovers with his second interception along with a fumble recovery. The Bears defense has come up big once again. The "Monsters of the Midway" have another takeaway, and the Bears have possession at their 27-yard line.

The time is down to 7:47 as Wade breaks from the huddle and comes to the line. He fades, looks . . . he's down, hit by Ladd and dropped for a 4-yard loss. Ladd came storming in and Wade could not get the throw away in time, so the Bears now face a 2nd and 14 from their own 23.

Wade throws a quick screen to Galimore who makes the catch and is brought down after 2 yards by Buncom, who is now backing up the line in place of Maguire.

It's 3rd and 12 as Wade drops deep with Gross applying pressure. Wade throws long for Galimore who has Karas beat, but it's just out of his reach and incomplete. That could have given the Bears some big yardage that time as Galimore just outran Karas while Ditka was occupying Blair and Harris with double coverage. So now the Bears will have to punt again.

Green nails it and Alworth has to fair catch this one; it was sky high but now we have a flag on the play. There's some pushing going on down there, and San Diego is going to be hit with an unnecessary roughness call which will move the ball back to their own 13-yard line.

Lowe and McDougall set up as the backs as Rote takes the ball and gives it to McDougall, who's into the line and stopped cold by Atkins and Leggett for a loss of 1, bringing up 2nd and 11.

Time is ticking with only 6:11 left. Rote gets set to pass, he throws to Kocourek, AND IT'S INTERCEPTED BY PETITBON at the 25, and he returns it down to the 15. Oh my, how many times can the Bears defense come up big like that! That is huge for Chicago, who is again deep in San Diego's end of the field.

The Bears offense lines up with Ditka set up tight right with Morris beyond him and Marconi and Bull behind Wade. Wade throws looking for Morris at the 8 but it falls incomplete. Good coverage that time by Dick Harris. Harris is active on that corner and is described by most AFL receivers as tough and feisty. So the Bears now have it a 2nd and 10 from the 15.

Wade gives to Casares up the middle where he's met by Ladd, Gross, and Allen, and it looks like he didn't make it back to the line. A loss of 1 yard for Chicago gives them a 3rd and 11 at the 16. The Bears definitely need to score here with time winding down.

Wade steps back on a play action pass—the Chargers are blitzing. Wade throws to Morris on a post pattern . . . AND IT'S INTERCEPTED BY McNEIL! He's to the sideline and past the 20 to the 30, the 40, and tackled by Ronnie Bull at the Chargers' 44-yard line. Wade is kicking himself for rushing that pass. He froze the blitzing Allen on the play action, but Ladd was right there and it looked like he threw the ball before he wanted to. That's an unbelievable turnover this late in the game as the Bears looked like they were certain to wrap this game up. San Diego now has the ball on their own 44 and we have less than five minutes to go in regulation. This game will not end in a tie, and just like the Colts and Giants did in 1958 and the Oilers and Texans last year, we will have extra time until somebody wins it.

Lincoln goes in motion, Rote turns and pitches to Lowe on a counter and Lowe is around the end and past the 50 to the Chicago 44 for a 12-yard pick-up and a first down for San Diego. Once more the Chargers have shown how quick they are as Lowe got a step on Atkins to the outside, which was all he needed. Lowe has now picked up 35 yards on 7 carries.

It's 1st and 10 from the 44, and here's Lowe on another sweep, where he picks up maybe 2 yards. Doug Atkins was in on the tackle for Chicago, making it 2nd and 8 with 3:24 to go in regulation.

Time is becoming a factor and the Bear defense has spent a lot of time on the field this half but have held the San Diego offense in check. They need to hold on here and keep them out of scoring range.

Rote fires a quick out to Alworth, but it falls incomplete. He was looking to give Alworth some running room by hitting him right off the line but he overthrew the pass and they'll face a 3rd and 8 from the 42.

Bill George is moving in toward the line. Taylor and Petitbon move up as well. Rote takes the snap and drops back to pass; he throws to Norton on a curl and . . . McRae knocks it away for an incomplete pass. The Bears have done it again, coming up big for Papa Bear Halas and their defensive leader George Allen. And with only 3:18 to go, this is well outside of George Blair's range and Sid Gillman is going to have to give the ball back to the Bears.

Paul Maguire is back to punt for San Diego. He takes the snap and boots it away and man, did he get a hold of that one. It rolls into the end zone for a touchback and the Bears will have it at the 20, a mere 80 yards away from the championship.

Now the question remains: Can that big Charger front four hold the Bears to a three-and-out to give their offence one last chance to take the Chargers into the end zone?

Wade hands to Galimore off tackle and there's Gross and Petrich to bring him down after only a 3-yard gain. The tension is mounting for both clubs and the crowd is buzzing louder and louder as we near the end. I don't think anyone is still sitting.

Wade on 2nd and 7 pitches to Galimore on a sweep, looking for an opening, but Faison is there to bring him down behind the line for a loss of 2, and that will stop the clock for the two-minute warning. This game between the two best teams from both leagues has surely lived up to the hype. But there can be only one winner, and the way this game has been played, it's a shame that someone has to walk away with a loss. Both teams have played their hearts out and have been great representatives of their respective leagues. We are still tied at 27 with only two minutes to go, and the Bears have possession with a 3rd and 9 from their 21-yard line.

Wade brings the Bears out of the huddle. He's taking his time looking over the Charger defense. Ladd and Faison are lined up on the Bears' right side. Harris and Westmoreland are giving Morris and Coia a few yards more than usual. Here's the snap, Wade to pass, to Casares over the middle, and it falls incomplete. He was hit by Chuck Allen just as the ball arrived and was not able to hold on, and the Chargers will be getting the ball back with just under two minutes remaining.

Bobby Joe Green is back to punt. Here's the snap and the kick is away to Alworth at his own 45 where he signals for a fair catch . . . but there's a flag back at the line of scrimmage, and it's holding on Chicago. That's a bad play by the Bears and mighty untimely at this point in the game. The penalty moves the ball back to the 11, and Green will be kicking from his own end zone.

The punt is away, and it's way up there as Green really got a hold of it. It heads for the sideline where it takes a Chicago bounce and Alworth lets it roll rather than risk a misplay. The Chargers will start from their own 43, so the penalty actually lost San Diego 2 yards. That was a clutch kick by Green. The Chargers take over on offense with only 1:38 left on the clock.

Rote walks to the line. He's in no hurry and needs to be careful with four interceptions already today. He steps back to pass and he throws for Lowe in the flat and it's off his hands and incomplete. That was a little high and he might have been distracted with Atkins bearing down on him.

Second down, and Rote gives it to Lowe on a sweep. He's got Shea in front and fights forward for 5 yards. With only 1:02 left, the Chargers are now faced with a 3rd down and 5 at the San Diego 48-yard line.

Rote brings the Chargers to the line. Chicago is in a 4–3 defense. Rote is taking his time, here's the snap, he throws short to Kocourek and it's incomplete . . . but there's another flag on the field. The call is passing interference on Chicago, and that will give the Chargers a first down at the Bears' 44-yard line. Larry Morris got to Kocourek before the ball did and that is another costly mistake for the otherwise brilliant Chicago defense.

The Chargers come out of the huddle and are ready, as the clock has ticked down to less than a minute left to play. Chicago digs in. Lincoln goes in motion to the right. Rote steps back and gives to Lowe on a quick trap and he's got running room! He's to the 35 and finally pulled down by Whitsell and Bill George at the 27 for a 17-yard gain. You are seeing one of the best and quickest runners in the AFL in Paul Lowe, folks. He just hit that opening and was gone as Ron Mix opened a hole by moving Stan Jones to the outside and picked up another first down.

The Chargers are now in field-goal range, but will Sid Gillman elect to kick one now or go for the end zone with 42 seconds left on the clock? Gerry McDougall is in for Lowe behind Rote. The give is to McDougall who lunges forward for 2 yards to the 25 and the clock moves down to 31 seconds before the Chargers call a time-out.

The question now is, can the Bears' defense come up with one more miracle and stop this Charger drive? Can they somehow force a turnover and give themselves another chance in overtime? Gillman is talking to Rote in front of the Chargers' bench as Halas on the other side is calling out encouragement to his defense while George Allen and Bill George are plotting their strategy.

One of the officials has now motioned to Gillman to get Rote back out to the huddle, and here he comes. Let's see if they go for the end zone or just try to get into field position and set up George Blair for a mid-range kick. But as we have all seen, there is nothing easy about a 30-yard field goal.

Rote brings the Chargers to the line and steps in under Rogers, the center. Here's the snap, and it's a give to Lowe who squeezes through the line to the 20 for another 5 yards. Lowe has had a superb game for the Chargers this afternoon. Both he and Lincoln have become the best backfield duo in the American Football League, and those who may be seeing them for the first time today have witnessed why. Gillman is pacing the sideline and looking toward the scoreboard. There are 16 ticks left and he still has two time-outs remaining, but it looks as though he's going to let the clock run down. The Chargers have a 3rd and 3 from the 20, but I don't think he wants to risk another play from scrimmage at this point. As the clock ticks to three seconds left he finally calls his second time-out. So after a hard-fought 59:57, it has all come down to one play, with everything riding on the right foot of San Diego kicker George Blair. No matter what has transpired on the field today, what people will remember about this game is what will happen on this play. Now Halas wants to talk to his captain again and calls for a time-out. It must seem like a lifetime for Blair as he sizes up the goalposts one more time. He has come out to attempt a 27-yard field goal to give the Chargers the unprecedented Championship of Pro Football. He's made six of seven from this distance during the season, but has never had one with this kind of pressure riding on it. The Bears huddle around Halas on the sideline as he gives them some last-second instructions. Now here's the official's whistle and the Bears jog back out on the field. This place is bedlam; it is so hard to hear right now as the noise of the crowd is deafening. Okay, they're ready, and here we go folks. This is for the championship of the world!

The Chargers come to the line. Tobin Rote will hold. The Bears are packing the middle, hoping to get a hand on the kick

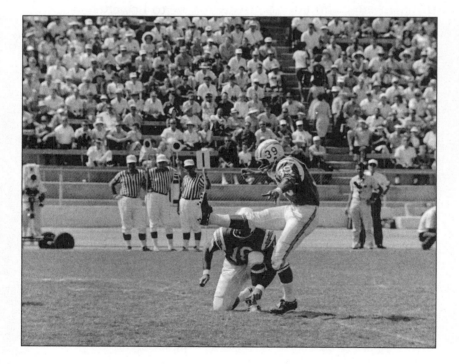

and take the game into overtime. Maybe to even cause a bad snap. Rogers is over the ball at center. Bill George is down in front of him.

Here we go, here's the snap from Rogers, the hold, the kick is up . . . IT'S GOOOOD! IT'S GOOD! GEORGE BLAIR HAS JUST KICKED A 27-YARD FIELD GOAL TO GIVE THE SAN DIEGO CHARGERS THE FIRST WORLD CHAMPIONSHIP OF PRO FOOTBALL! THE CHARGERS WIN, 30–27!

Oh, what an epic battle this has been. It's hard to put into words how riveting and entertaining this game was. Hard fought, neck-and-neck, nip-and-tuck, back-and-forth, you can pick as many of the great sports clichés as you can muster and you still wouldn't truly capture the intensity and emotion of this incredible contest. This game will be talked about for years, endlessly analyzed, agonized over, and celebrated again and again. These two champions really put on a remarkable show today and fought gallantly. It was a game that was as closely contested as anyone could have asked for, with the outcome in question right up to the very last play. Halas and Gillman are meeting at the middle of the field, with both coaches congratulating each other. The players are moving to midfield as well and they all appear to be physically drained but still hugging and shaking hands. This, folks, was a game for the ages and undoubtedly the most tension-packed and electrifying game in either league all season. We have just seen history made and a giant leap forward for the AFL. What we witnessed today is proof positive that when the two best teams from each league meet, on any given day, the best team from the AFL can hold their own and even beat the best team from the NFL. After four years of banter between the leagues, the debate has finally ended. On this day, now and for all time, the San Diego Chargers can say that they are 1963's BEST TEAM IN PRO FOOTBALL! Thanks for joining us, folks, as it has been our pleasure to bring you this historic game. And we hope you have enjoyed it as much as we have, in bringing it to you.

	1	2	3	4	Total
SAN DIEGO	7	13	7	3	30
CHICAGO	13	7	7	0	27

1st 9:35 Chicago TD Wade 5 pass to Casares (Jencks Kick)	0–7
1st 6:25 San Diego TD Rote 39 to Alworth (Blair Kick)	7–7
1st 0:38 Chicago TD Wade 9 to Farrington (Jencks Kick)	7–14
2nd 13:36 Chicago TD Galimore 9 Run (No Good)	7–20
2nd 8:56 San Diego TD Rote 5 to Alworth (No Good)	13–20
2nd 2:36 San Diego TD Rote 13 to Norton (Blair Kick)	20–20
3rd 9:36 Chicago TD Bull 1 Run (Jencks Kick)	20–27
3rd 5:59 San Diego TD Lowe 4 Run (Blair Kick)	27–27
4th 0:00 San Diego Fg Blair 27	30–27

FINAL STATISTICS

	SD	CHI
1st Downs	24	17
Rushes	29–152	33–66
Passes	35–18–325	29–18–216
Sacked	1–3	1–4
Fumbles	1	0
Penalties	6–46	6–49
Turnovers	5	1
Time Of Pos.	27:07	32:53
3rd Down	6–11	10–16
4th Down	1–2	0–0
Net Offense	474	278

SAN DIEGO

Passing	ATT	Cmp	%	Yds	Sk	Int	Td	Rate
Rote	34	18	52.9	322	1	4	3	75.9
Lowe	1	0						

Rushing	Att	Yds	Avg	Td	Lg				
Lincoln	10	63	6.3	0	15				
Lowe	11	64	5.8	1	17				
Rote	4	13	3.3	0	6				
Jackson	1	8	8	0	8				
McDougall	3	4	1.3		3				
Receiving	**No**	**Yds**	**Avg**	**Td**	**Lg**				
Lowe	6	106	17.7	0	32				
Alworth	5	81	16.2	2	39				
Lincoln	3	51	17	0	27				
Norton	3	63	21.0	1	31				
Jackson	1	25	25	0	25				
CHICAGO									
Passing	**Att**	**Cmp**	**%**	**Yds**	**Sk**	**Int**	**Td**	**Rate**	
Wade	29	18	62.0	212	1	1	2	93.5	
Rushing	**Att**	**Yds**	**Avg**	**Td**	**Lg**				
Marconi	10	22	2.2	0	4				
Bull	10	19	1.9	1	6				
Wade	3	12	4	0	10				
Galimore	8	12	1.5	1	9				
Casares	2	1	.5	0	2				
Receiving	**No**	**Yds**	**Avg**	**Td**	**Lg**				
Marconi	5	52	10.4	0	21				
Ditka	4	68	17	0	40				
Morris	3	57	19	0	34				
Galimore	2	7	3.5	0	5				
Casares	2	15	7.5	0	10				
Farrington	1	9	9	1	9				
Coia	1	8	8	0	8				

And there you have it. The game has finally been played, the results are in, and the stats have been posted. No one could ask for more than a game that went down to the wire and was won on the last play as time ran out. It says a lot about the quality and caliber of both great teams. And whether you like or dislike the outcome, we hope you enjoyed the game, and at the very least agree that the 1963 San Diego Chargers were one outstanding football team that should take a back seat to no one. Here's to the champions!

8

WOULD THE CHARGERS HAVE WON IF THE GAME WERE REPLAYED?

Some may say that a one-game sampling is not enough to declare one league's champion better than the other leagues. Additionally, you may be wondering what program was used and how it was programmed to manage such a simulation. So here are the facts to set your minds at ease.

Thanks to detailed and professional formatting abilities from Dave Koch Sports and the Action! PC football game program, offensive and defensive game plans were formulated using play-calling tendencies based on down, distance, field position, and match-ups.

ACTION! PC

SPORTS GAMES

Beyond the game you just read about, in which the Chargers beat the Bears, 30–27, the Championship Game was run 99 more times. Each time it was on a neutral field with an average temperature of 71 degrees. The teams alternated between being the designated home and away team with no advantage or disadvantage to either.

The Results

Running the simulation one hundred times, the results came out with the Chargers winning 54 times and the Bears winning 46. There was one overtime game (Chicago won, 17–14), and the average score between the two teams was the Chargers 18.08 points per game to the Bears 16.35.

In Memoriam
Deceased Chargers

Frank Buncom, Linebacker, November 2, 1939–September 14, 1969
Reg Carolan, Tight End, October 25, 1939–January 2, 1983
Sam DeLuca Guard May 2, 1936–September 13, 2011
Sid Gillman, Head Coach/General Manager, October 26,
    1911–January 3, 2003
George Gross, Defensive Tackle, January 26, 1941–April 27, 2010
Sam Gruneisen, Guard, January 16, 1941–September 28, 2012
Emil Karas, Linebacker, December 13, 1933–November 25, 1974
Dave Kocourek, Tight End, August 20, 1937–April 24, 2013
Ernie Ladd, Defensive Tackle, November 28, 1938–March 10, 2007
Jacque MacKinnon, End, November 10, 1938–March 6, 1975
Joe Madro, Asst. Coach, March 21, 1913–September 22, 1994
Bob Mitinger, Linebacker, February 13, 1940–September 25, 2004
Chuck Noll, Asst. Coach, January 5, 1932–June 13, 2014
Don Norton, Split End, March 13, 1938–June 23, 1997
Tobin Rote, Quarterback, January 18, 1928–June 27, 2000
Pat Shea, Guard, June 28, 1939–May 22, 2013
Walt Sweeney, Guard, Defensive End, April 18, 1941–
    February 2, 2013
Hugh "Bones" Taylor, Asst. Coach, July 6, 1923–October 31, 1992
Ernie Wright, Tackle, November 6, 1939–March 20, 2007

SEASON STATISTICS

1963 SAN DIEGO CHARGERS STATISTICS

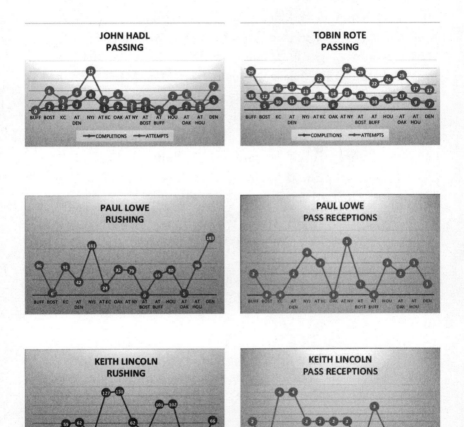

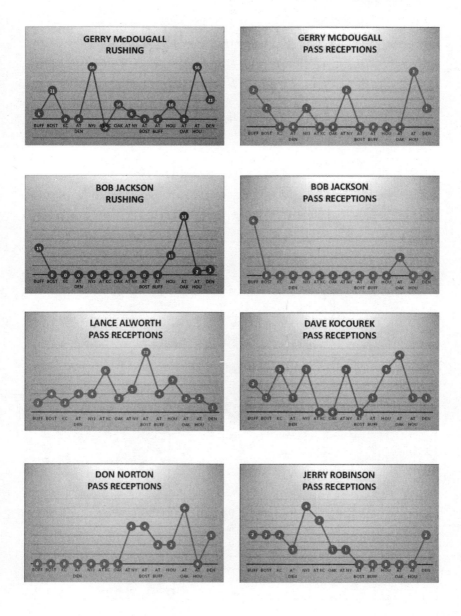

THE UNCROWNED CHAMPS

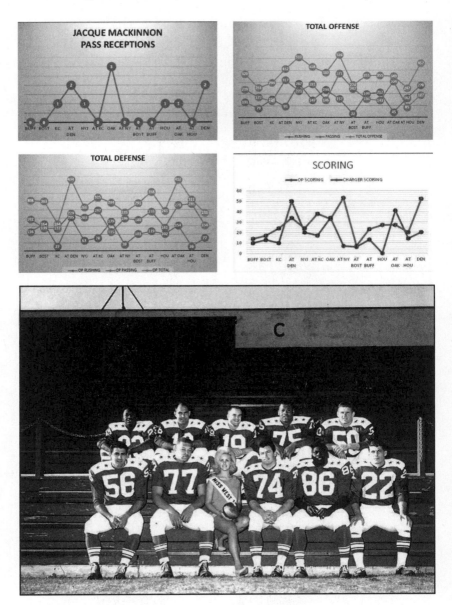

Chargers All-Stars.

Front Row—Emil Karas, Ernie Ladd, Miss West, Ron Mix, Earl Faison, Keith Lincoln

Back Row—Paul Lowe, Tobin Rote, Lance Alworth, Ernie Wright, Chuck Allen

Tobin Rote avoids pressure from the East All-Stars.

Tobin Rote receives the AFL's Player of the Year Award at the All-Star Game.

THE UNCROWNED CHAMPS

Lance Alworth catches a pass in the All-Star Game.

Keith Lincoln greets All-Stars Lance Alworth, Art Powell, and Paul Lowe.

FINAL STATISTICS							
PASSING	**COMP**	**ATT**	**%**	**YDS**	**TD**	**INT**	**RATE**
Tobin Rote	170	286	59.4	2510	20	17	86.7
John Hadl	28	64	43.8	502	6	6	63.4
Paul Lowe	2	4	50	100	1	1	95.8
Keith Lincoln	0	1	0	0	0	0	
G. McDougall	1	1	11	11	1	0	
Don Norton	1	1	15	15	0	0	
RUSHING	**ATT**	**YDS**	**AVG**	**TD**			
Paul Lowe	177	1010	5.7	8			
Keith Lincoln	128	826	6.5	5			
G. McDougall	38	199	5.2	1			
Bob Jackson	18	64	3.6	4			
Tobin Rote	24	62	2.6	2			
John Hadl	8	26	3.3	0			
Lance Alworth	2	14	7	0			
RECEIVING	**REC**	**YDS**	**AVG**	**TD**			
Lance Alworth	61	1205	19.8	11			
Paul Lowe	26	191	7.3	2			
Keith Lincoln	24	325	13.5	3			
Dave Kocourek	23	359	15.6	5			
Don Norton	21	281	13.4	1			
Jerry Robinson	18	315	17.5	2			
Jacque Mackinnon	11	262	23.8	4			
Gerry McDougall	10	115	11.5	0			
Bob Jackson	8	85	10.6	0			
INTERCEPTIONS	**NO**	**YDS**	**TD**				
Dick Harris	8	83	1				
Chuck Allen	5	37	0				
Paul Maguire	4	47	0				
Charlie McNeil	4	40	0				
Bob Mitinger	3	26	0				
Emil Karas	2	30	0				
George Blair	1	40	0				
Gary Glick	1	13	0				
Bud Whitehead	1	0	0				

THE UNCROWNED CHAMPS

Kicking	FGATT	MADE	PCT	PAT	ATT	MADE	PCT	
George Blair	28	17	60.7		48	44	91.7	
PUNTING	**NO**	**YDS**	**AVG**					
Paul Maguire	58	2241	38.6					
John Hadl	2	75	37.5					
KICK OFF & PUNT RETURNS	**PUNTS**	**RET**	**YDS**	**AVG**	**KO**	**RET**	**YDS**	**RET**
Keith Lincoln		7	98	14		17	439	25.8
Lance Alworth		11	120	10.9		10	216	21.6
Dick Westmoreland		-	-	-		10	204	20.4
Dick Harris		4	43	10.8		2	34	17
Paul Lowe		-	-	-		5	132	26.4
Gerry McDougall		-	-	-		3	77	25.7

ACKNOWLEDGMENTS

It was quite amazing to me when I started doing research for this book how few former AFL teams had organized archives chronicling their team's history. Some didn't even have a contact list of former AFL players. Photos, articles, game films, if they existed, were described by media departments as thrown in boxes and unedited for content and chronology.

Were it not for former Chargers intern Todd Tobias and his appreciation of football history, his ability and passion to archive and catalog the history of the Chargers in the 1960s, this book would never have been started. His friendship and generosity in helping me track down the essentials needed for this project gave me the motivation to pursue it and see it through to the end.

He also put me in touch with the many former players who graciously and enthusiastically consented to be interviewed, even after I explained that I would be taxing their memories about events that happened more than fifty years ago. I am thankful and indebted to all of them for their kindness and willingness to remember the past with such interesting and vivid recall. Talking to them was surreal. The same players that I adored, whose football cards I collected, and who I watched religiously week after week, were now talking to me as if we were old pals who had reunited. They were pros then, and they are still pros today.

THE UNCROWNED CHAMPS

Thanks to the following players:
Hank Schmidt

Bob Petrich

John Hadl

Chuck Allen

Chris Burford

Fred Arbanas

Ed Budde

Dave Hill

Bobby Bell

Art Powell

Billy Joe

Len Dawson

Charley Hennigan

Bobby Hunt

Their stories and conversation were not only interesting and informative, they were filled with passion and feelings of admiration for their friends and love for the AFL.

Special thanks also to Jamaal LeFrance and the San Diego Chargers for their gracious supply of photos and program covers that add tremendous aesthetic value with their content. To Dwight Spadlin of the Tennessee Titans (Houston Oilers) and Christy Berkery of the New England Patriots, Will Kiss and the Oakland Raiders for additional photos, and Bob Moore of the Kansas City

ACKNOWLEDGMENTS

Chiefs for work above and beyond. Also, thanks go out to Craig Wheeler for the helmets that appear and the NFL for allowing the inclusion of the team logos, to Charlie Butler of *Runners World* magazine for his advice and connections to the publishing world, to Ken Samelson for his keen eye while fact-checking my work, and to Skyhorse Publishing editor Jason Katzman for his professional and expert guidance in making this book come to life. Finally, it was a great honor to connect with the AFL's first Hall of Fame inductee, Lance Alworth, whose genuine interest, enthusiasm, and friendship during this project kept me energized throughout. Our many phone conversations were always insightful, nostalgic, and the highlight of my days. I am especially proud to have his foreword be part of this book. He is HOF all the way.

ABOUT THE AUTHOR

Dave Steidel is the author of *Remember the AFL: The Ultimate Fan's Guide to the American Football League*, and appears in Showtime's production *Full Color Football*, celebrating the history of the AFL. An AFL fan from its inception in 1960, he continues to research and write about the league. Many of his articles can be found at talesfromtheamericanfootballleague.com.